THE HYPERNATURALS™

VOLUME TWO

ROSS RICHIE Chief Executive Officer • **MATT GAGNON** Editor-in-Chief • **FILIP SABLIK** VP-Publishing & Marketing • **LANCE KREITER** VP-Licensing & Merchandising • **PHIL BARBARO** Director of Finance • **BRYCE CARLSON** Managing Editor
DAFNA PLEBAN Editor • **SHANNON WATTERS** Editor • **ERIC HARBURN** Editor • **CHRIS ROSA** Assistant Editor • **ALEX GALER** Assistant Editor • **STEPHANIE GONZAGA** Graphic Designer • **KASSANDRA HELLER** Production Designer
MIKE LOPEZ Production Designer • **JASMINE AMIRI** Operations Coordinator • **DEVIN FUNCHES** E-Commerce & Inventory Coordinator • **VINCE FREDERICK** Event Coordinator • **BRIANNA HART** Executive Assistant

THE HYPERNATURALS Volume Two — August 2013. Published by BOOM! Studios, a division of Boom Entertainment, Inc. The Hypernaturals is Copyright © 2013 Boom Entertainment, Inc. Originally published in single magazine form as THE HYPERNATURALS 4-8. Copyright © 2012, 2013 Boom Entertainment, Inc. All rights reserved. BOOM! Studios™ and the BOOM! Studios logo are trademarks of Boom Entertainment, Inc., registered in various countries and categories. All characters, events, and institutions depicted herein are fictional. Any similarity between any of the names, characters, persons, events, and/or institutions in this publication to actual names, characters, and persons, whether living or dead, events, and/ or institutions is unintended and purely coincidental. BOOM! Studios does not read or accept unsolicited submissions of ideas, stories, or artwork.

A catalog record of this book is available from OCLC and from the BOOM! Studios website, www.boom-studios.com, on the Librarians Page.

BOOM! Studios, 5670 Wilshire Boulevard, Suite 450, Los Angeles, CA 90036-5679. Printed in China. First Printing. ISBN: 978-1-60886-319-8

THE HYPERNATURALS

WRITTEN BY
DAN ABNETT & ANDY LANNING

ART BY
TOM DERENICK
ANDRES GUINALDO WITH INKS BY BIT

COLORS BY
STEPHEN DOWNER

LETTERS BY
ED DUKESHIRE

COVER BY
FRANCESCO MATTINA

EDITOR
DAFNA PLEBAN

MANAGING EDITOR
BRYCE CARLSON

TRADE DESIGN BY
MIKE LOPEZ

QUANTINUUM CONTENT DESIGNS BY
STEPHANIE GONZAGA
MIKE LOPEZ

CREATED BY
ABNETT, LANNING & WALKER

CHAPTER FOUR

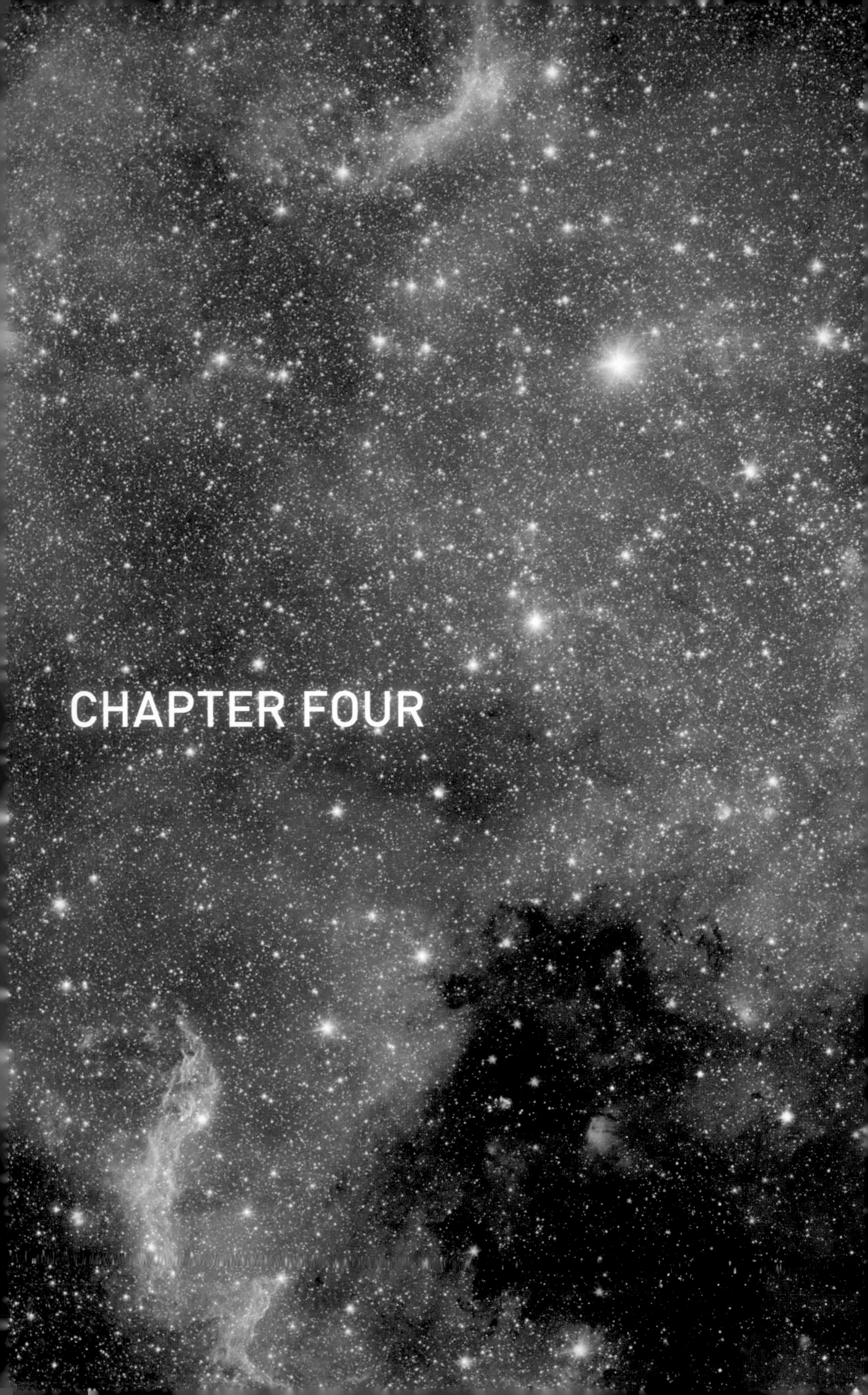

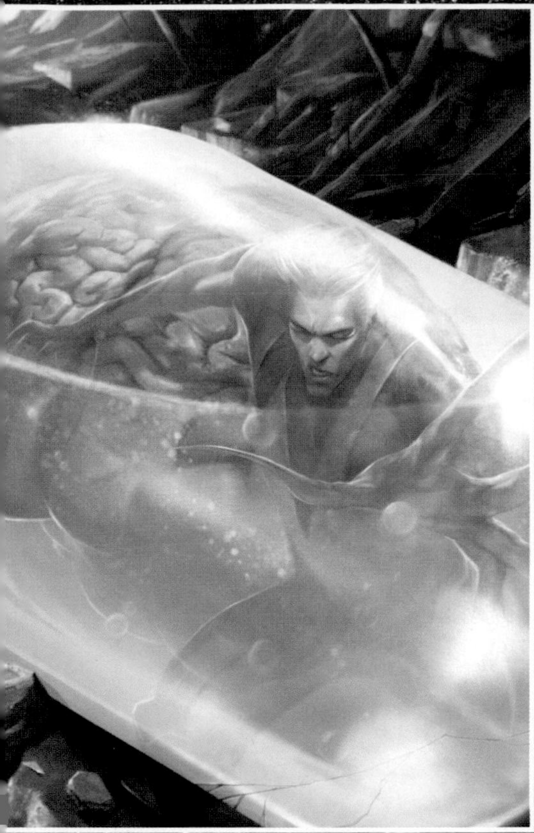

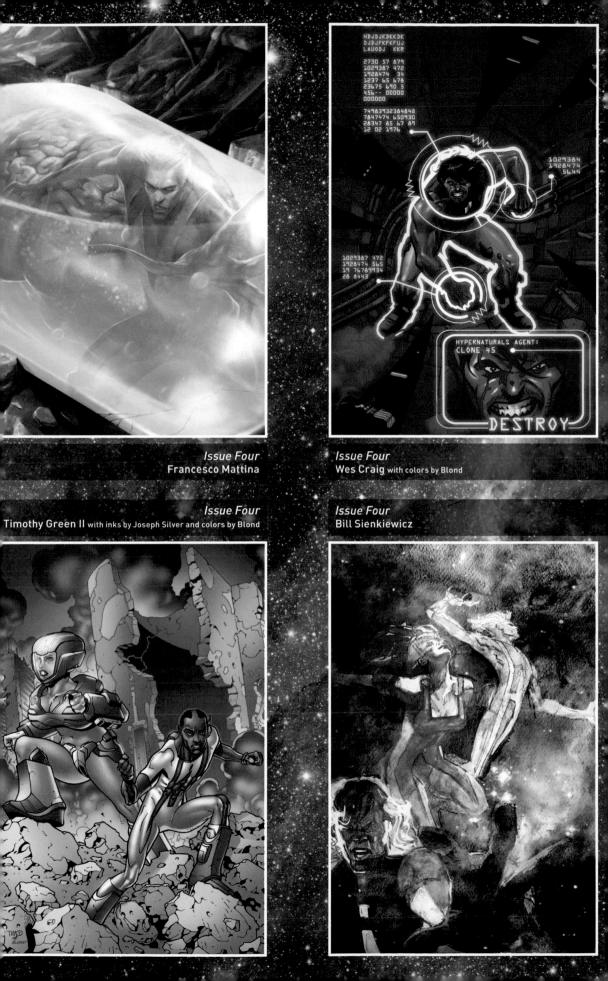

Issue Four
Francesco Mattina

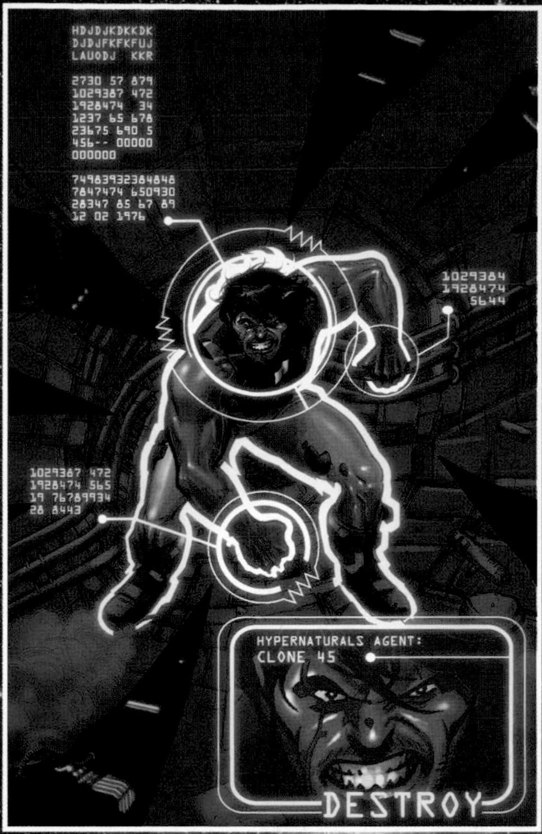
HDJDJKDKKDK
DJDJFKFKFUJ
LAUODJ KKR
2730 57 879
1029387 472
1928474 34
1237 65 678
23675 690 5
456-- 00000
000000
74983932384848
7847474 650930
28347 85 67 89
12 02 1976
1029384
1928474
5644
1029387 472
1928474 565
19 76789934
28 8443
HYPERNATURALS AGENT:
CLONE 45
DESTROY

Issue Four
Wes Craig with colors by Blond

Issue Four
Timothy Green II with inks by Joseph Silver and colors by Blond

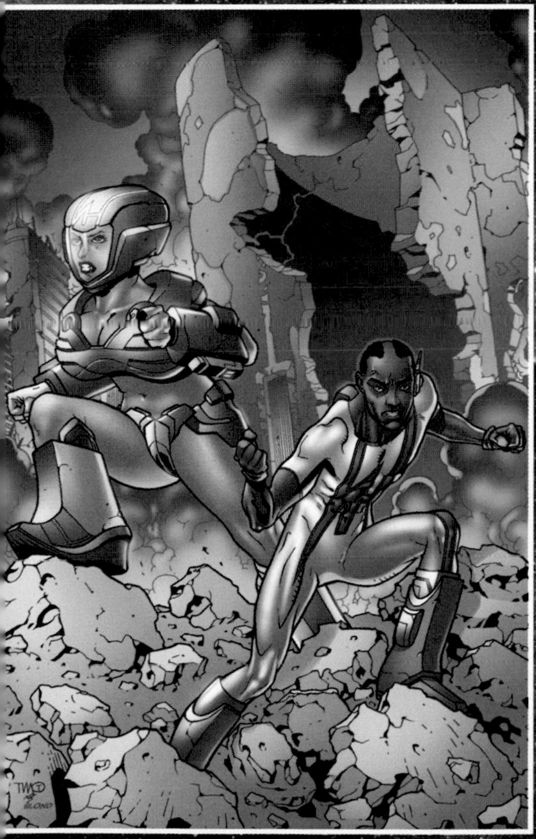

Issue Four
Bill Sienkiewicz

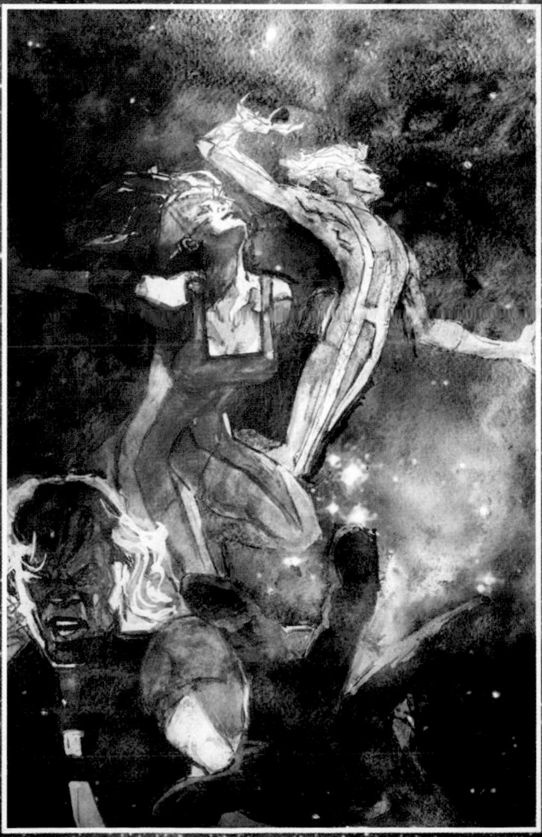

• You have selected Q-Data link.

• It is the 11th of January in the year **100 A.Q.**
- Touch here to select an alternative to the **Anno Quantinuum** calendar system.
- Touch here to load local weather reports for your **current cosmic location.**
- Touch here to access **Q-Data newsflows** from planets near your current cosmic location.
- Touch here for latest **Quantum Trip transit times.**

• Q-Data entry: The Quantinuum

• The Quantinuum is the name for the **human galactic culture,** and also for the **artificial intelligence** that controls its function.

• The Quantinuum was created 100 years ago at the start of the **Nanocene Era.** The Nanocene began when the Quantinuum AI achieved Singularity and refashioned human galactic culture. Succeeding the **Holocene Era,** the Nanocene is the next progression of human evolution and...

(to read this entry in full, touch here)

• You have selected live feed newsflow.

- Cyclonic super-storm hits **22 Hassan**
- **Askala Inc** announces breakthrough new nano-tube process
- **Forvolund AC** to merge with **Systemware,** jobs may suffer
- **Kelman** and **Falk** clinch **aeroball** doubles title in dramatic final
- **AI Law** starlet Allie Albers mutates at awards ceremony, doctors say no cause for concern
- Public still awaiting statement from Hypernaturals Central concerning fate of the Centennial Year Iteration of the Team, apparently lost during an emergency response mission to 28 Kosov. Concern remains high

• The Hypernaturals are the Quantinuum's foremost champions. Famous across the entirety of human galactic culture, the team members are selected on the basis of their hypernatural powers and their strength of character, and serve for five-year terms. In honor of the start of the twenty-first term, the line-up of the team's so-called "Centennial Year Iteration" has recently been announced amid huge publicity and--

...BREAKING NEWS... unconfirmed sources report the entire Hypernatural Team has vanished on its inaugural mission to 28 Kosov... according to a spokesperson at Hypernaturals Central, San Diego, a special reserve formation of Hypernaturals, including now retired team members Bewilder and Thinkwell from the classic "Nineteenth Tour" line-up, has investigated the site on 28 Kosov... rumors of a survivor have circulated... an unnamed source says other avenues of inquiry are being followed regarding the event...

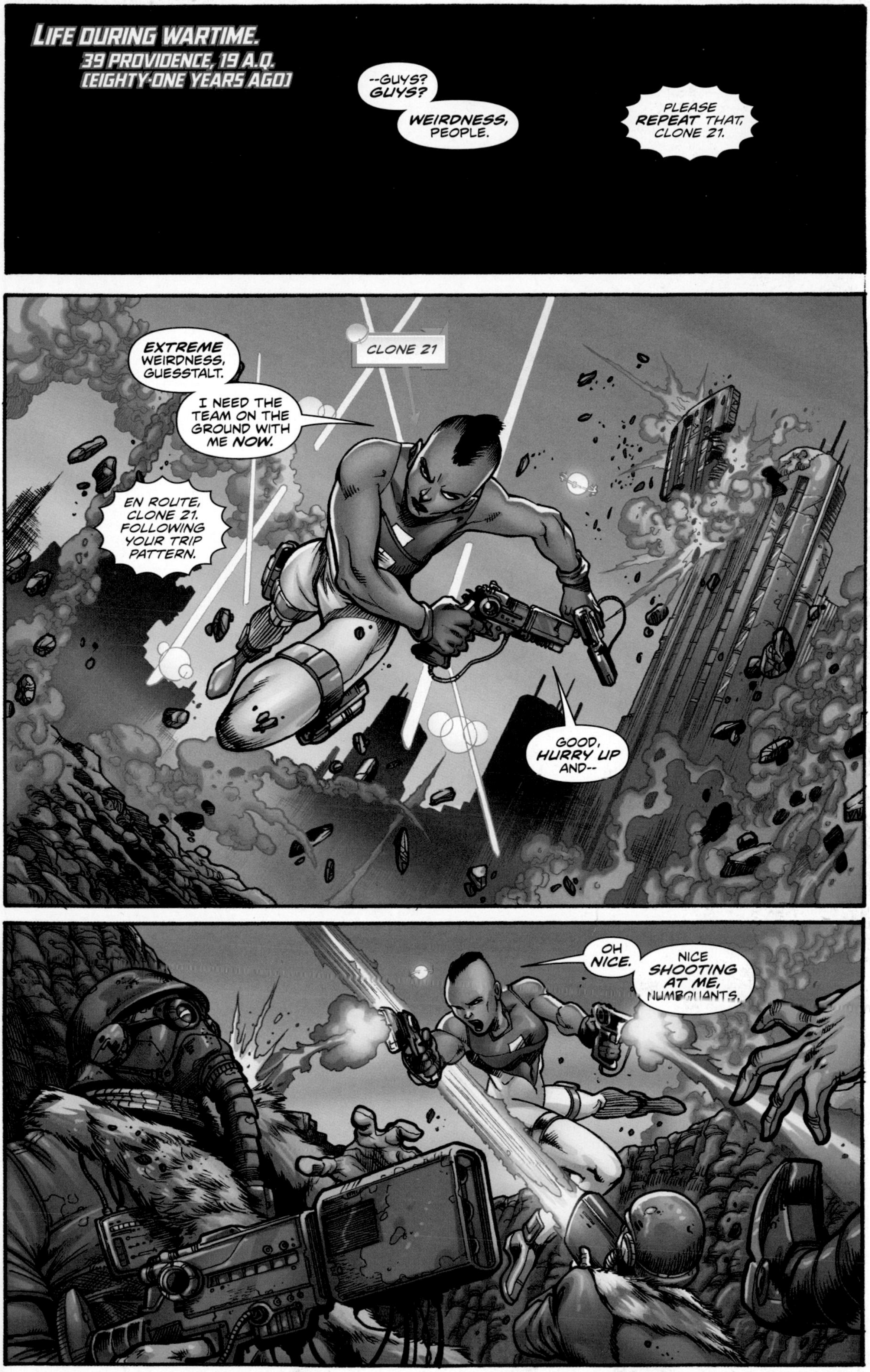
LIFE DURING WARTIME.
39 PROVIDENCE, 19 A.Q.
[EIGHTY-ONE YEARS AGO]
--GUYS? GUYS?
WEIRDNESS, PEOPLE.
PLEASE REPEAT THAT, CLONE 21.
CLONE 21
EXTREME WEIRDNESS, GUESSTALT.
I NEED THE TEAM ON THE GROUND WITH ME NOW.
EN ROUTE, CLONE 21. FOLLOWING YOUR TRIP PATTERN.
GOOD, HURRY UP AND--
OH NICE.
NICE SHOOTING AT ME, NUMBQUANTS.

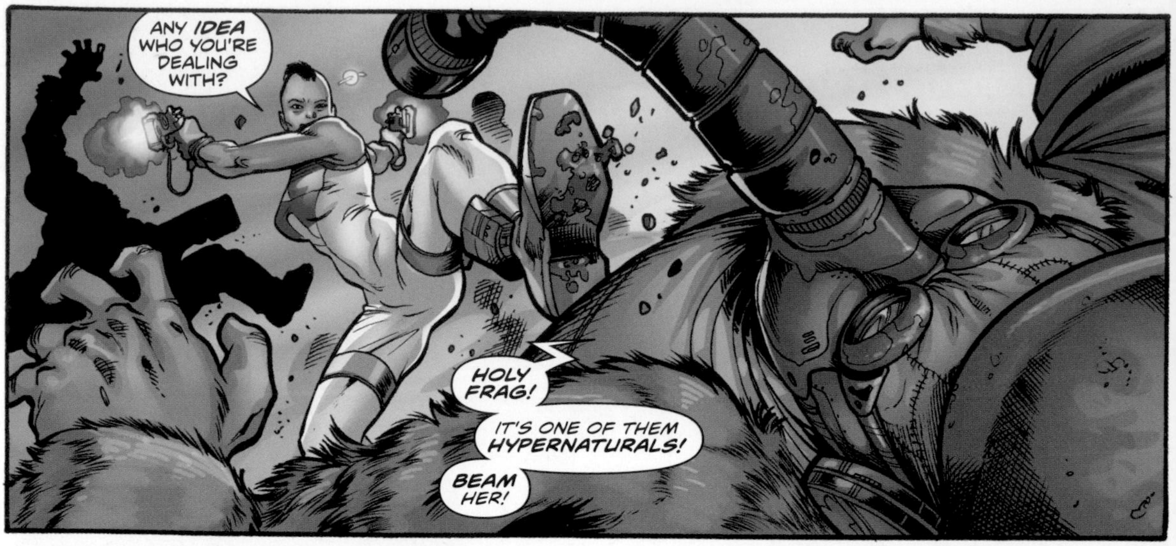
ANY IDEA WHO YOU'RE DEALING WITH?
HOLY FRAG!
IT'S ONE OF THEM HYPERNATURALS!
BEAM HER!

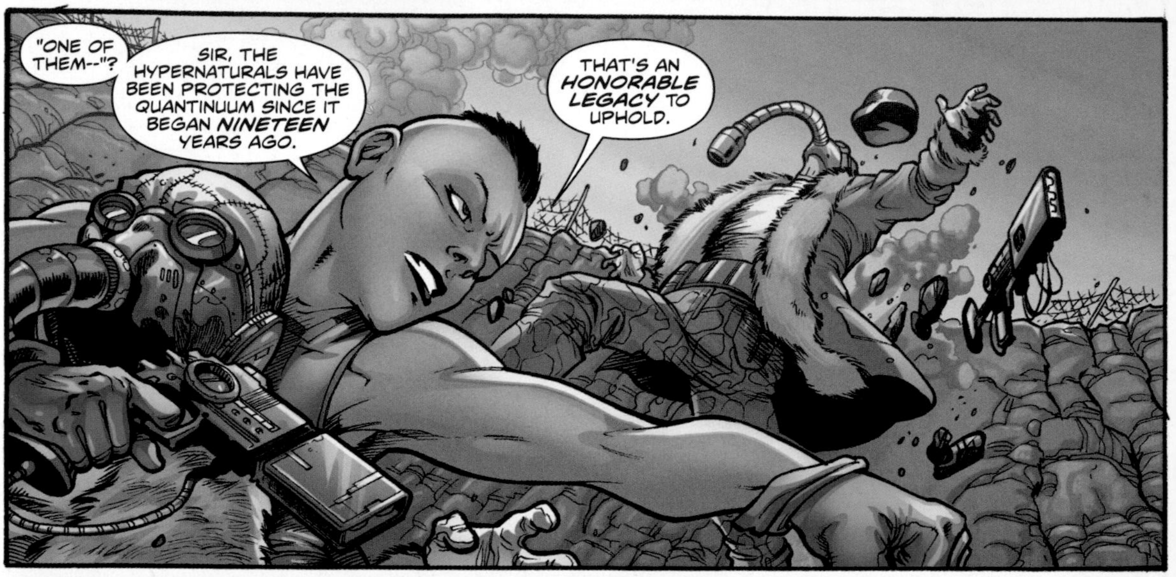
"ONE OF THEM--"?
SIR, THE HYPERNATURALS HAVE BEEN PROTECTING THE QUANTINUUM SINCE IT BEGAN NINETEEN YEARS AGO.
THAT'S AN HONORABLE LEGACY TO UPHOLD.

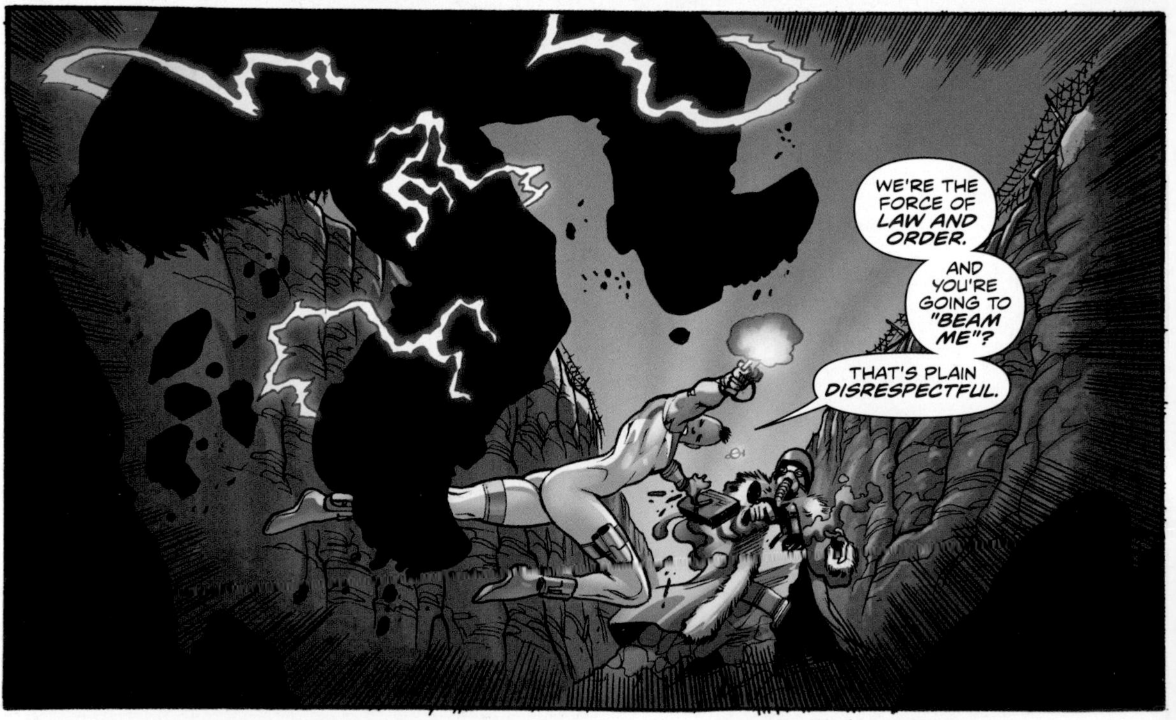
WE'RE THE FORCE OF LAW AND ORDER.
AND YOU'RE GOING TO "BEAM ME"?
THAT'S PLAIN DISRESPECTFUL.

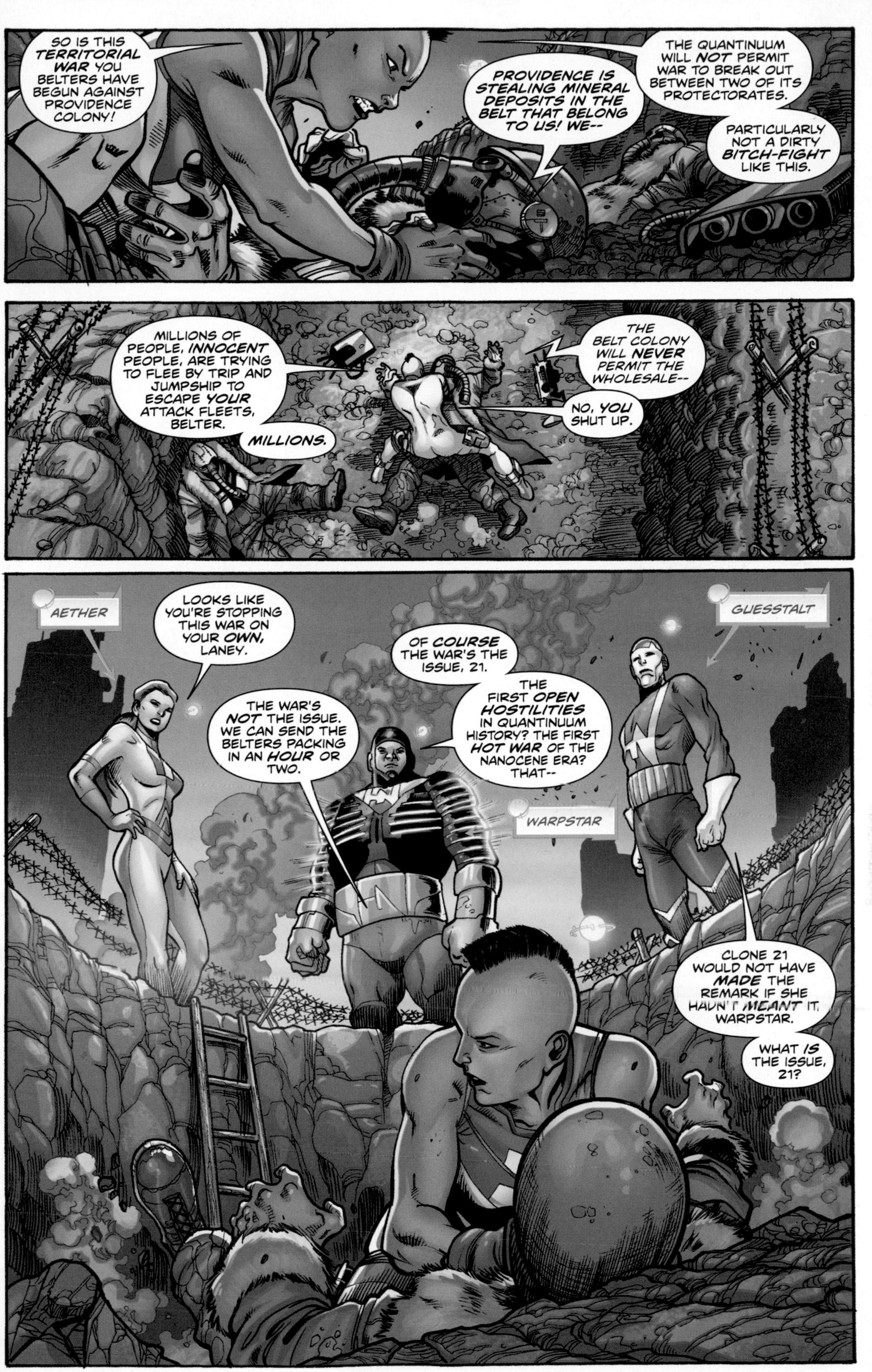
SO IS THIS TERRITORIAL WAR YOU BELTERS HAVE BEGUN AGAINST PROVIDENCE COLONY!
PROVIDENCE IS STEALING MINERAL DEPOSITS IN THE BELT THAT BELONG TO US! WE--
THE QUANTINUUM WILL NOT PERMIT WAR TO BREAK OUT BETWEEN TWO OF ITS PROTECTORATES.
PARTICULARLY NOT A DIRTY BITCH-FIGHT LIKE THIS.
MILLIONS OF PEOPLE, INNOCENT PEOPLE, ARE TRYING TO FLEE BY TRIP AND JUMPSHIP TO ESCAPE YOUR ATTACK FLEETS, BELTER.
MILLIONS.
THE BELT COLONY WILL NEVER PERMIT THE WHOLESALE--
NO, YOU SHUT UP.
AETHER
LOOKS LIKE YOU'RE STOPPING THIS WAR ON YOUR OWN, LANEY.
GUESSTALT
WARPSTAR
THE WAR'S NOT THE ISSUE. WE CAN SEND THE BELTERS PACKING IN AN HOUR OR TWO.
OF COURSE THE WAR'S THE ISSUE, 21.
THE FIRST OPEN HOSTILITIES IN QUANTINUUM HISTORY? THE FIRST HOT WAR OF THE NANOCENE ERA? THAT--
CLONE 21 WOULD NOT HAVE MADE THE REMARK IF SHE HADN'T MEANT IT, WARPSTAR.
WHAT IS THE ISSUE, 21?

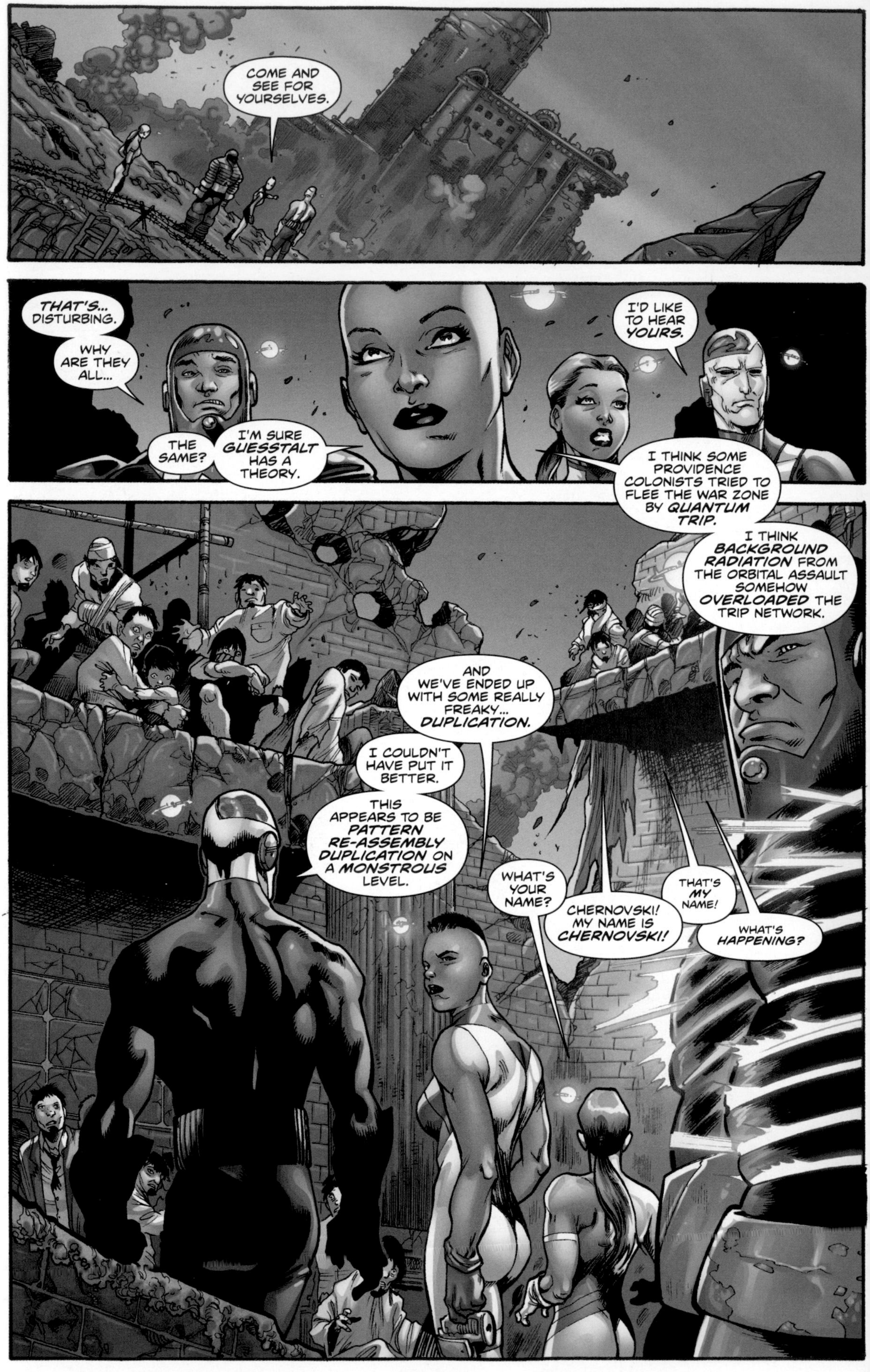
COME AND SEE FOR YOURSELVES.
THAT'S... DISTURBING.
WHY ARE THEY ALL...
THE SAME?
I'M SURE GUESSTALT HAS A THEORY.
I'D LIKE TO HEAR YOURS.
I THINK SOME PROVIDENCE COLONISTS TRIED TO FLEE THE WAR ZONE BY QUANTUM TRIP.
I THINK BACKGROUND RADIATION FROM THE ORBITAL ASSAULT SOMEHOW OVERLOADED THE TRIP NETWORK.
AND WE'VE ENDED UP WITH SOME REALLY FREAKY... DUPLICATION.
I COULDN'T HAVE PUT IT BETTER.
THIS APPEARS TO BE PATTERN RE-ASSEMBLY DUPLICATION ON A MONSTROUS LEVEL.
WHAT'S YOUR NAME?
CHERNOVSKI! MY NAME IS CHERNOVSKI!
THAT'S MY NAME!
WHAT'S HAPPENING?

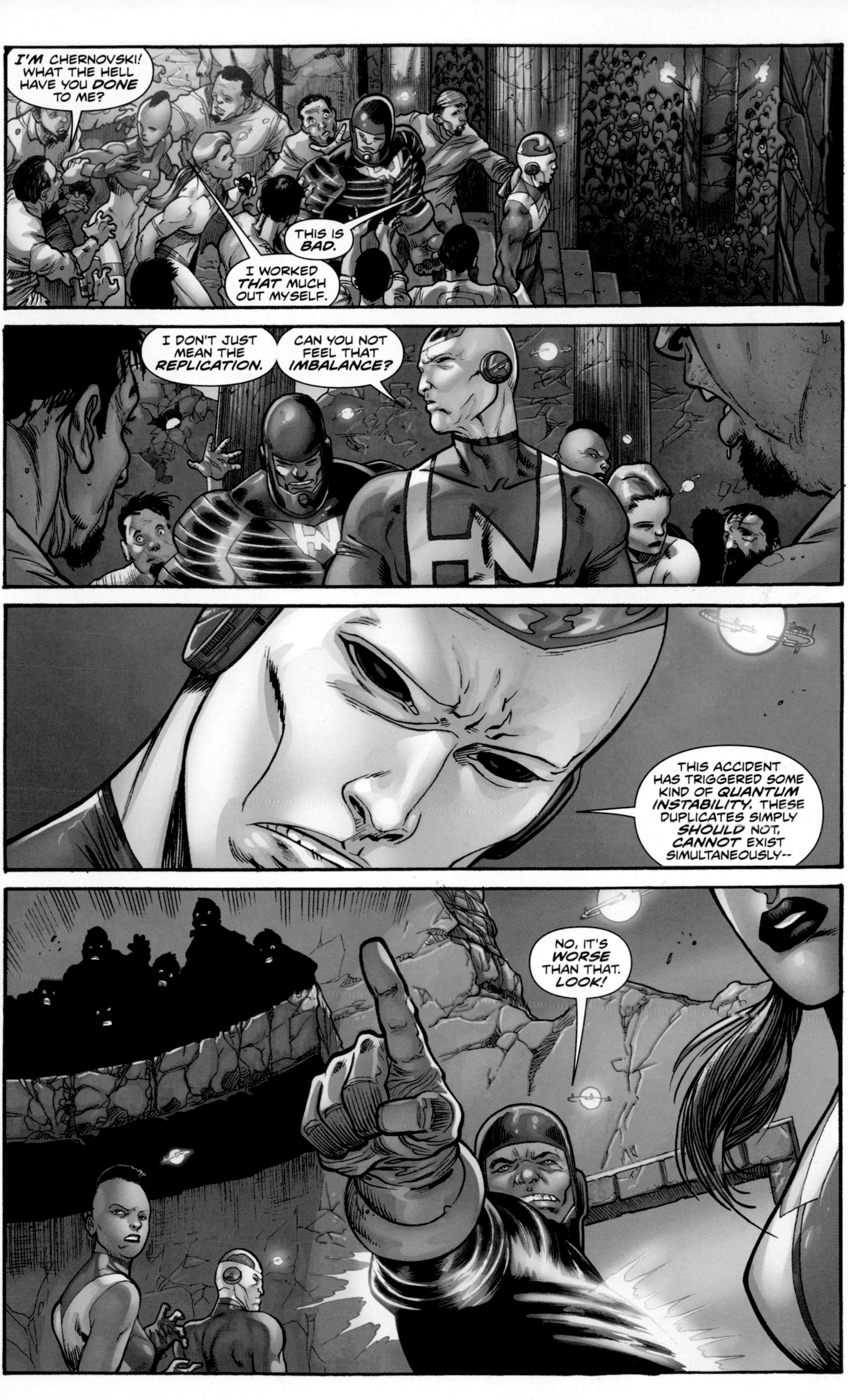

I'M CHERNOVSKI! WHAT THE HELL HAVE YOU DONE TO ME?
THIS IS BAD.
I WORKED THAT MUCH OUT MYSELF.
I DON'T JUST MEAN THE REPLICATION.
CAN YOU NOT FEEL THAT IMBALANCE?
THIS ACCIDENT HAS TRIGGERED SOME KIND OF QUANTUM INSTABILITY. THESE DUPLICATES SIMPLY SHOULD NOT, CANNOT EXIST SIMULTANEOUSLY--
NO, IT'S WORSE THAN THAT. LOOK!

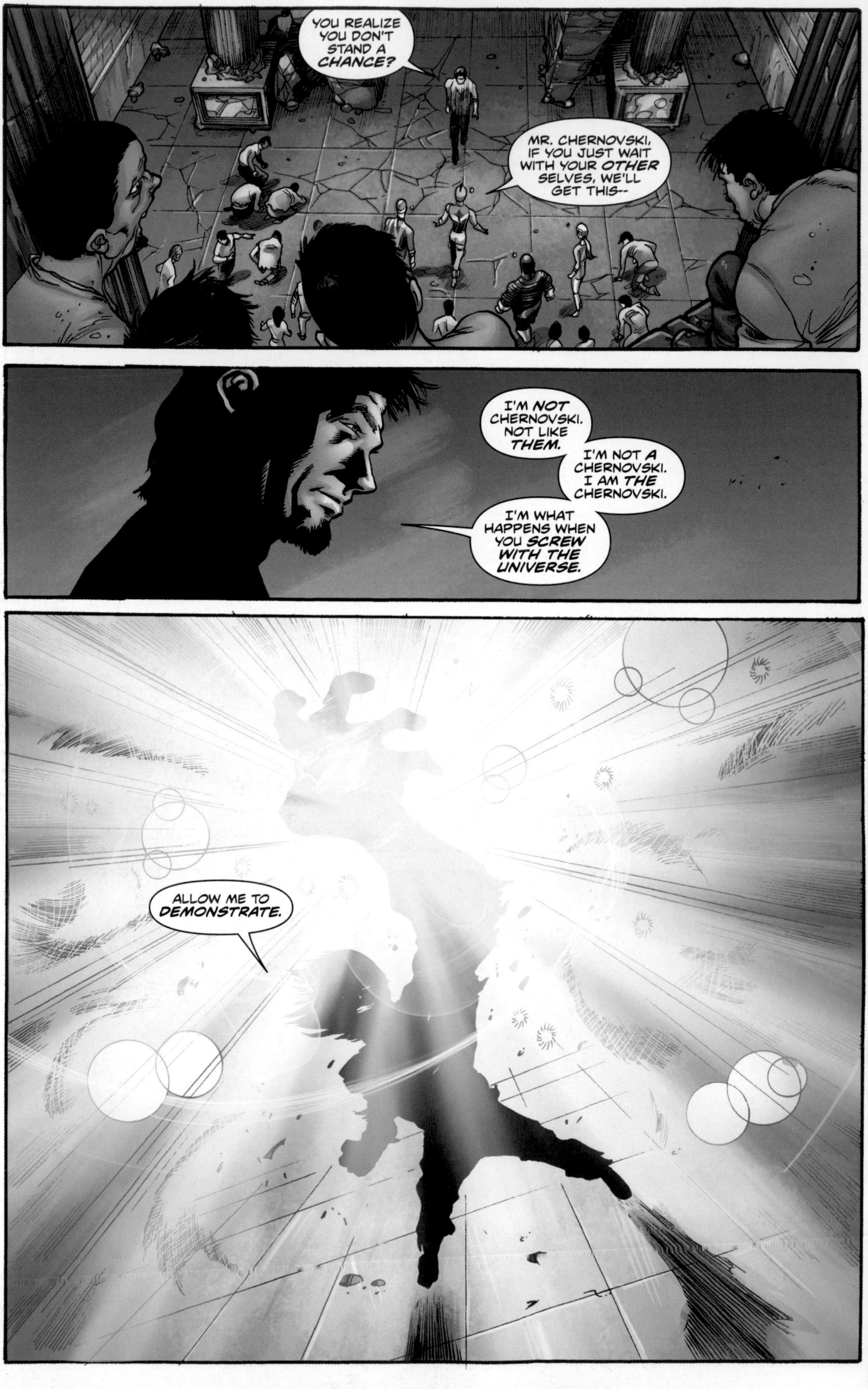
YOU REALIZE YOU DON'T STAND A CHANCE?
MR. CHERNOVSKI, IF YOU JUST WAIT WITH YOUR OTHER SELVES, WE'LL GET THIS--
I'M NOT CHERNOVSKI. NOT LIKE THEM.
I'M NOT A CHERNOVSKI. I AM THE CHERNOVSKI.
I'M WHAT HAPPENS WHEN YOU SCREW WITH THE UNIVERSE.
ALLOW ME TO DEMONSTRATE.

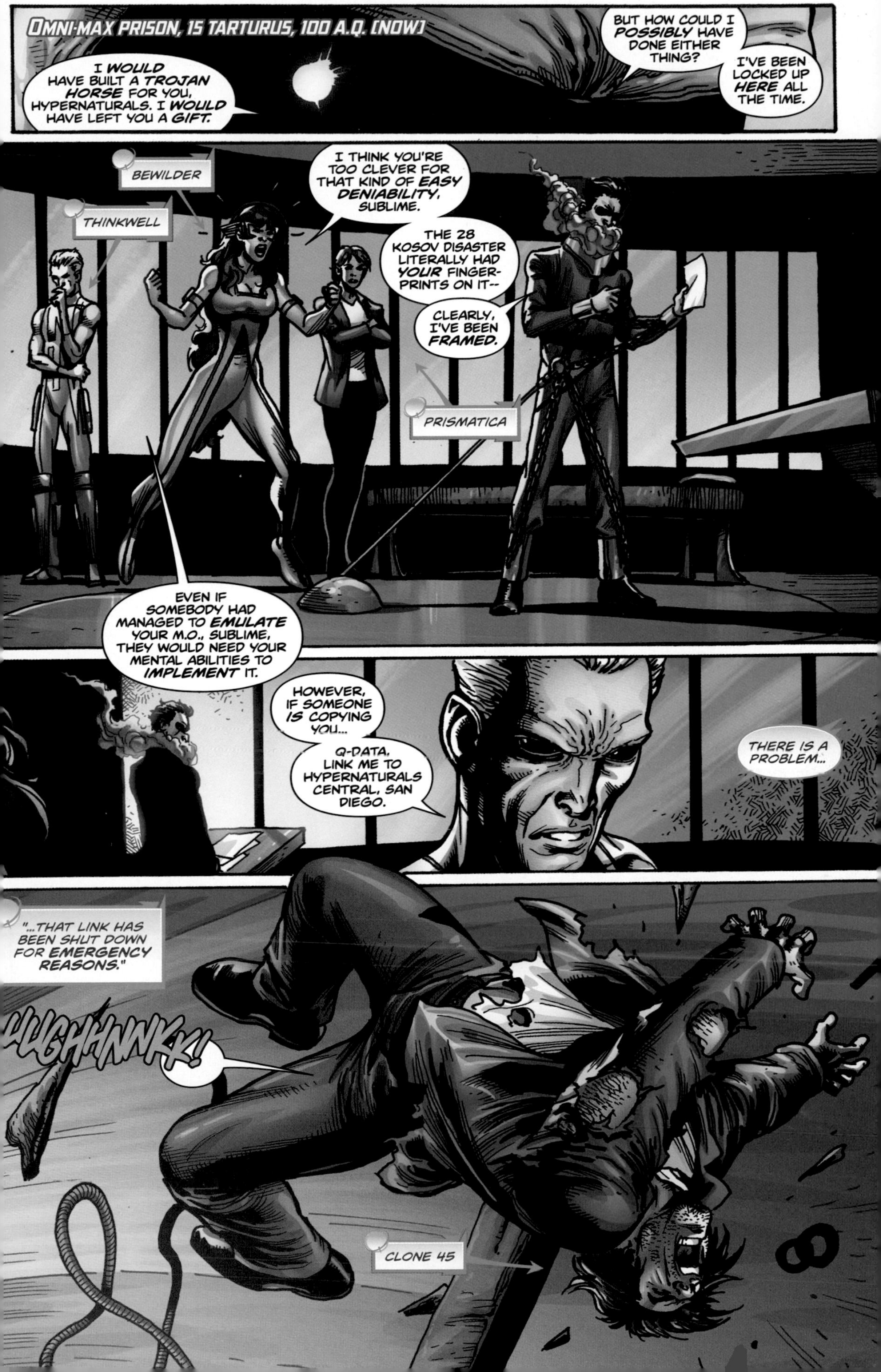

OMNI-MAX PRISON, 15 TARTURUS, 100 A.Q. [NOW]
I WOULD HAVE BUILT A TROJAN HORSE FOR YOU, HYPERNATURALS. I WOULD HAVE LEFT YOU A GIFT.
BUT HOW COULD I POSSIBLY HAVE DONE EITHER THING?
I'VE BEEN LOCKED UP HERE ALL THE TIME.
BEWILDER
THINKWELL
I THINK YOU'RE TOO CLEVER FOR THAT KIND OF EASY DENIABILITY, SUBLIME.
THE 28 KOSOV DISASTER LITERALLY HAD YOUR FINGER-PRINTS ON IT--
CLEARLY, I'VE BEEN FRAMED.
PRISMATICA
EVEN IF SOMEBODY HAD MANAGED TO EMULATE YOUR M.O., SUBLIME, THEY WOULD NEED YOUR MENTAL ABILITIES TO IMPLEMENT IT.
HOWEVER, IF SOMEONE IS COPYING YOU...
Q-DATA, LINK ME TO HYPERNATURALS CENTRAL, SAN DIEGO.
THERE IS A PROBLEM...
"...THAT LINK HAS BEEN SHUT DOWN FOR EMERGENCY REASONS."
UUGHHNNKK!
CLONE 45

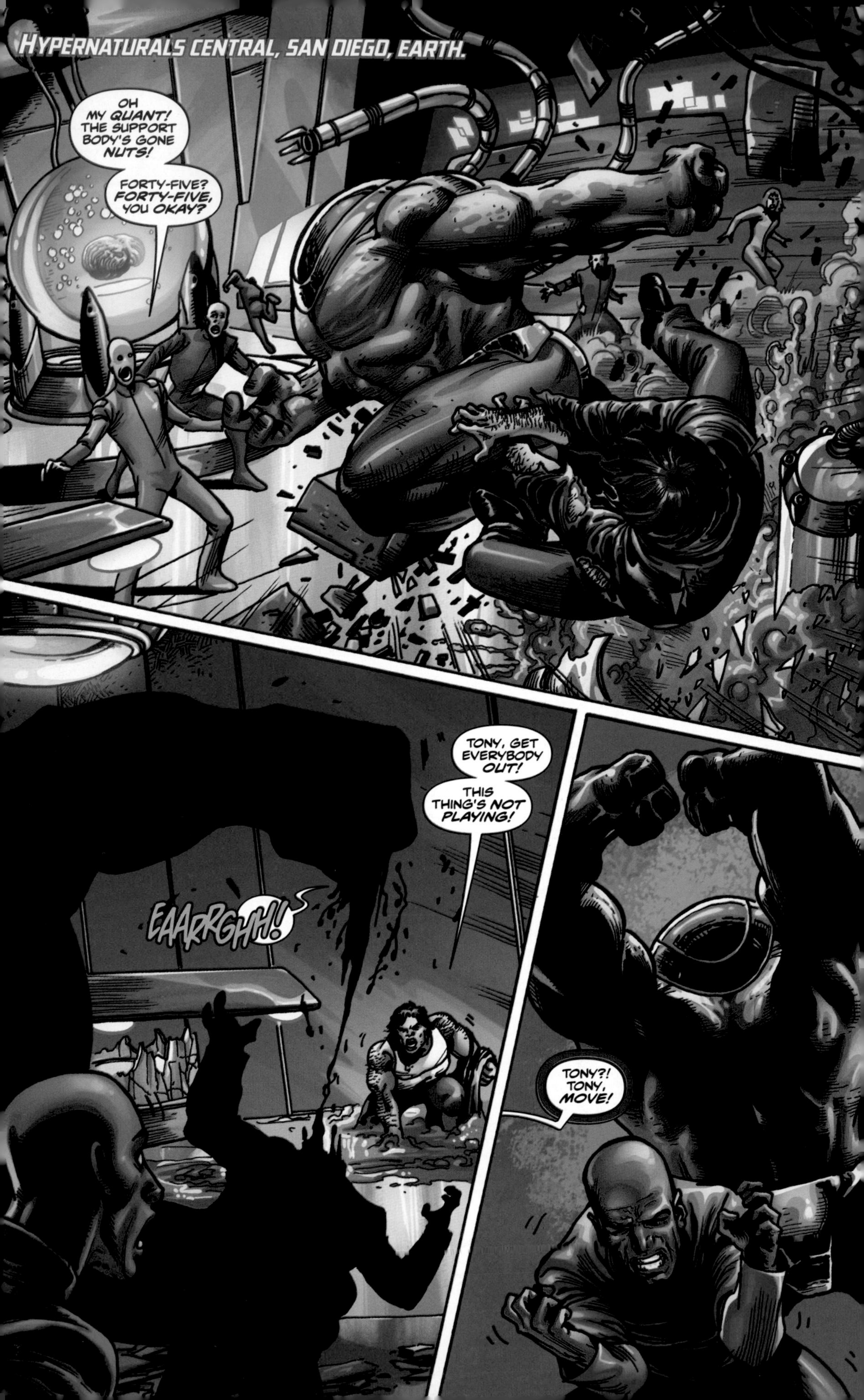
HYPERNATURALS CENTRAL, SAN DIEGO, EARTH.
OH MY QUANT! THE SUPPORT BODY'S GONE NUTS!
FORTY-FIVE? FORTY-FIVE, YOU OKAY?
TONY, GET EVERYBODY OUT!
THIS THING'S NOT PLAYING!
EAARRGHH!
TONY?! TONY, MOVE!

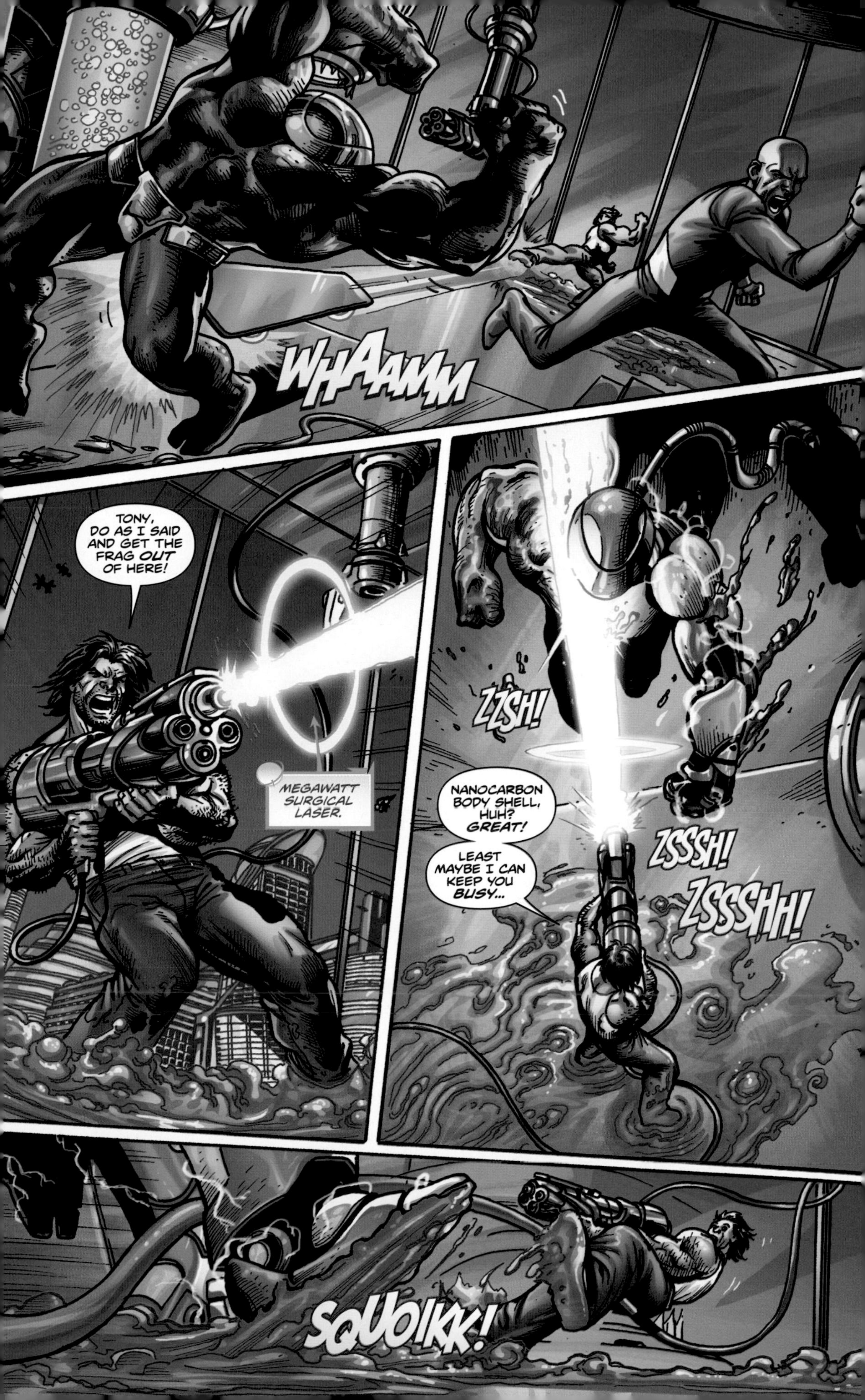
WHAAMM
TONY, DO AS I SAID AND GET THE FRAG *OUT* OF HERE!
MEGAWATT SURGICAL LASER.
ZZSH!
NANOCARBON BODY SHELL, HUH? *GREAT!*
LEAST MAYBE I CAN KEEP YOU *BUSY*...
ZSSSH!
ZSSSHH!
SQUOIKK!

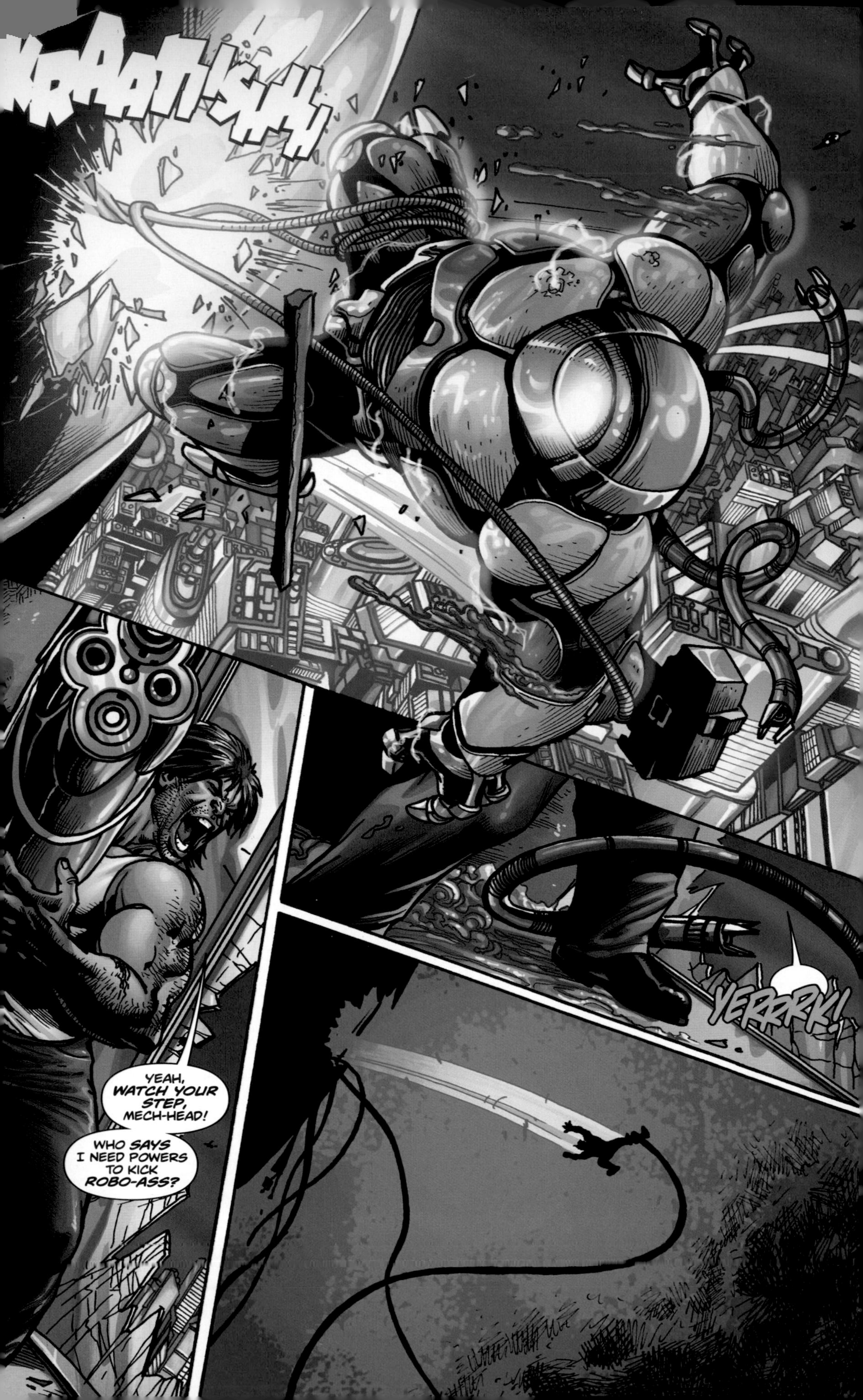
KRAAASHKKH
YERRRK!
YEAH, WATCH YOUR STEP, MECH-HEAD!
WHO SAYS I NEED POWERS TO KICK ROBO-ASS?

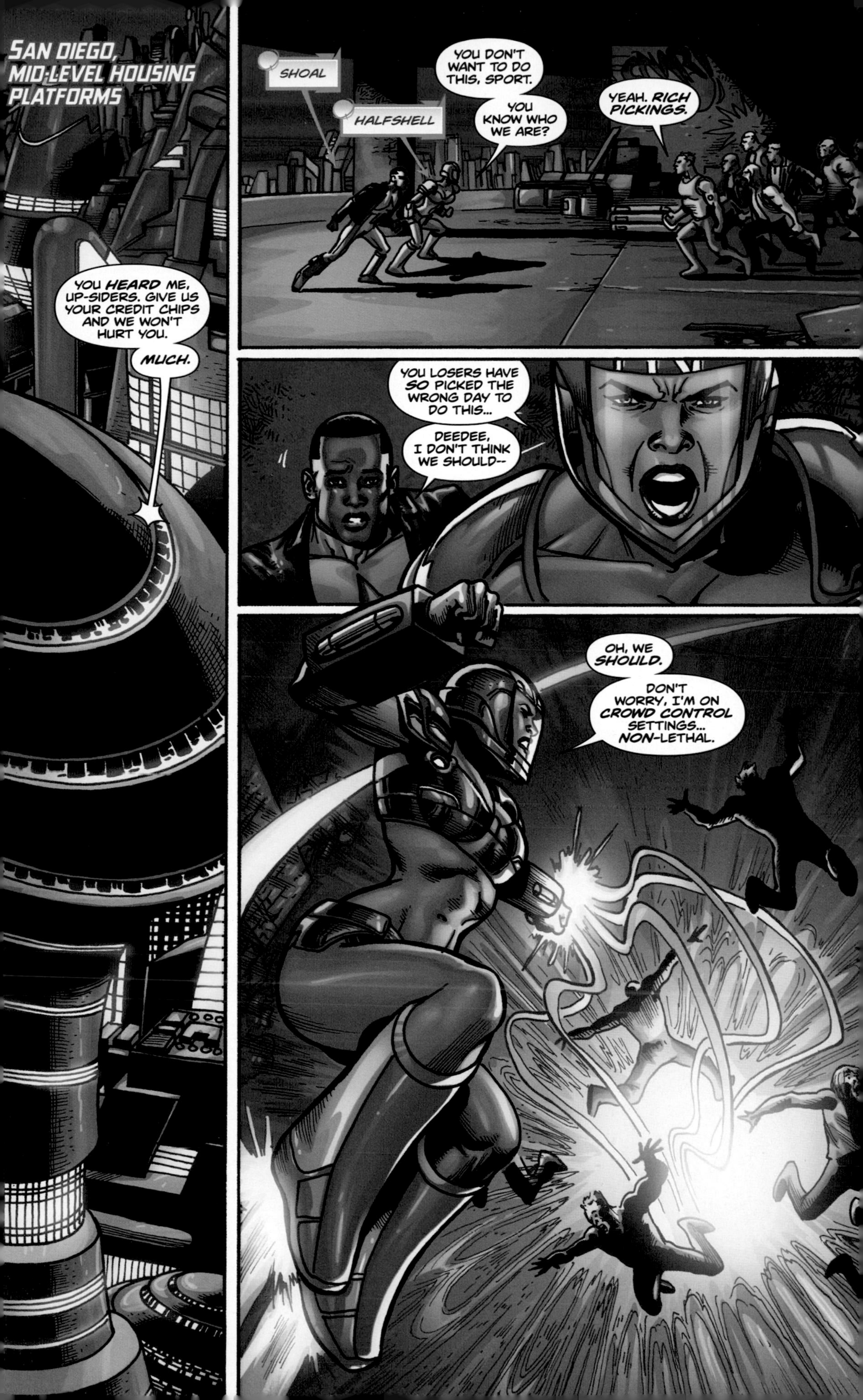
SAN DIEGO, MID-LEVEL HOUSING PLATFORMS
YOU HEARD ME, UP-SIDERS. GIVE US YOUR CREDIT CHIPS AND WE WON'T HURT YOU.
MUCH.
SHOAL
HALFSHELL
YOU DON'T WANT TO DO THIS, SPORT.
YOU KNOW WHO WE ARE?
YEAH. RICH PICKINGS.
YOU LOSERS HAVE SO PICKED THE WRONG DAY TO DO THIS...
DEEDEE, I DON'T THINK WE SHOULD--
OH, WE SHOULD.
DON'T WORRY, I'M ON CROWD CONTROL SETTINGS... NON-LETHAL.

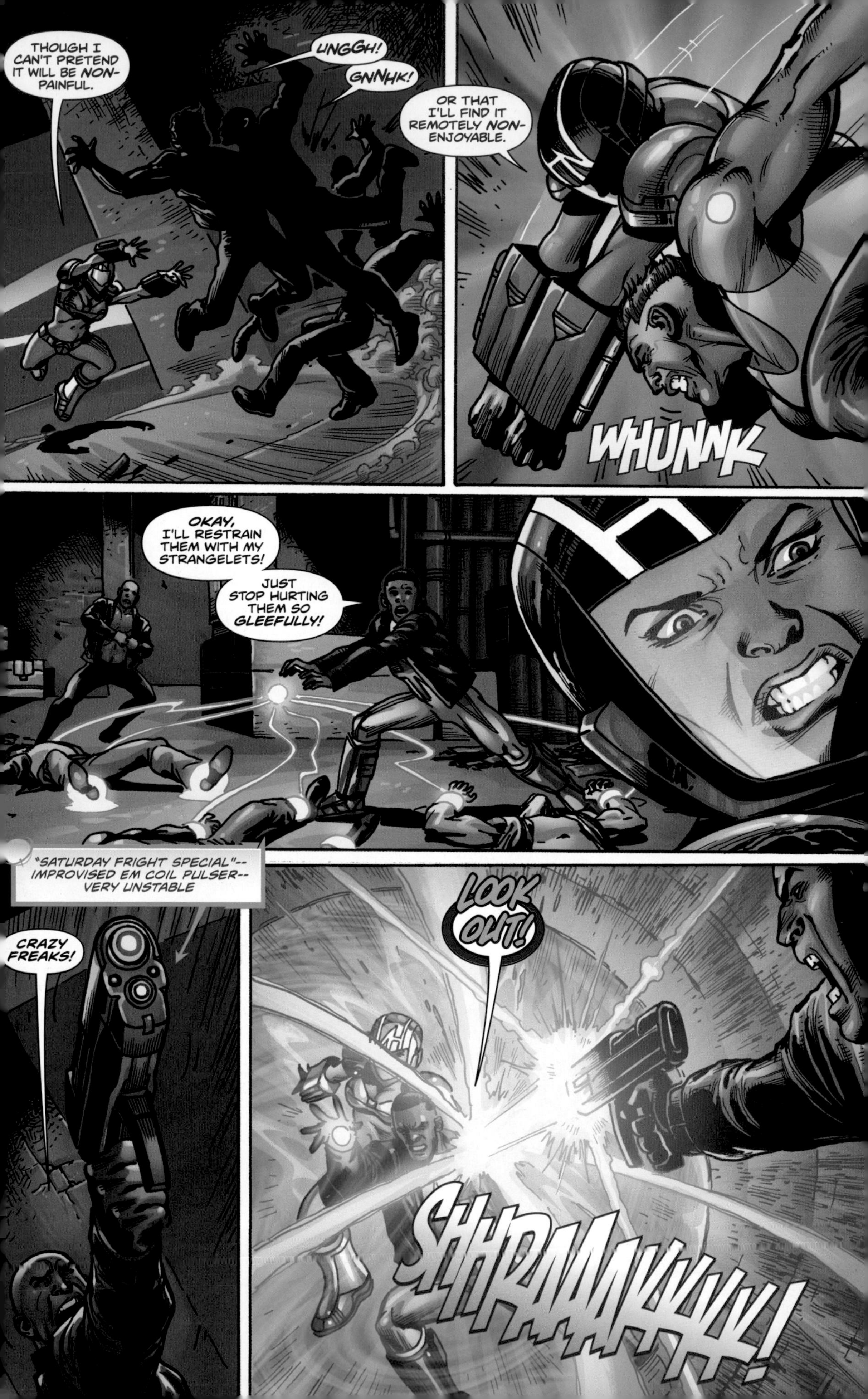
THOUGH I CAN'T PRETEND IT WILL BE NON-PAINFUL.
UNGGH!
GNNHK!
OR THAT I'LL FIND IT REMOTELY NON-ENJOYABLE.
WHUNNK
OKAY, I'LL RESTRAIN THEM WITH MY STRANGELETS!
JUST STOP HURTING THEM SO GLEEFULLY!
"SATURDAY FRIGHT SPECIAL"-- IMPROVISED EM COIL PULSER-- VERY UNSTABLE
CRAZY FREAKS!
LOOK OUT!
SHRAAKKKK!

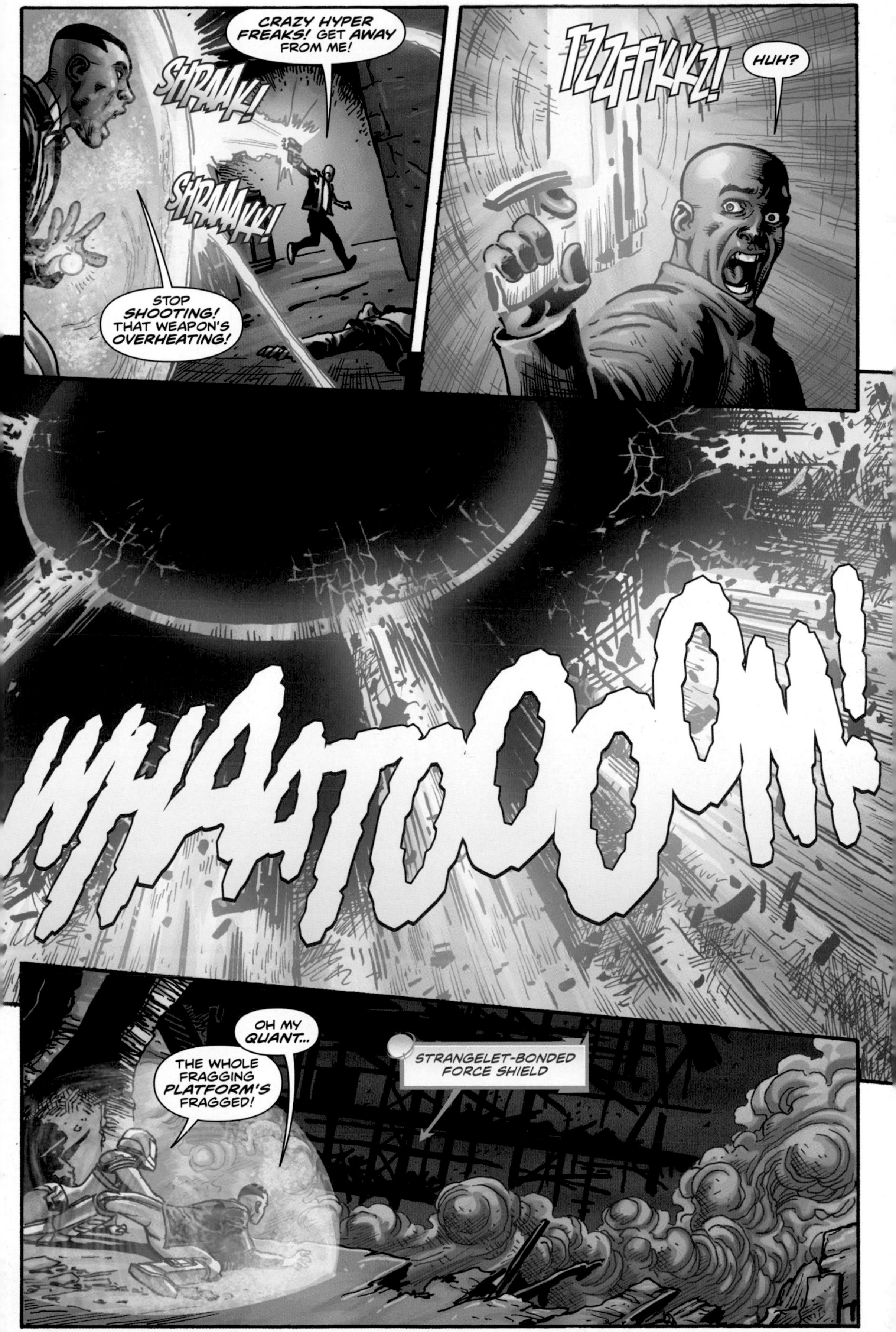
CRAZY HYPER FREAKS! GET AWAY FROM ME!
SHRAAK!
SHRAAAKK!
STOP SHOOTING! THAT WEAPON'S OVERHEATING!
TZZFFKKZ!
HUH?
WHATOOOM!
OH MY QUANT...
THE WHOLE FRAGGING PLATFORM'S FRAGGED!
STRANGELET-BONDED FORCE SHIELD

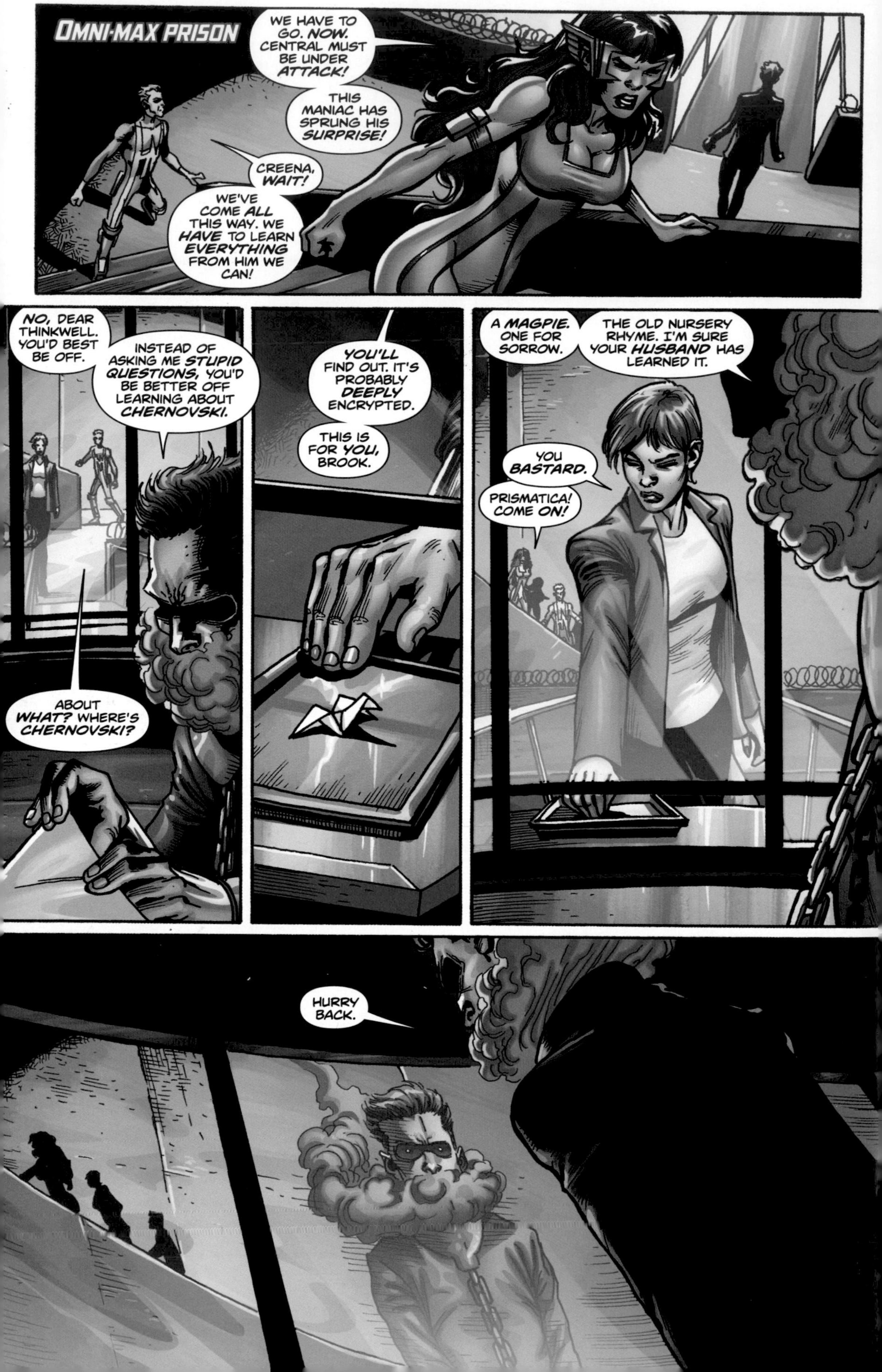
OMNI-MAX PRISON
WE HAVE TO GO. NOW. CENTRAL MUST BE UNDER ATTACK!
THIS MANIAC HAS SPRUNG HIS SURPRISE!
CREENA, WAIT!
WE'VE COME ALL THIS WAY. WE HAVE TO LEARN EVERYTHING FROM HIM WE CAN!
NO, DEAR THINKWELL. YOU'D BEST BE OFF.
INSTEAD OF ASKING ME STUPID QUESTIONS, YOU'D BE BETTER OFF LEARNING ABOUT CHERNOVSKI.
ABOUT WHAT? WHERE'S CHERNOVSKI?
YOU'LL FIND OUT. IT'S PROBABLY DEEPLY ENCRYPTED.
THIS IS FOR YOU, BROOK.
A MAGPIE. ONE FOR SORROW.
THE OLD NURSERY RHYME. I'M SURE YOUR HUSBAND HAS LEARNED IT.
YOU BASTARD.
PRISMATICA! COME ON!
HURRY BACK.

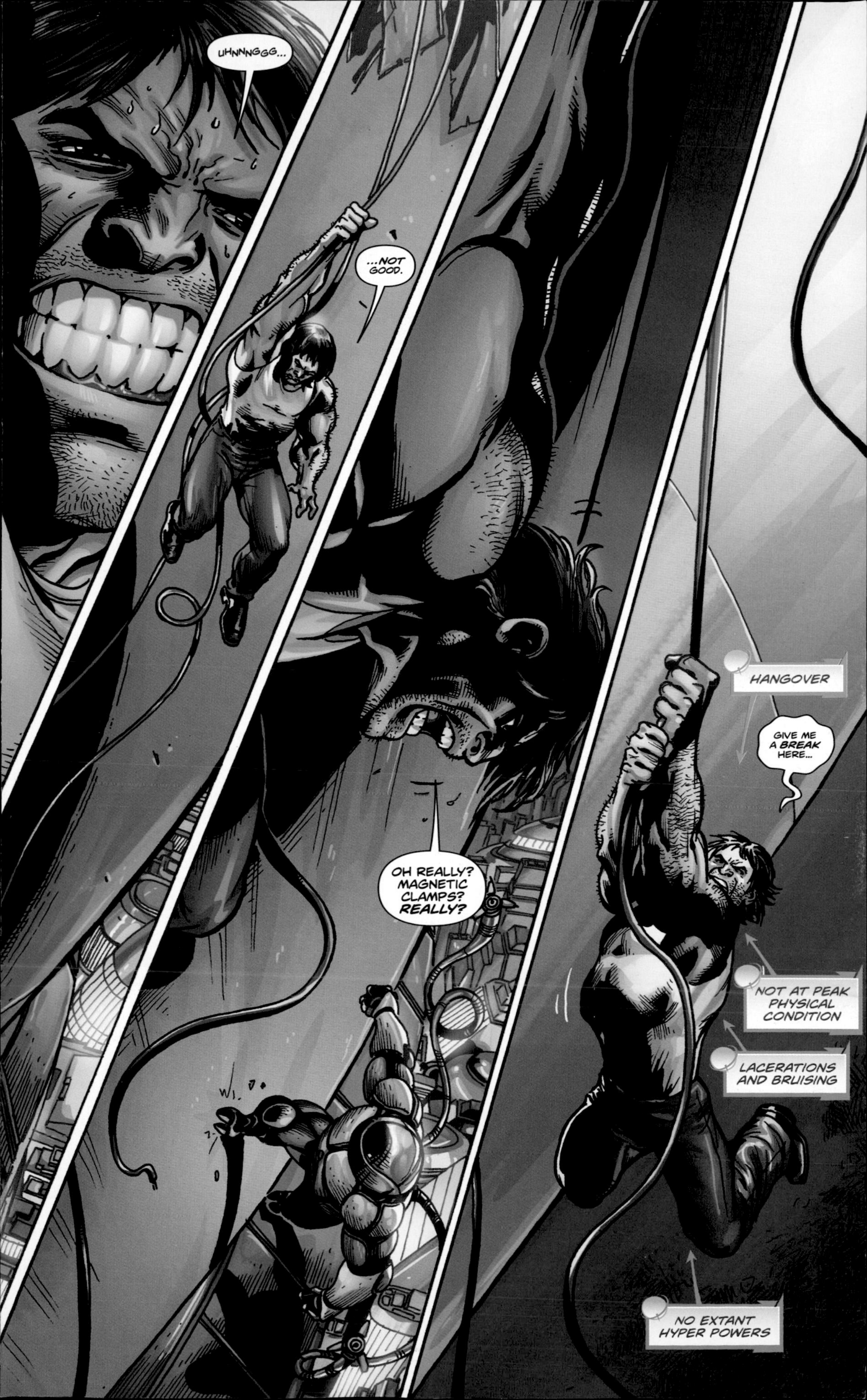
UHNNNGGG...
...NOT GOOD.
OH REALLY? MAGNETIC CLAMPS? REALLY?
HANGOVER
GIVE ME A BREAK HERE...
NOT AT PEAK PHYSICAL CONDITION
LACERATIONS AND BRUISING
NO EXTANT HYPER POWERS

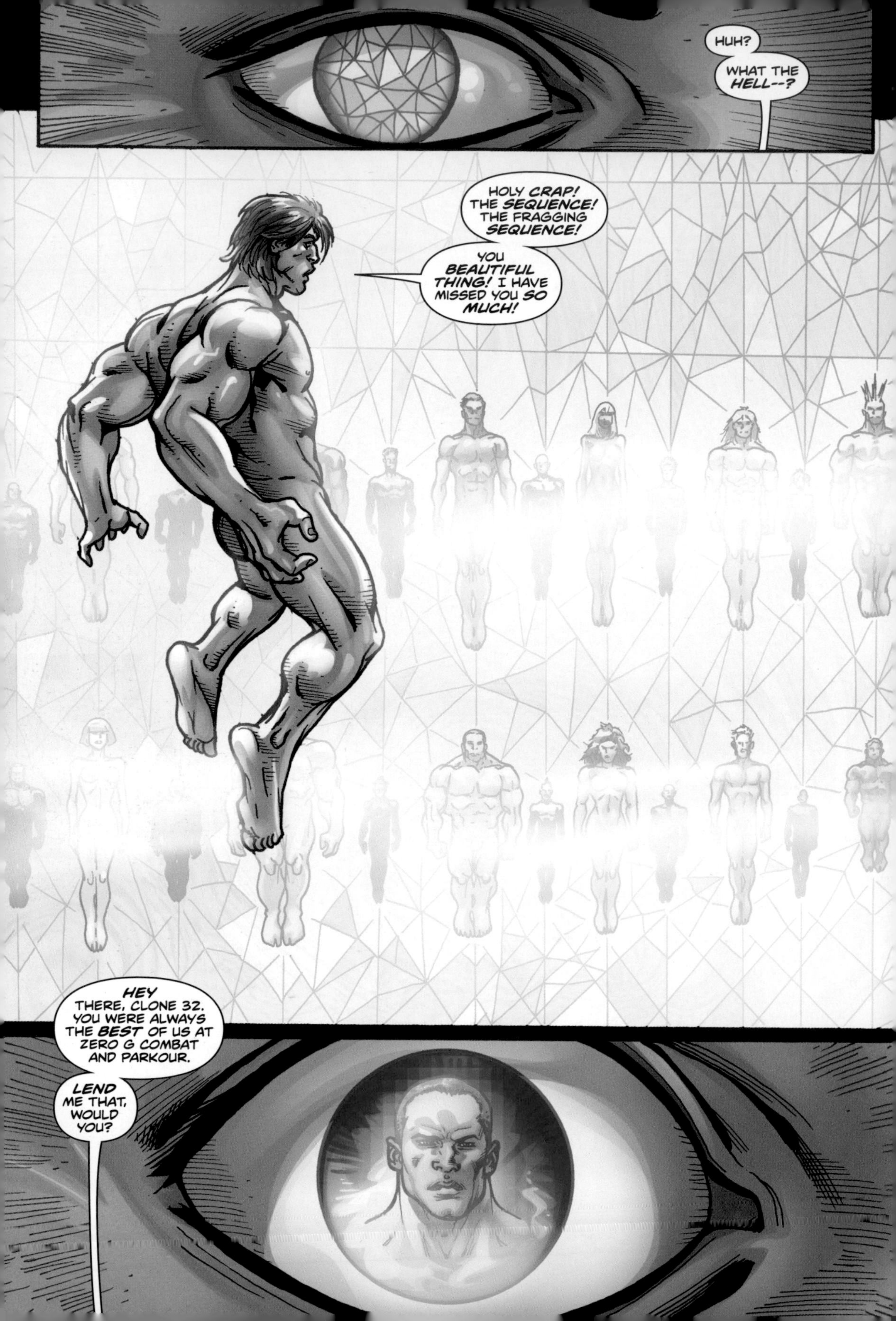
HUH?
WHAT THE HELL--?
HOLY CRAP! THE SEQUENCE! THE FRAGGING SEQUENCE!
YOU BEAUTIFUL THING! I HAVE MISSED YOU SO MUCH!
HEY THERE, CLONE 32. YOU WERE ALWAYS THE BEST OF US AT ZERO G COMBAT AND PARKOUR.
LEND ME THAT, WOULD YOU?

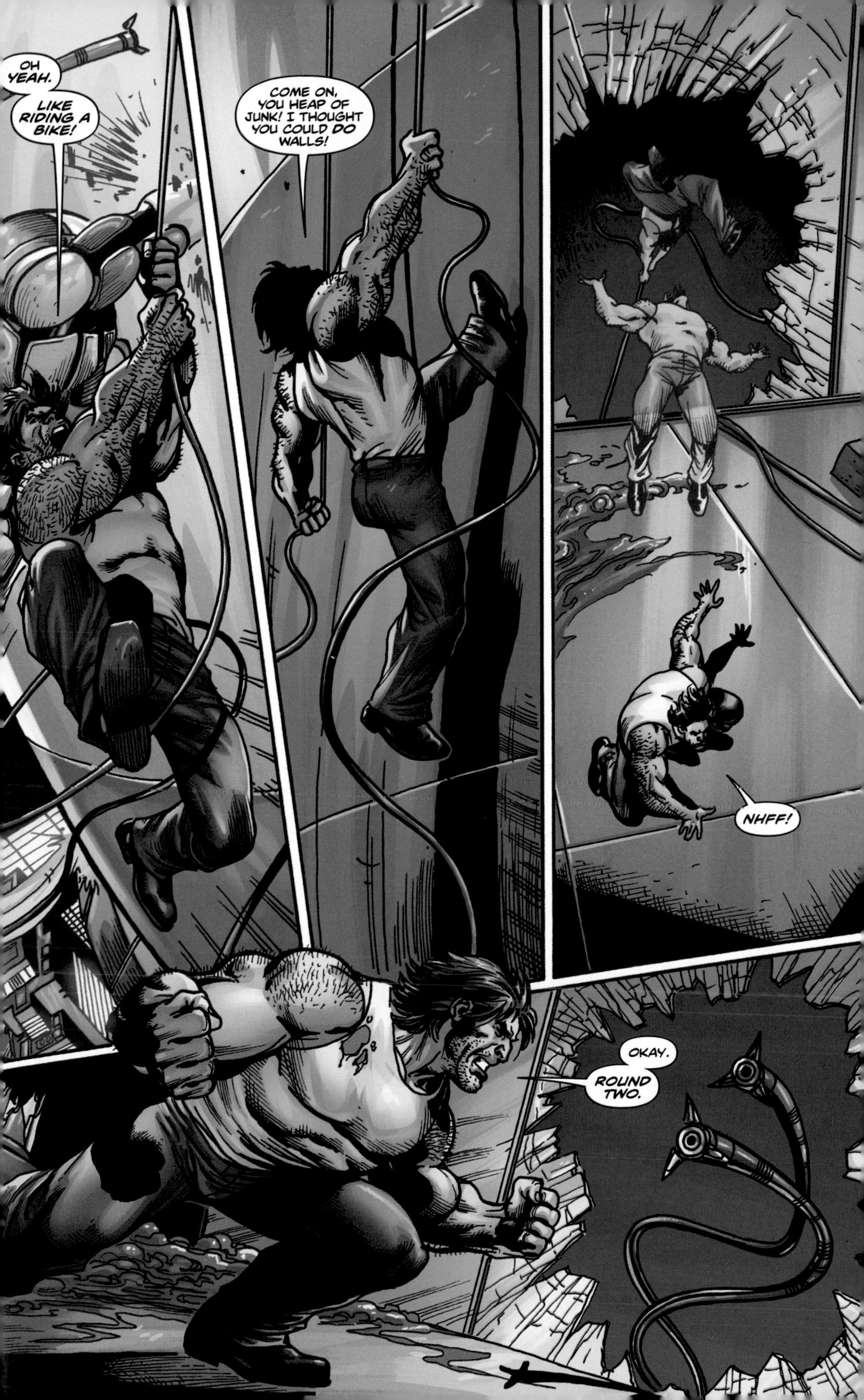
OH YEAH.
LIKE RIDING A BIKE!
COME ON, YOU HEAP OF JUNK! I THOUGHT YOU COULD DO WALLS!
NHFF!
OKAY.
ROUND TWO.

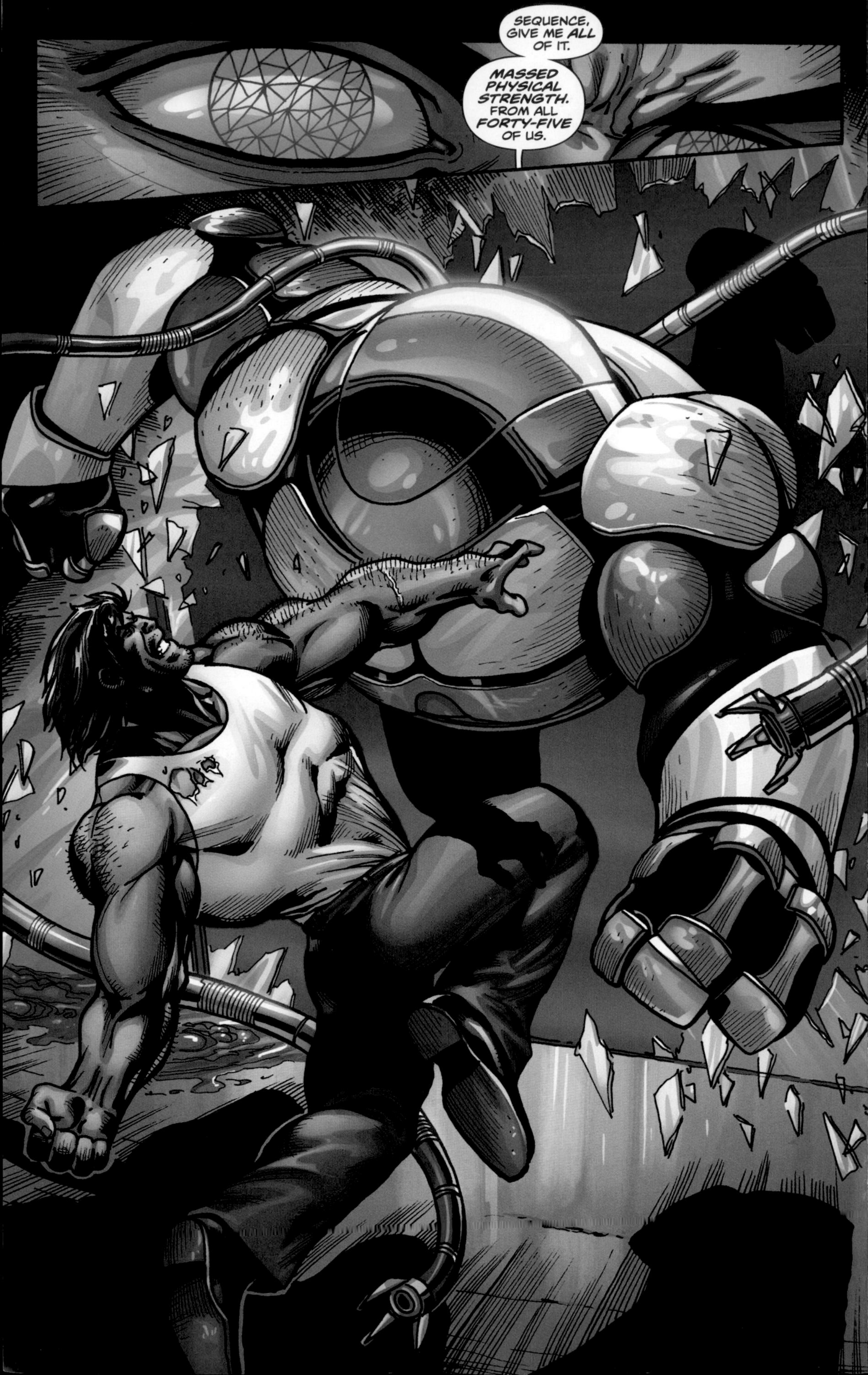
SEQUENCE, GIVE ME ALL OF IT.
MASSED PHYSICAL STRENGTH. FROM ALL FORTY-FIVE OF US.

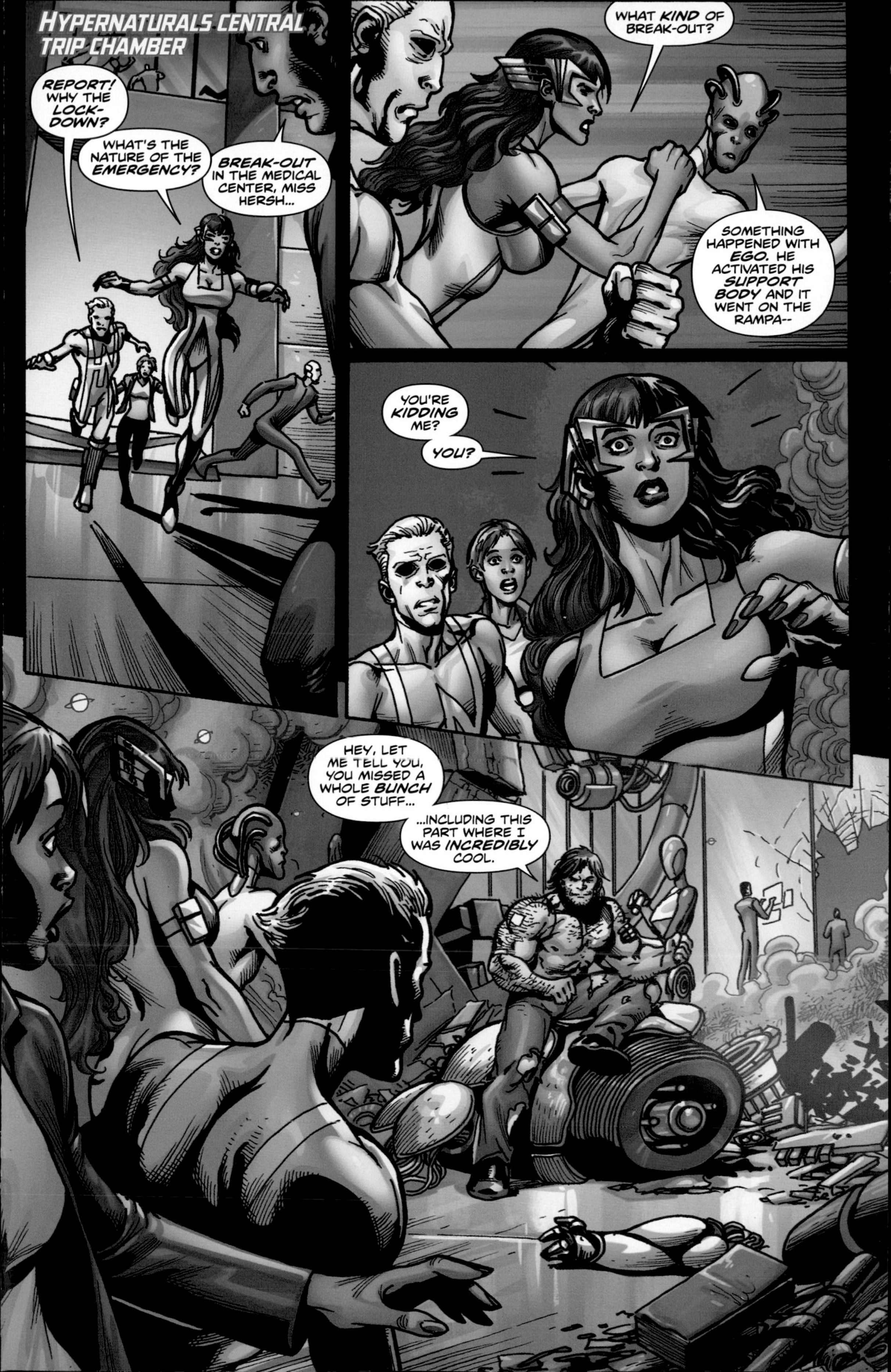
HYPERNATURALS CENTRAL TRIP CHAMBER
REPORT! WHY THE LOCK-DOWN?
WHAT'S THE NATURE OF THE EMERGENCY?
BREAK-OUT IN THE MEDICAL CENTER, MISS HERSH...
WHAT KIND OF BREAK-OUT?
SOMETHING HAPPENED WITH EGO. HE ACTIVATED HIS SUPPORT BODY AND IT WENT ON THE RAMPA--
YOU'RE KIDDING ME?
YOU?
HEY, LET ME TELL YOU, YOU MISSED A WHOLE BUNCH OF STUFF...
...INCLUDING THIS PART WHERE I WAS INCREDIBLY COOL.

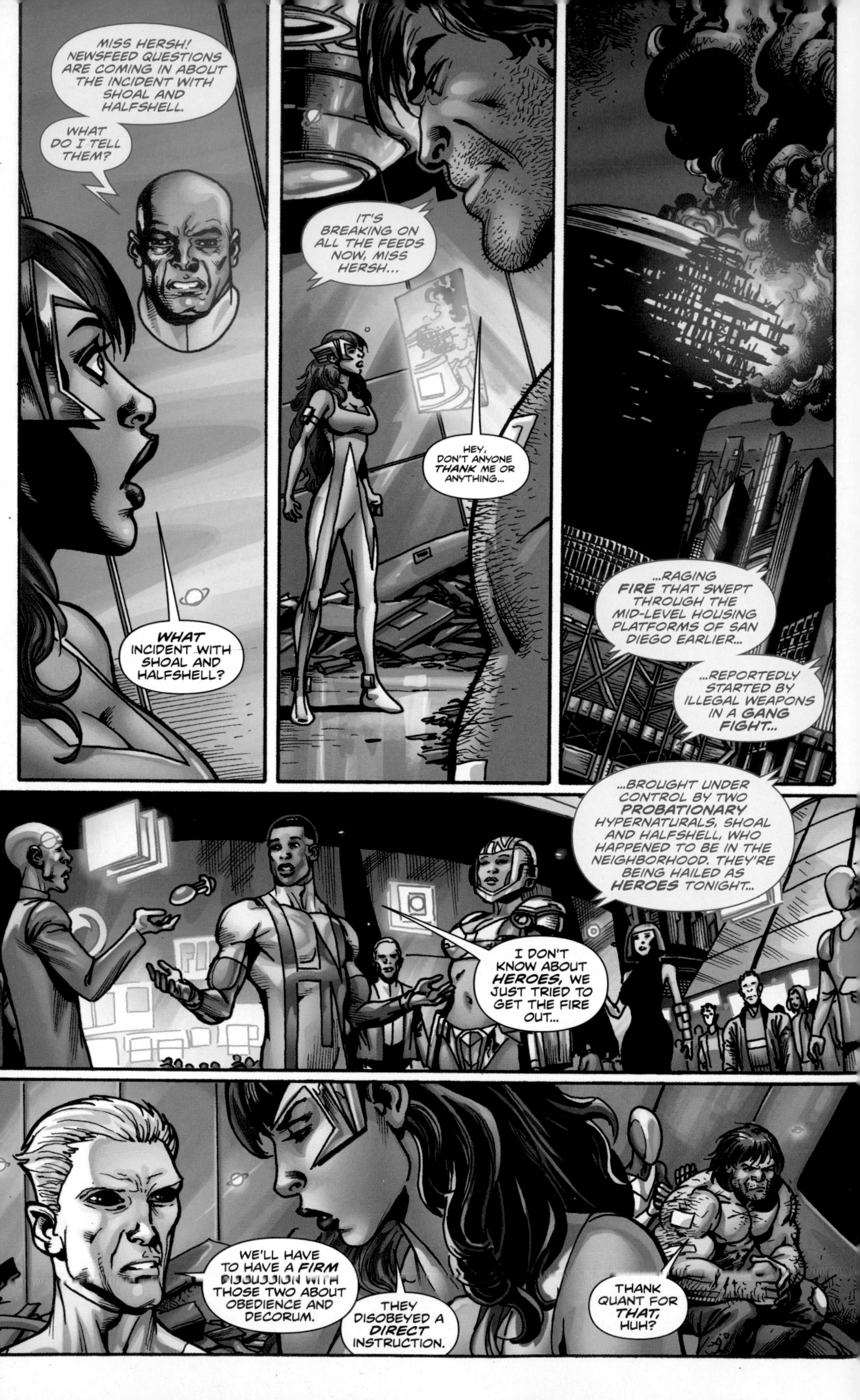
MISS HERSH! NEWSFEED QUESTIONS ARE COMING IN ABOUT THE INCIDENT WITH SHOAL AND HALFSHELL.
WHAT DO I TELL THEM?
WHAT INCIDENT WITH SHOAL AND HALFSHELL?
IT'S BREAKING ON ALL THE FEEDS NOW, MISS HERSH...
HEY, DON'T ANYONE THANK ME OR ANYTHING...
...RAGING FIRE THAT SWEPT THROUGH THE MID-LEVEL HOUSING PLATFORMS OF SAN DIEGO EARLIER...
...REPORTEDLY STARTED BY ILLEGAL WEAPONS IN A GANG FIGHT...
...BROUGHT UNDER CONTROL BY TWO PROBATIONARY HYPERNATURALS, SHOAL AND HALFSHELL, WHO HAPPENED TO BE IN THE NEIGHBORHOOD. THEY'RE BEING HAILED AS HEROES TONIGHT...
I DON'T KNOW ABOUT HEROES, WE JUST TRIED TO GET THE FIRE OUT...
WE'LL HAVE TO HAVE A FIRM DISCUSSION WITH THOSE TWO ABOUT OBEDIENCE AND DECORUM.
THEY DISOBEYED A DIRECT INSTRUCTION.
THANK QUANT FOR THAT, HUH?

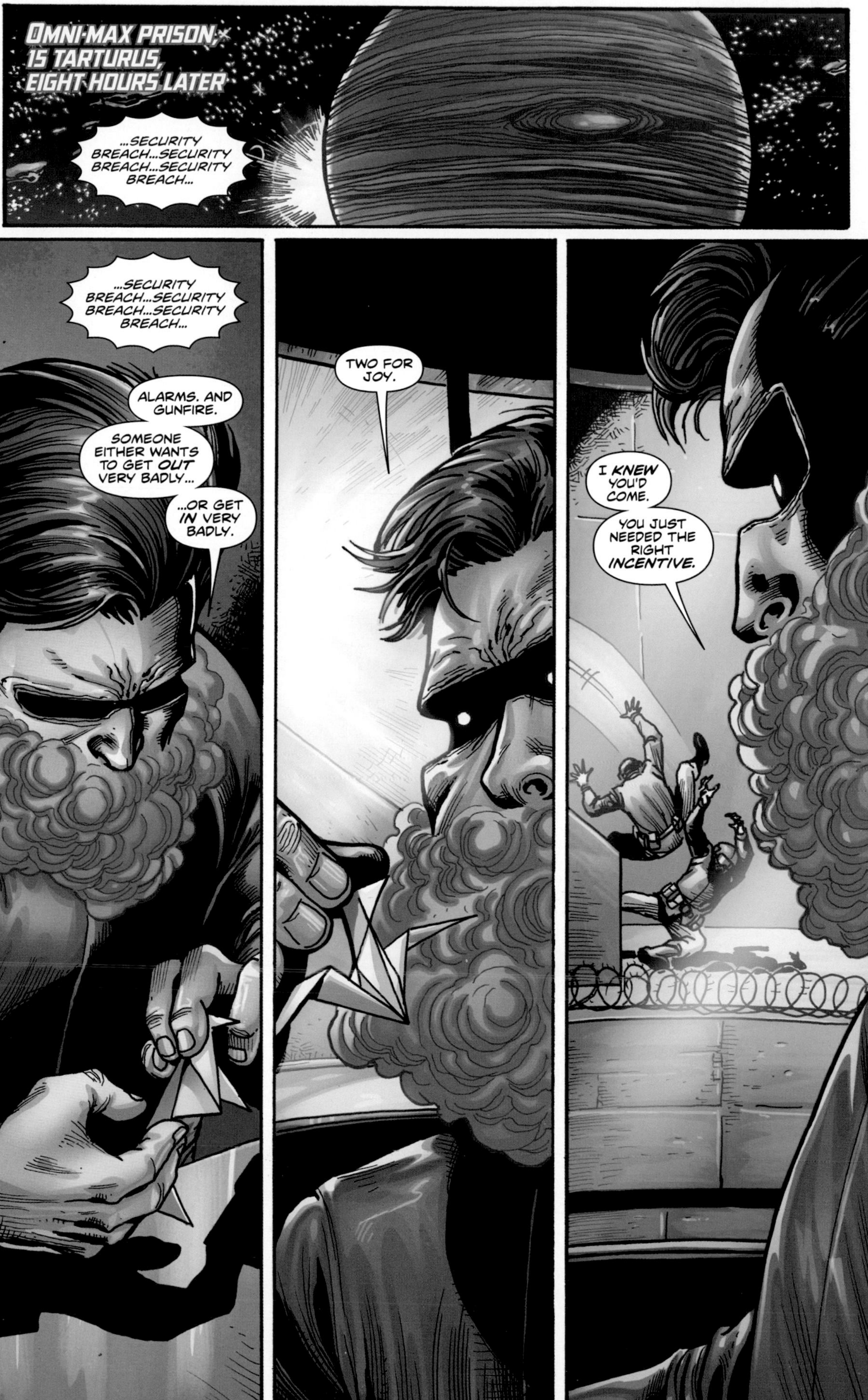
OMNI-MAX PRISON, 15 TARTURUS, EIGHT HOURS LATER
...SECURITY BREACH...SECURITY BREACH...SECURITY BREACH...
...SECURITY BREACH...SECURITY BREACH...SECURITY BREACH...
ALARMS. AND GUNFIRE.
SOMEONE EITHER WANTS TO GET OUT VERY BADLY...
...OR GET IN VERY BADLY.
TWO FOR JOY.
I KNEW YOU'D COME.
YOU JUST NEEDED THE RIGHT INCENTIVE.

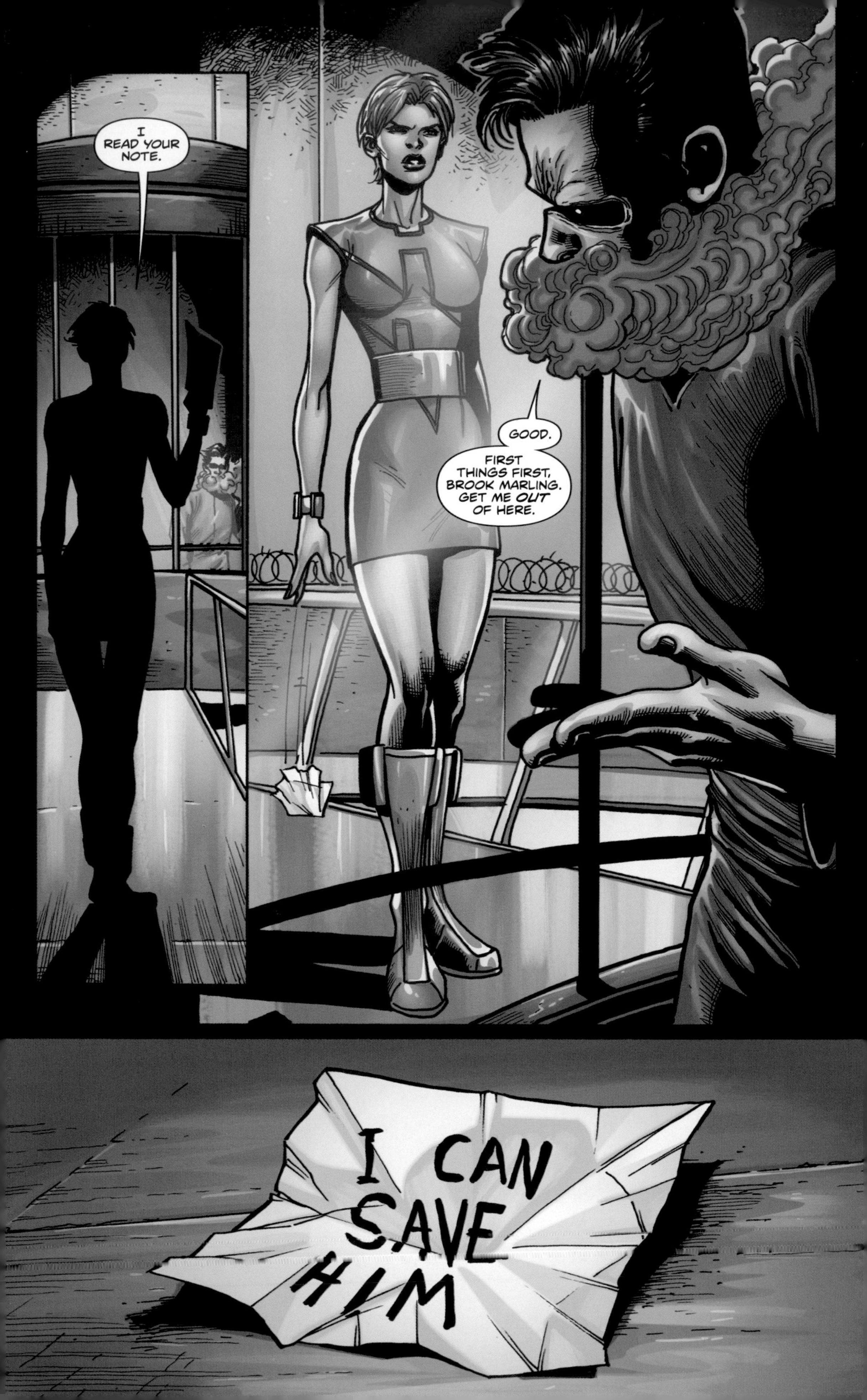
I READ YOUR NOTE.
GOOD.
FIRST THINGS FIRST, BROOK MARLING. GET ME *OUT* OF HERE.
I CAN SAVE HIM

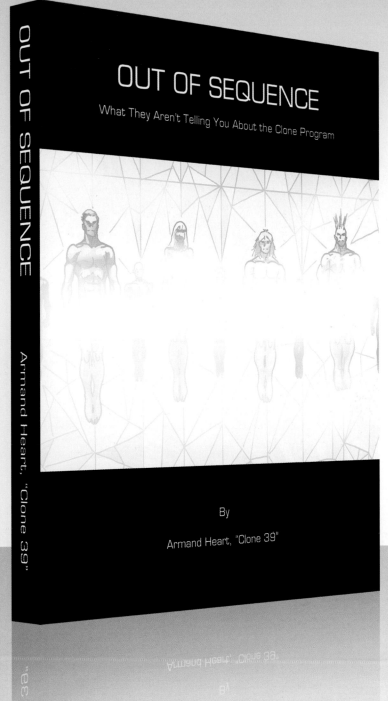

OUT OF SEQUENCE
What They Aren't Telling You About the Clone Program
By
Armand Heart, "Clone 39"
OUT OF SEQUENCE
Armand Heart, "Clone 39"

The Clones have been the backbone of Quantinuum defense and the Hypernaturals team for decades...but what are the secrets they aren't telling you? What really happens with the Sequence? And what ever became of the missing Clone 21?

Clone 39 himself, fan-favorite Armand Heart, reveals all in his shocking new autobiography.

Quantinuum House Press. From all good bookloaders now.

THE SEQUENCE

THE SEQUENCE IS THE SHARED AND INHERITED BACKGROUND NOOSPHERE THAT CONNECTS ALL CLONES, ALLOWING THEM TO INTUITIVELY ACCESS AND ACQUIRE SKILLS, TALENTS AND KNOWLEDGE FROM PREVIOUS CLONES IN THE LINE. THE SEQUENCE WAS NOT PART OF THE ORIGINAL PROGRAM DESIGNED, BUT IS A PHENOMENA THAT EVOLVED SPONTANEOUSLY AND MYSTERIOUSLY AS THE PROGRAM GREW, THANKS TO SUBTLE QUANTUM CONNECTIONS IN THE SHARED GENETIC BASE OF THE CLONES, A PROCESS THAT IS STILL NOT UNDERSTOOD.

CLONE 45

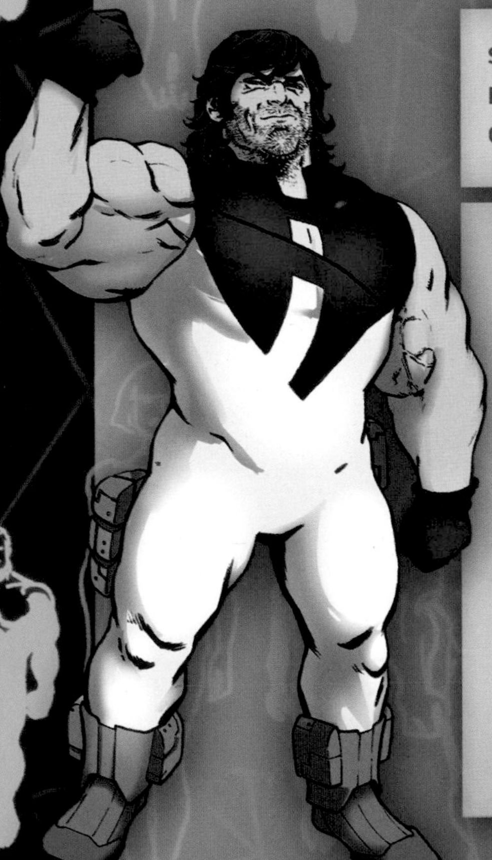

SERVED ON: THE NINETEENTH TOUR
REAL NAME: HATCH GROMAN
CURRENT LOCATION: SINK CITY, 31 GLIESE

He was the team's bruiser/combat specialist. He is the 45th in a line of clones taken from an ultimate soldier program that has produced a long line of universally loved super soldiers.

He has all the abilities and experience of his predecessors and can utilize any fighting technique and weapon and operate any vehicle or equipment.

He is super strong and super tough -- with heightened reflexes and healing factor.

Retired from the Hypernaturals after his third and final term, Clone 45 has been replaced by Clone 46.

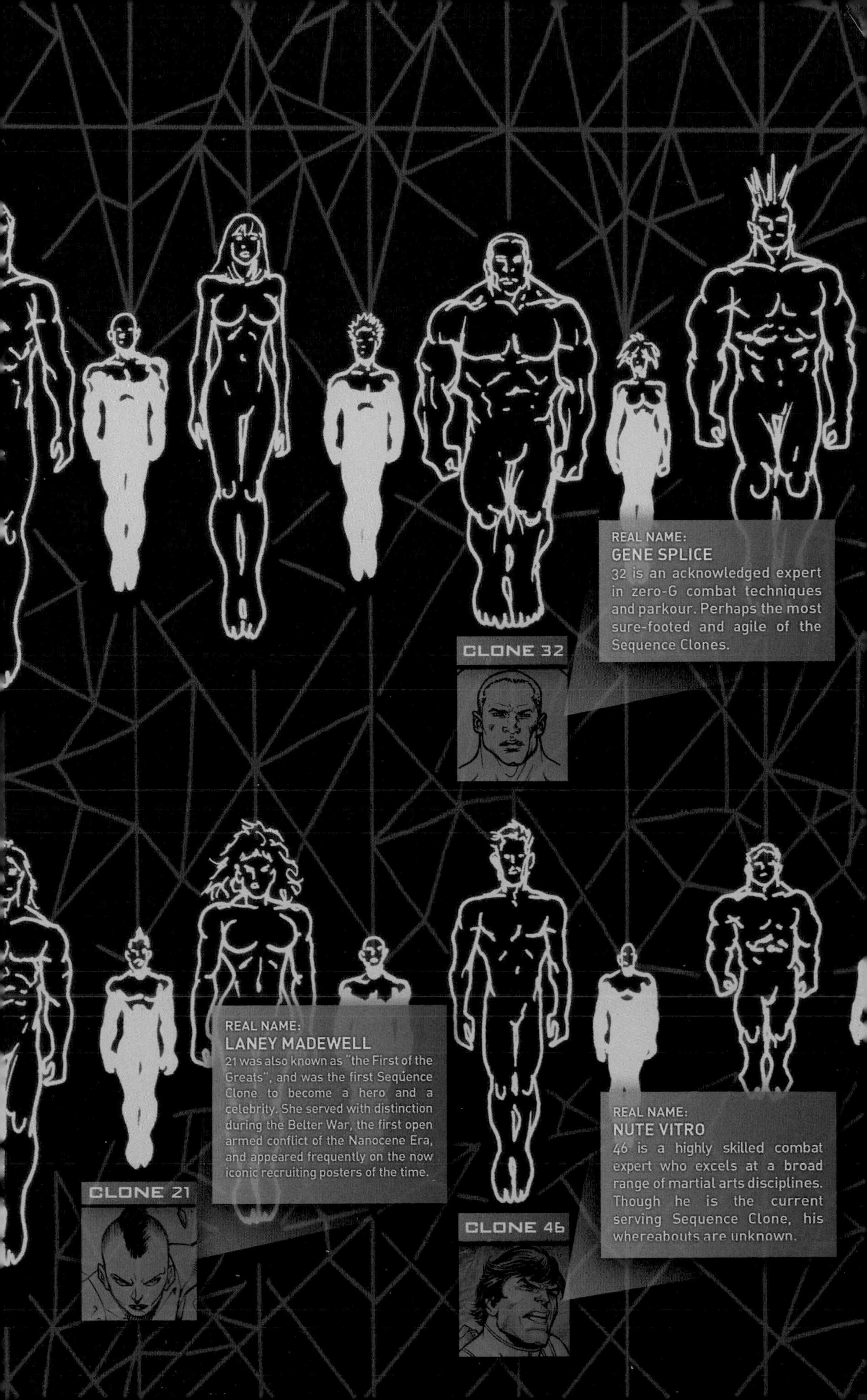

REAL NAME:
GENE SPLICE
32 is an acknowledged expert in zero-G combat techniques and parkour. Perhaps the most sure-footed and agile of the Sequence Clones.
CLONE 32
REAL NAME:
LANEY MADEWELL
21 was also known as "the First of the Greats", and was the first Sequence Clone to become a hero and a celebrity. She served with distinction during the Belter War, the first open armed conflict of the Nanocene Era, and appeared frequently on the now iconic recruiting posters of the time.
CLONE 21
REAL NAME:
NUTE VITRO
46 is a highly skilled combat expert who excels at a broad range of martial arts disciplines. Though he is the current serving Sequence Clone, his whereabouts are unknown.
CLONE 46

CHAPTER FIVE

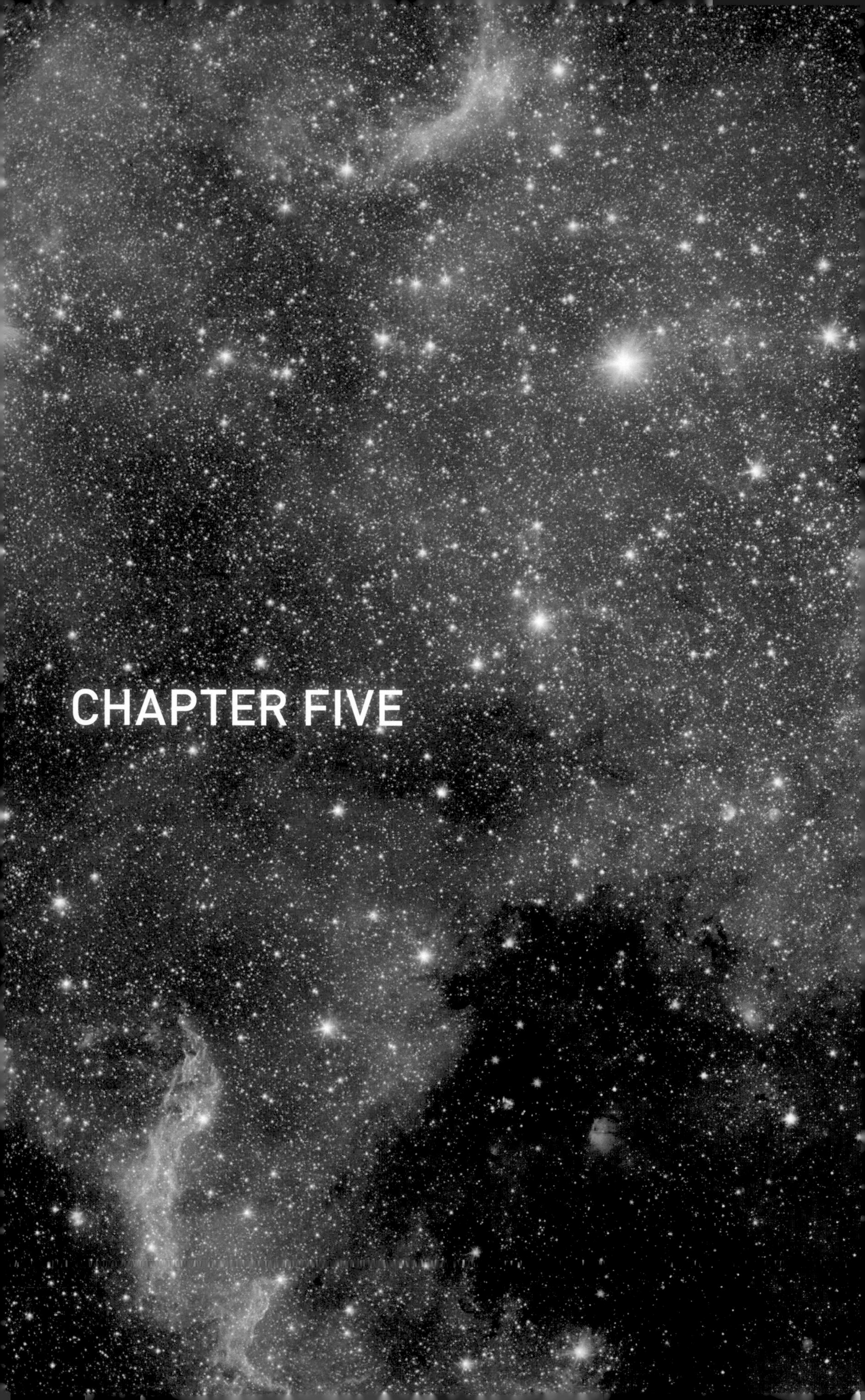

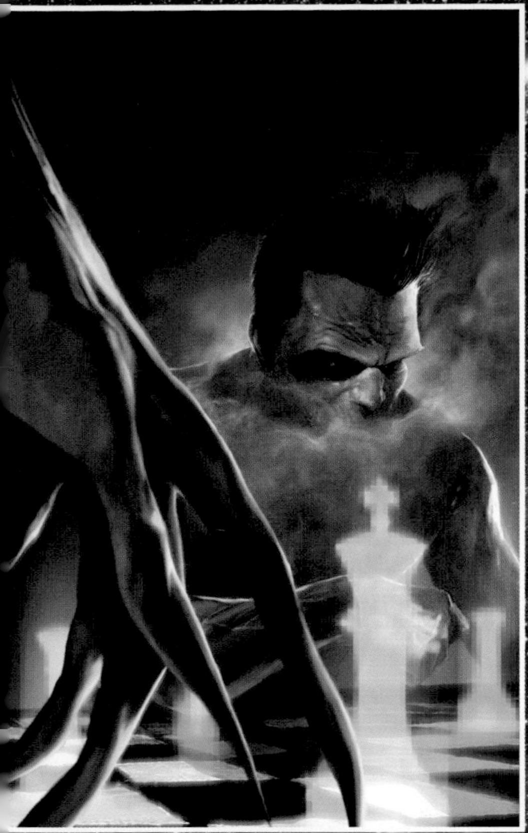

Issue Five
Francesco Mattina

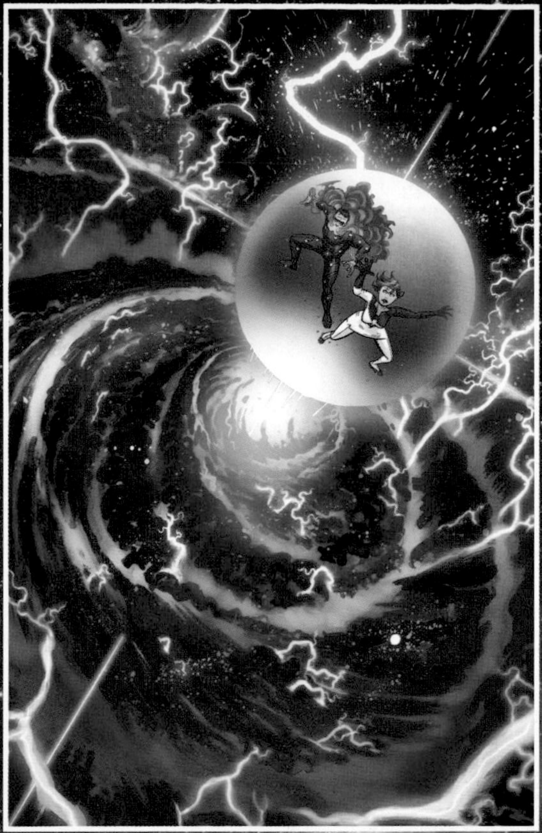

Issue Five
Wes Craig with colors by Blond

Issue Five
Tom Derenick with colors by Blond

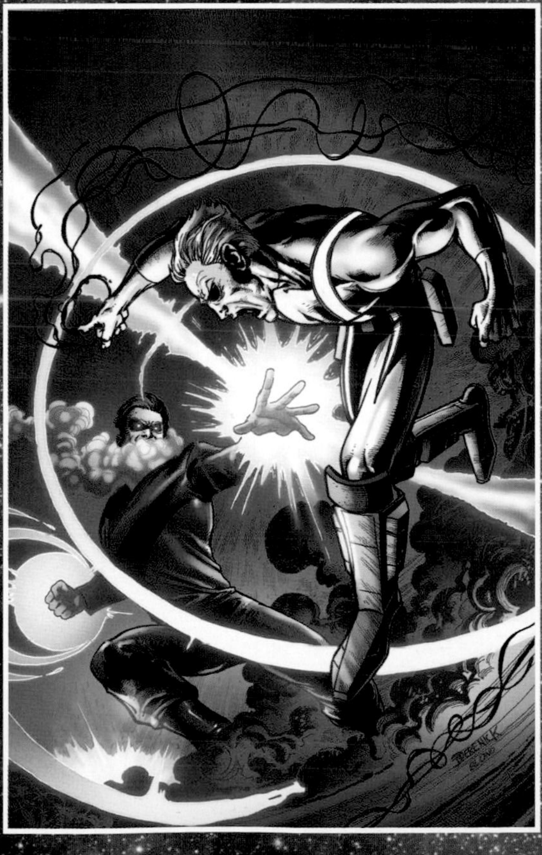

• You have selected Q-Data link.

• We... ...ndred years of the
Hype... ...w, but it's a huge
resp... ...t stopped Bioerror.
The team that saved 356 Barnard from the Replicator crisis. This is the team that put Sublime
in iso, for Quant's sake! Big shoes. Big, big shoes.

- It is the 12th of January in the year **100 A.Q.**
  - Touch here to select an alternative to the **Anno Quantinuum** calendar system.
  - Touch here to load local weather reports for your **current cosmic location.**
  - Touch here to access **Q-Data newsflows** from planets near your current cosmic location.
  - Touch here for latest **Quantum Trip** transit times.

- Q-Data entry: The Quantinuum

- The Quantinuum is the name for the **human galactic culture,** and also for the **artificial intelligence** that controls its function.

- The Quantinuum was created 100 years ago at the start of the **Nanocene Era.** The Nanocene began when the Quantinuum AI achieved Singularity and refashioned human galactic culture. Succeeding the **Holocene Era,** the Nanocene is the next progression of human evolution and...

(to read this entry in full, touch here)

- You have selected live feed newsflow.

- Moabtown Migraines take the pennant in overtime
- Orbus Baxulund completes first solo circumnavigation of Transtrontian Black Warp
- **Forvolund AC** to merge with **Systemware,** jobs may suffer
- Farningham Foxweed to close asteroid belt factories, thousands laid off. Company blames import tariffs making it too hard to compete with Algolian Mining Consortium
- **AI Law** producers announce that audience favourite Bill Frooper of Doctor Heuristics is to join show as a hard-hitting cyber-attorney
- Incident reported at Hypernaturals Central, San Diego. Speculation mounts that the incident is connected with the still unexplained fate of the Centennial Year Iteration of the Team, lost during an emergency response mission to 28 Kosov two days ago

- The Hypernaturals are the Quantinuum's foremost champions. Famous across the entirety of human galactic culture, the team members are selected on the basis of their hypernatural powers and their strength of character, and serve for five-year terms. In honor of the start of the twenty-first term, the line-up of the team's so-called "Centennial Year Iteration" has recently been announced amid huge publicity and--

...BREAKING NEWS... the entire Hypernatural Team has vanished on its inaugural mission to 28 Kosov... according to a spokesperson at Hypernaturals Central, San Diego, a special reserve formation of Hypernaturals, including now retired team members Bewilder, Clone 45 and Thinkwell from the classic "Nineteenth Tour" line-up are now working urgently to find the missing team members and resolve the crisis...

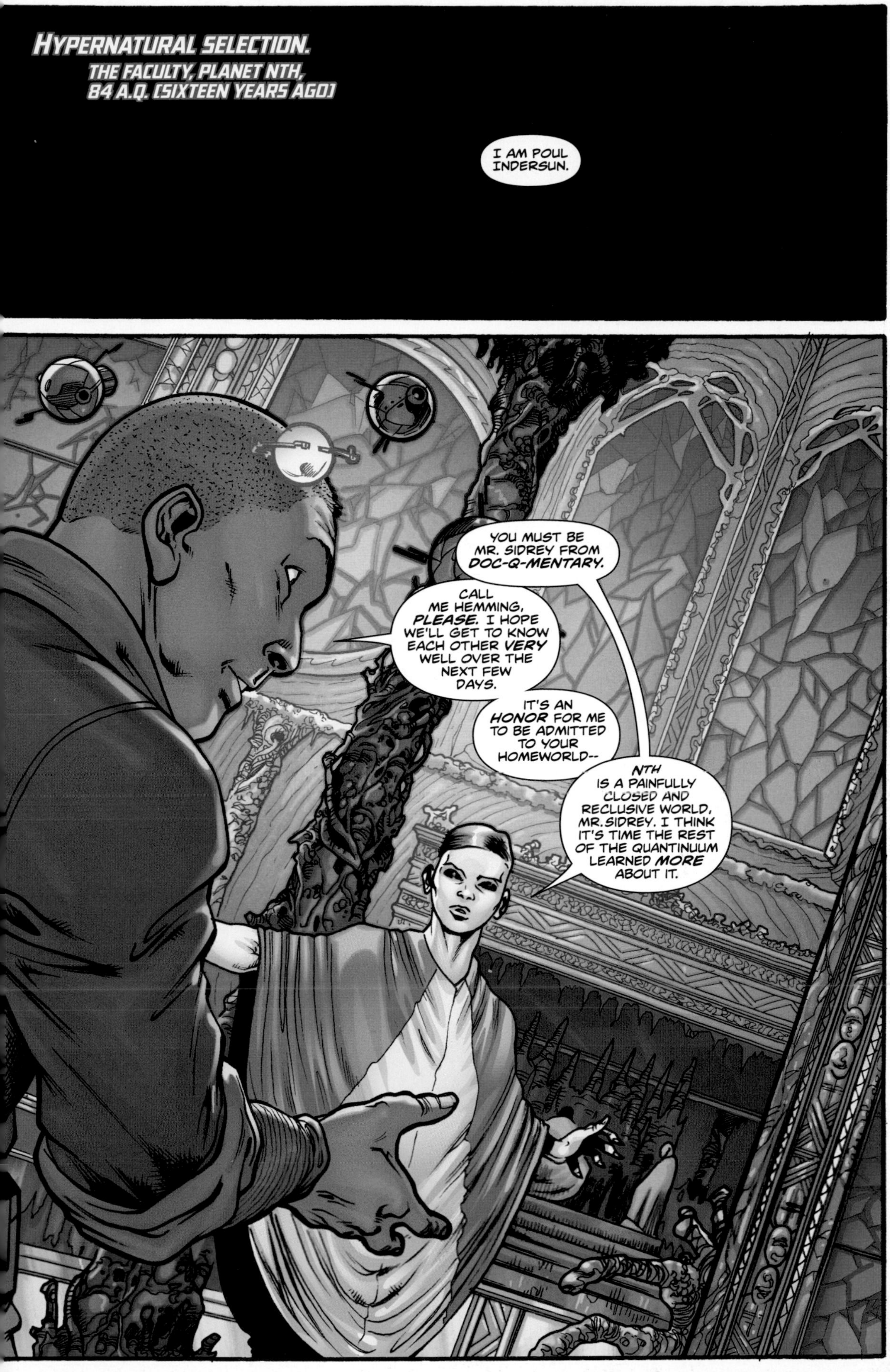
HYPERNATURAL SELECTION.
THE FACULTY, PLANET NTH, 84 A.Q. [SIXTEEN YEARS AGO]
I AM POUL INDERSUN.
YOU MUST BE MR. SIDREY FROM DOC-Q-MENTARY.
CALL ME HEMMING, PLEASE. I HOPE WE'LL GET TO KNOW EACH OTHER VERY WELL OVER THE NEXT FEW DAYS.
IT'S AN HONOR FOR ME TO BE ADMITTED TO YOUR HOMEWORLD--
NTH IS A PAINFULLY CLOSED AND RECLUSIVE WORLD, MR. SIDREY. I THINK IT'S TIME THE REST OF THE QUANTINUUM LEARNED MORE ABOUT IT.

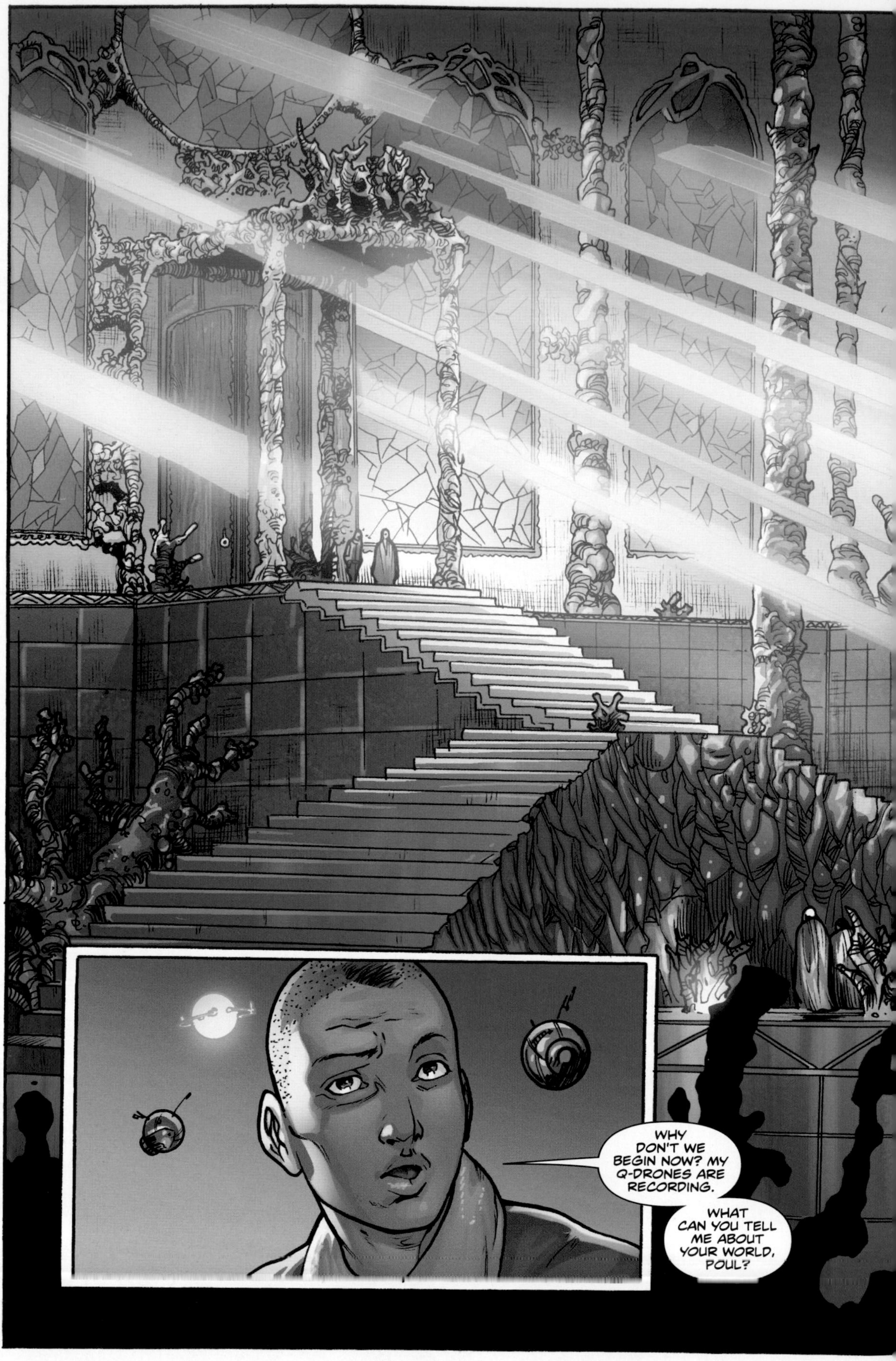
WHY DON'T WE BEGIN NOW? MY Q-DRONES ARE RECORDING.
WHAT CAN YOU TELL ME ABOUT YOUR WORLD, POUL?

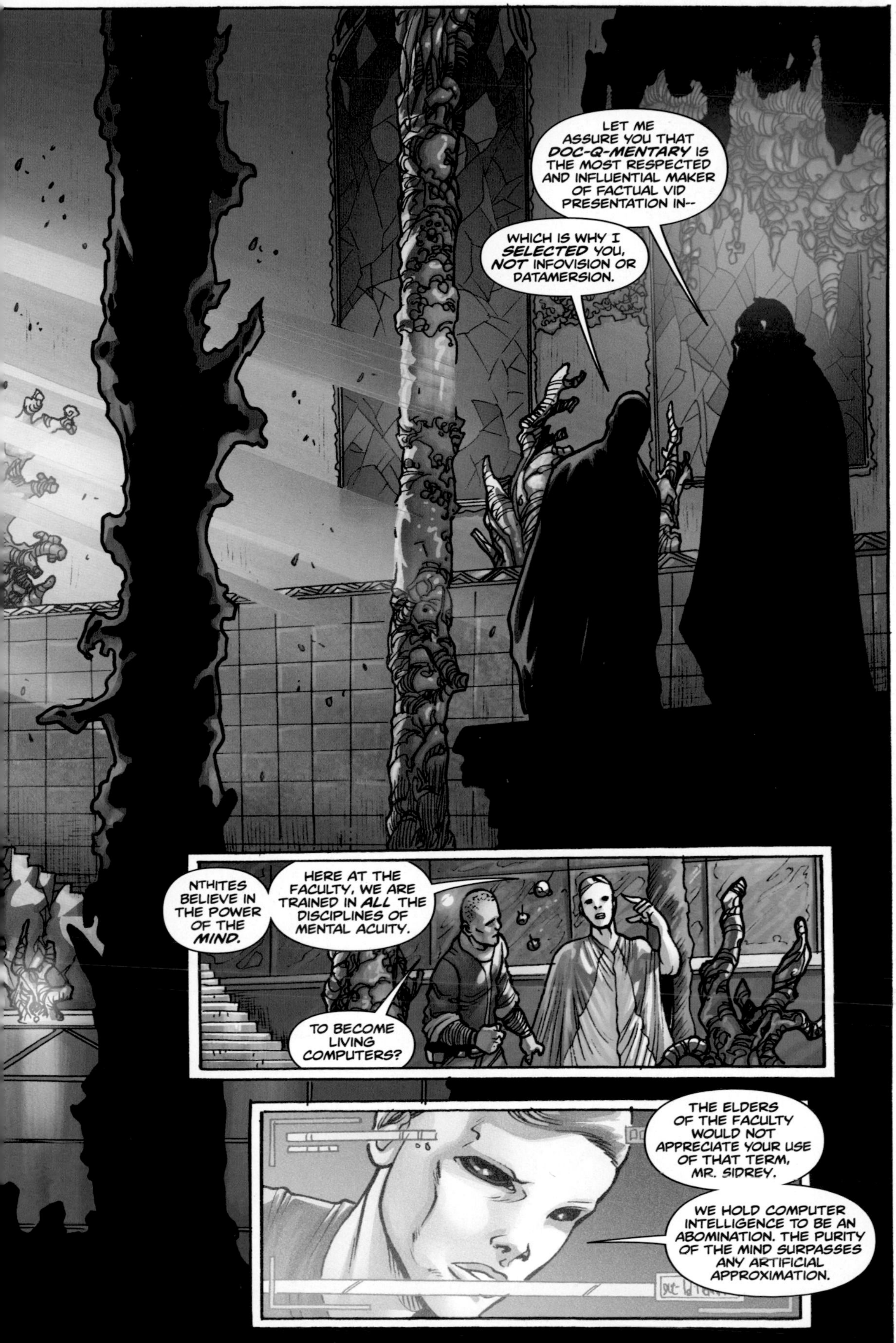
LET ME ASSURE YOU THAT DOC-Q-MENTARY IS THE MOST RESPECTED AND INFLUENTIAL MAKER OF FACTUAL VID PRESENTATION IN--
WHICH IS WHY I SELECTED YOU, NOT INFOVISION OR DATAMERSION.
NTHITES BELIEVE IN THE POWER OF THE MIND.
HERE AT THE FACULTY, WE ARE TRAINED IN ALL THE DISCIPLINES OF MENTAL ACUITY.
TO BECOME LIVING COMPUTERS?
THE ELDERS OF THE FACULTY WOULD NOT APPRECIATE YOUR USE OF THAT TERM, MR. SIDREY.
WE HOLD COMPUTER INTELLIGENCE TO BE AN ABOMINATION. THE PURITY OF THE MIND SURPASSES ANY ARTIFICIAL APPROXIMATION.

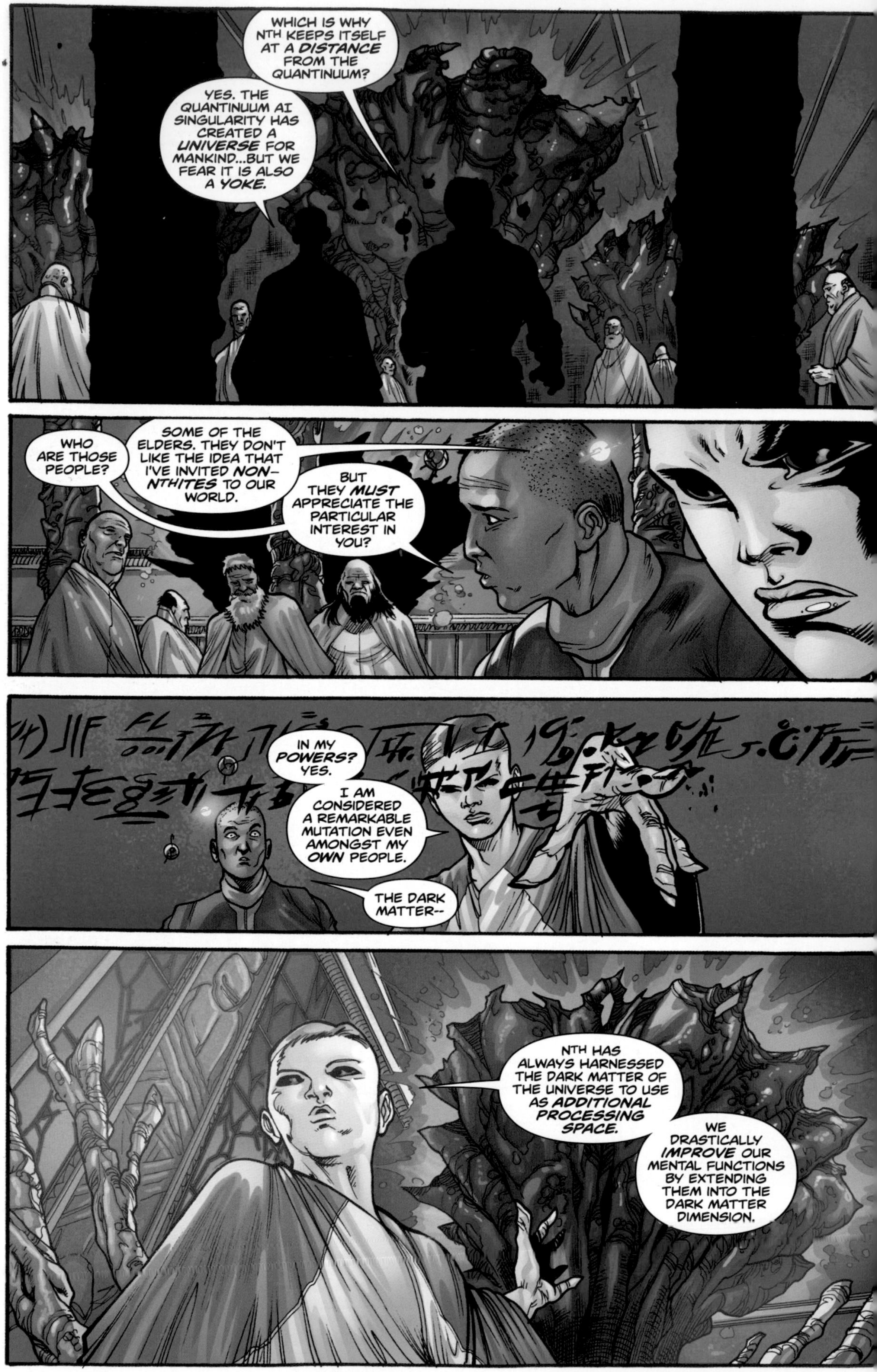
WHICH IS WHY NTH KEEPS ITSELF AT A DISTANCE FROM THE QUANTINUUM?
YES. THE QUANTINUUM AI SINGULARITY HAS CREATED A UNIVERSE FOR MANKIND...BUT WE FEAR IT IS ALSO A YOKE.
WHO ARE THOSE PEOPLE?
SOME OF THE ELDERS. THEY DON'T LIKE THE IDEA THAT I'VE INVITED NON-NTHITES TO OUR WORLD.
BUT THEY MUST APPRECIATE THE PARTICULAR INTEREST IN YOU?
IN MY POWERS? YES.
I AM CONSIDERED A REMARKABLE MUTATION EVEN AMONGST MY OWN PEOPLE.
THE DARK MATTER--
NTH HAS ALWAYS HARNESSED THE DARK MATTER OF THE UNIVERSE TO USE AS ADDITIONAL PROCESSING SPACE.
WE DRASTICALLY IMPROVE OUR MENTAL FUNCTIONS BY EXTENDING THEM INTO THE DARK MATTER DIMENSION.

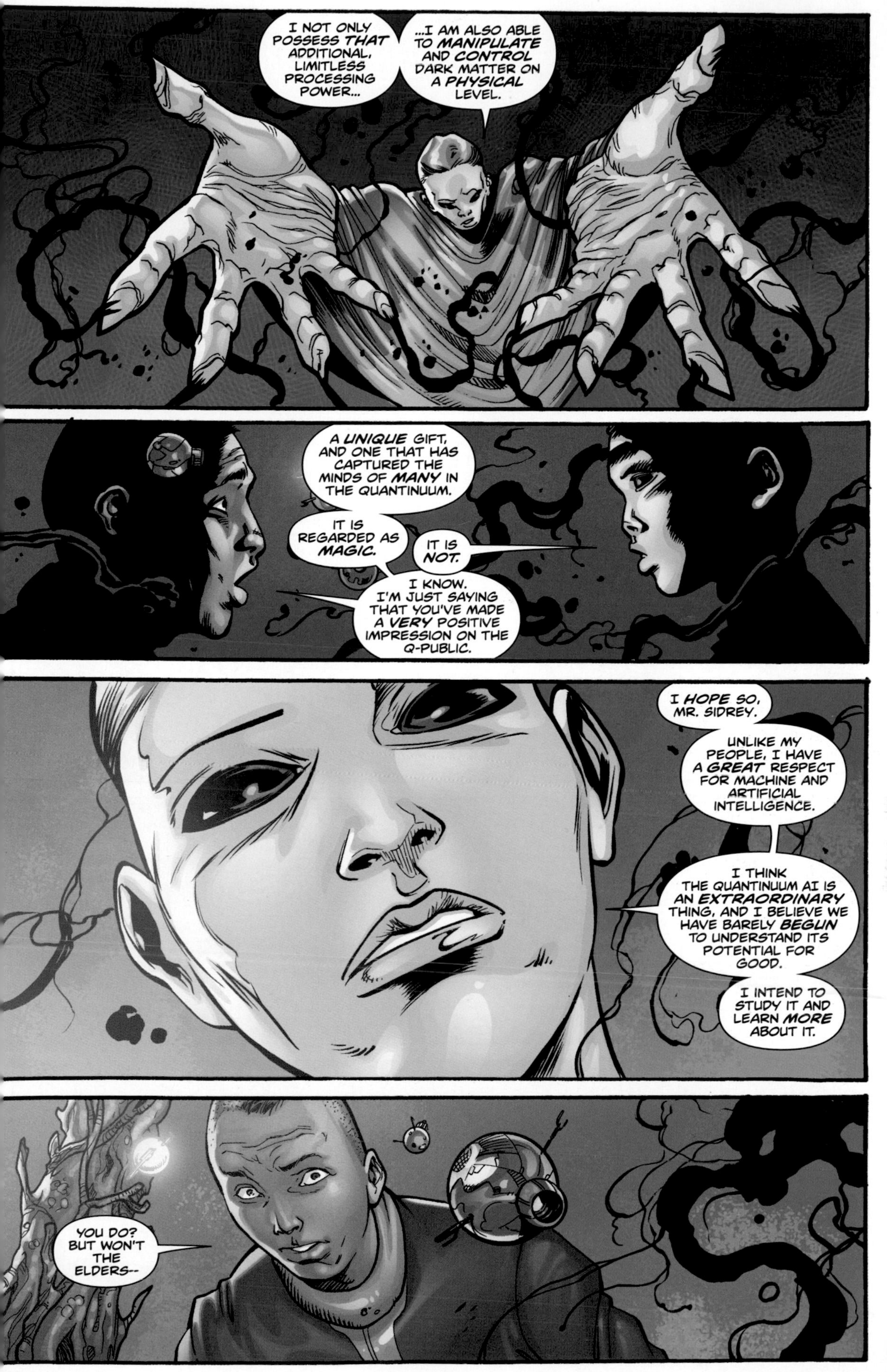
I NOT ONLY POSSESS *THAT* ADDITIONAL, LIMITLESS PROCESSING POWER...
...I AM ALSO ABLE TO *MANIPULATE* AND *CONTROL* DARK MATTER ON A *PHYSICAL* LEVEL.
A *UNIQUE* GIFT, AND ONE THAT HAS CAPTURED THE MINDS OF *MANY* IN THE QUANTINUUM.
IT IS REGARDED AS *MAGIC.*
IT IS *NOT.*
I KNOW. I'M JUST SAYING THAT YOU'VE MADE A *VERY* POSITIVE IMPRESSION ON THE Q-PUBLIC.
I *HOPE* SO, MR. SIDREY.
UNLIKE MY PEOPLE, I HAVE A *GREAT* RESPECT FOR MACHINE AND ARTIFICIAL INTELLIGENCE.
I THINK THE QUANTINUUM AI IS AN *EXTRAORDINARY* THING, AND I BELIEVE WE HAVE BARELY *BEGUN* TO UNDERSTAND ITS POTENTIAL FOR GOOD.
I INTEND TO STUDY IT AND LEARN *MORE* ABOUT IT.
YOU DO? BUT WON'T THE ELDERS--

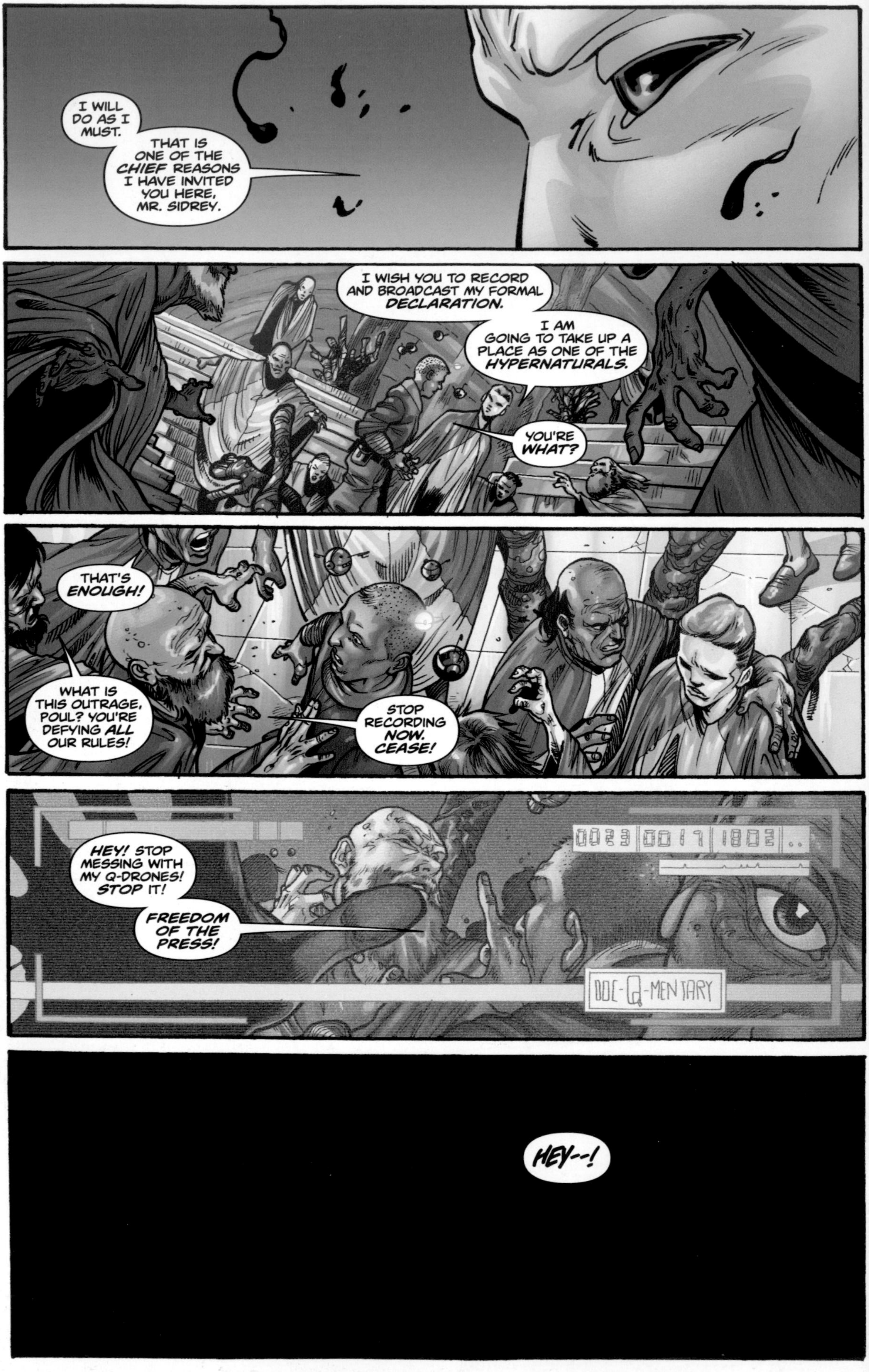

I WILL DO AS I MUST.
THAT IS ONE OF THE CHIEF REASONS I HAVE INVITED YOU HERE, MR. SIDREY.
I WISH YOU TO RECORD AND BROADCAST MY FORMAL DECLARATION.
I AM GOING TO TAKE UP A PLACE AS ONE OF THE HYPERNATURALS.
YOU'RE WHAT?
THAT'S ENOUGH!
WHAT IS THIS OUTRAGE, POUL? YOU'RE DEFYING ALL OUR RULES!
STOP RECORDING NOW. CEASE!
0023 0017 1802
HEY! STOP MESSING WITH MY Q-DRONES! STOP IT!
FREEDOM OF THE PRESS!
DOC-Q-MENTARY
HEY--!

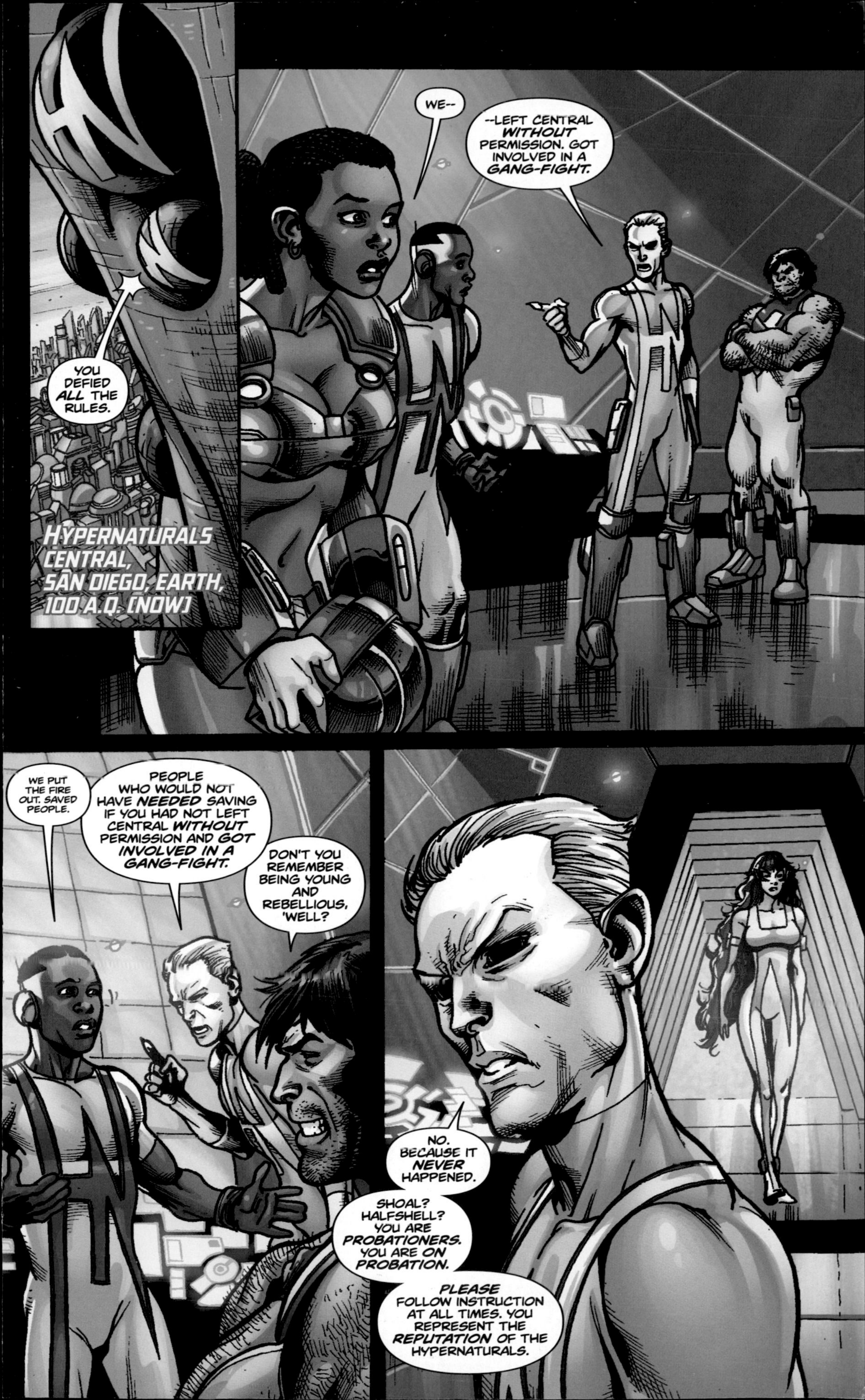

HYPERNATURALS CENTRAL, SAN DIEGO, EARTH, 100 A.Q. [NOW]
YOU DEFIED ALL THE RULES.
WE--
--LEFT CENTRAL WITHOUT PERMISSION. GOT INVOLVED IN A GANG-FIGHT.
WE PUT THE FIRE OUT. SAVED PEOPLE.
PEOPLE WHO WOULD NOT HAVE NEEDED SAVING IF YOU HAD NOT LEFT CENTRAL WITHOUT PERMISSION AND GOT INVOLVED IN A GANG-FIGHT.
DON'T YOU REMEMBER BEING YOUNG AND REBELLIOUS, 'WELL?
NO. BECAUSE IT NEVER HAPPENED.
SHOAL? HALFSHELL? YOU ARE PROBATIONERS. YOU ARE ON PROBATION.
PLEASE FOLLOW INSTRUCTION AT ALL TIMES. YOU REPRESENT THE REPUTATION OF THE HYPERNATURALS.

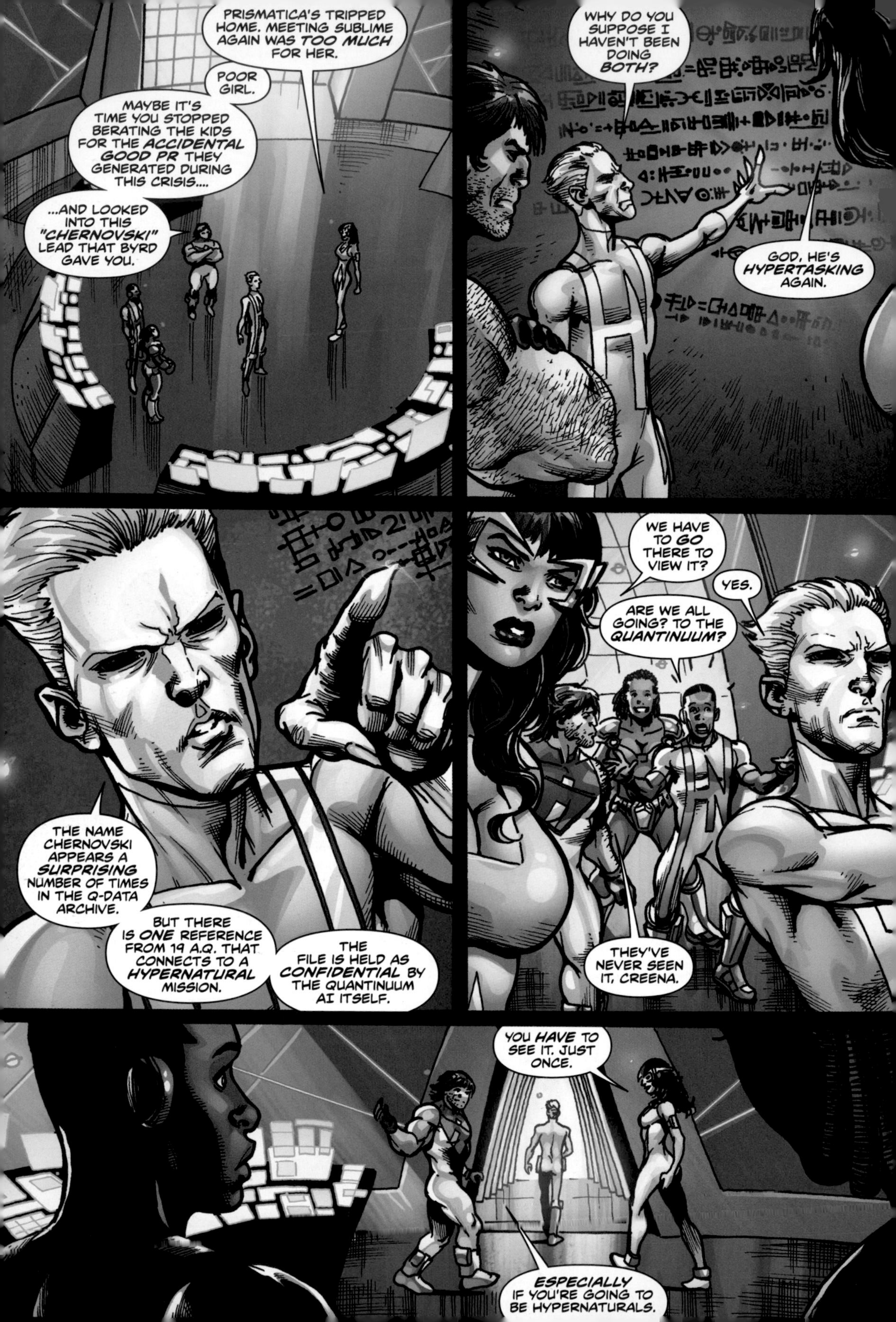
PRISMATICA'S TRIPPED HOME. MEETING SUBLIME AGAIN WAS TOO MUCH FOR HER.
POOR GIRL.
MAYBE IT'S TIME YOU STOPPED BERATING THE KIDS FOR THE ACCIDENTAL GOOD PR THEY GENERATED DURING THIS CRISIS....
...AND LOOKED INTO THIS "CHERNOVSKI" LEAD THAT BYRD GAVE YOU.
WHY DO YOU SUPPOSE I HAVEN'T BEEN DOING BOTH?
GOD, HE'S HYPERTASKING AGAIN.
THE NAME CHERNOVSKI APPEARS A SURPRISING NUMBER OF TIMES IN THE Q-DATA ARCHIVE.
BUT THERE IS ONE REFERENCE FROM 19 A.Q. THAT CONNECTS TO A HYPERNATURAL MISSION.
THE FILE IS HELD AS CONFIDENTIAL BY THE QUANTINUUM AI ITSELF.
WE HAVE TO GO THERE TO VIEW IT?
YES.
ARE WE ALL GOING? TO THE QUANTINUUM?
THEY'VE NEVER SEEN IT, CREENA.
YOU HAVE TO SEE IT. JUST ONCE.
ESPECIALLY IF YOU'RE GOING TO BE HYPERNATURALS.

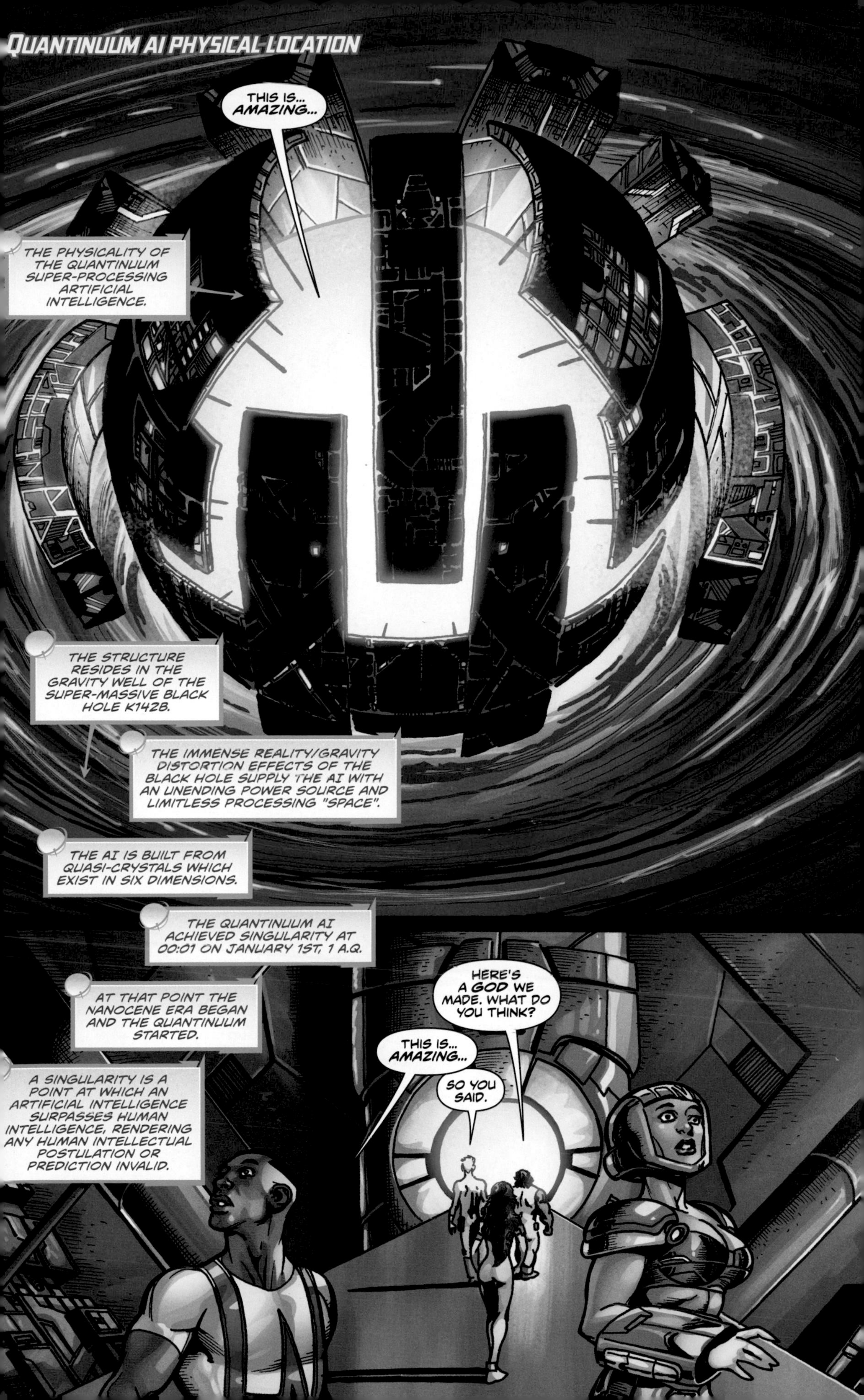
QUANTINUUM AI PHYSICAL LOCATION
THIS IS... AMAZING...
THE PHYSICALITY OF THE QUANTINUUM SUPER-PROCESSING ARTIFICIAL INTELLIGENCE.
THE STRUCTURE RESIDES IN THE GRAVITY WELL OF THE SUPER-MASSIVE BLACK HOLE K142B.
THE IMMENSE REALITY/GRAVITY DISTORTION EFFECTS OF THE BLACK HOLE SUPPLY THE AI WITH AN UNENDING POWER SOURCE AND LIMITLESS PROCESSING "SPACE".
THE AI IS BUILT FROM QUASI-CRYSTALS WHICH EXIST IN SIX DIMENSIONS.
THE QUANTINUUM AI ACHIEVED SINGULARITY AT 00:01 ON JANUARY 1ST, 1 A.Q.
AT THAT POINT THE NANOCENE ERA BEGAN AND THE QUANTINUUM STARTED.
A SINGULARITY IS A POINT AT WHICH AN ARTIFICIAL INTELLIGENCE SURPASSES HUMAN INTELLIGENCE, RENDERING ANY HUMAN INTELLECTUAL POSTULATION OR PREDICTION INVALID.
HERE'S A GOD WE MADE. WHAT DO YOU THINK?
THIS IS... AMAZING...
SO YOU SAID.

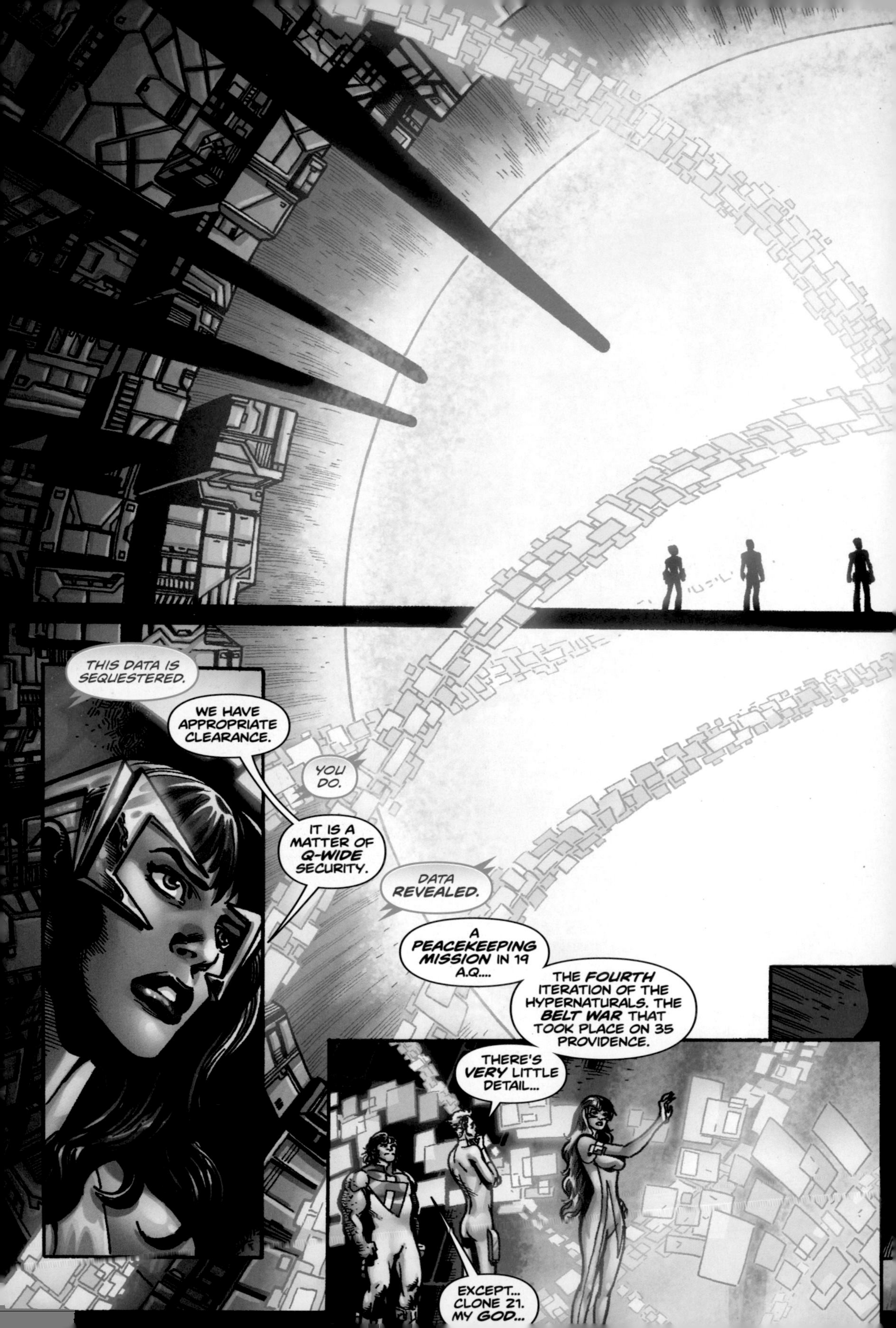
THIS DATA IS SEQUESTERED.
WE HAVE APPROPRIATE CLEARANCE.
YOU DO.
IT IS A MATTER OF Q-WIDE SECURITY.
DATA REVEALED.
A PEACEKEEPING MISSION IN 19 A.Q....
THE FOURTH ITERATION OF THE HYPERNATURALS. THE BELT WAR THAT TOOK PLACE ON 35 PROVIDENCE.
THERE'S VERY LITTLE DETAIL...
EXCEPT... CLONE 21. MY GOD...

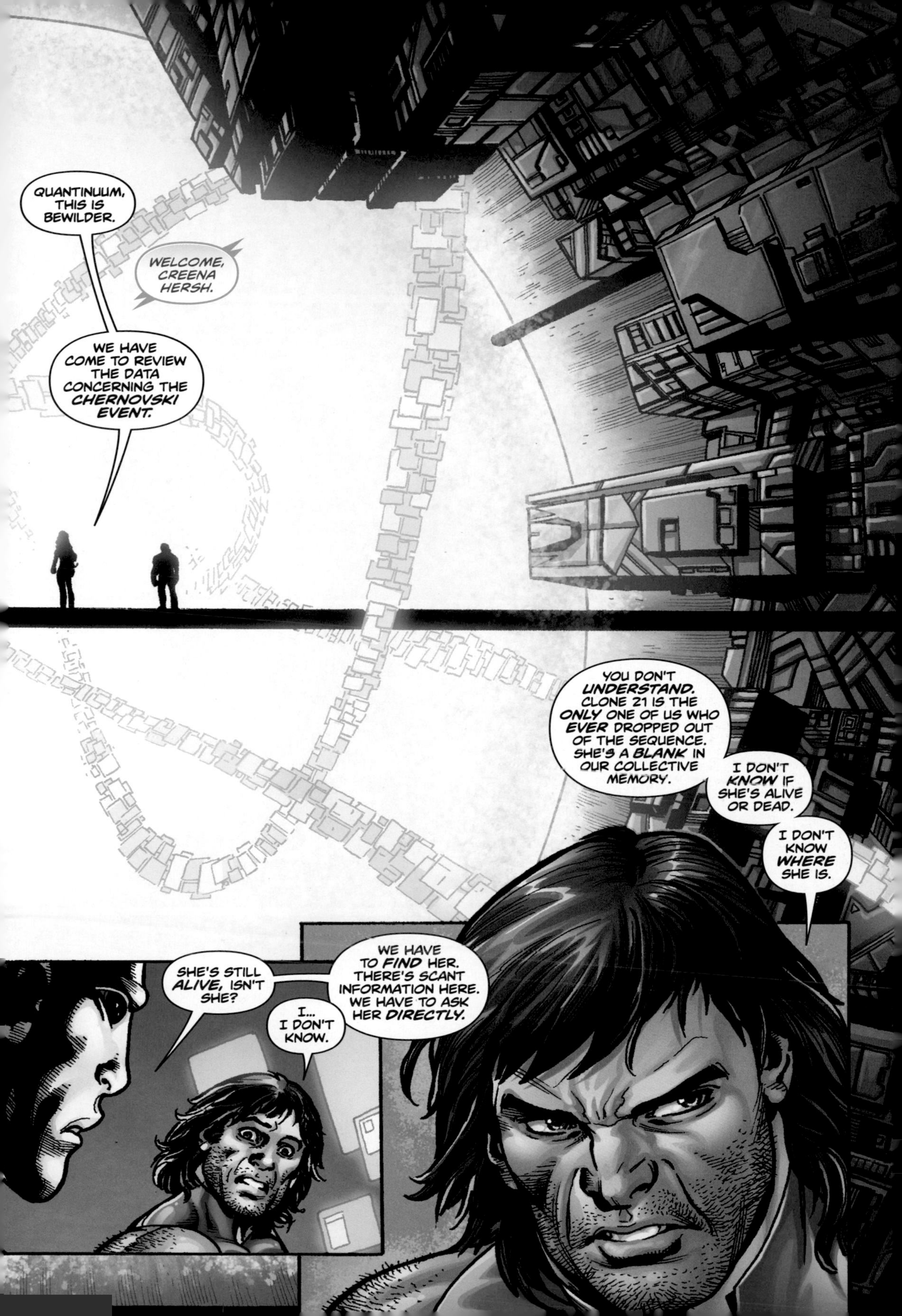
QUANTINUUM, THIS IS BEWILDER.
WELCOME, CREENA HERSH.
WE HAVE COME TO REVIEW THE DATA CONCERNING THE CHERNOVSKI EVENT.
YOU DON'T UNDERSTAND. CLONE 21 IS THE ONLY ONE OF US WHO EVER DROPPED OUT OF THE SEQUENCE. SHE'S A BLANK IN OUR COLLECTIVE MEMORY.
I DON'T KNOW IF SHE'S ALIVE OR DEAD.
I DON'T KNOW WHERE SHE IS.
SHE'S STILL ALIVE, ISN'T SHE?
I... I DON'T KNOW.
WE HAVE TO FIND HER. THERE'S SCANT INFORMATION HERE. WE HAVE TO ASK HER DIRECTLY.

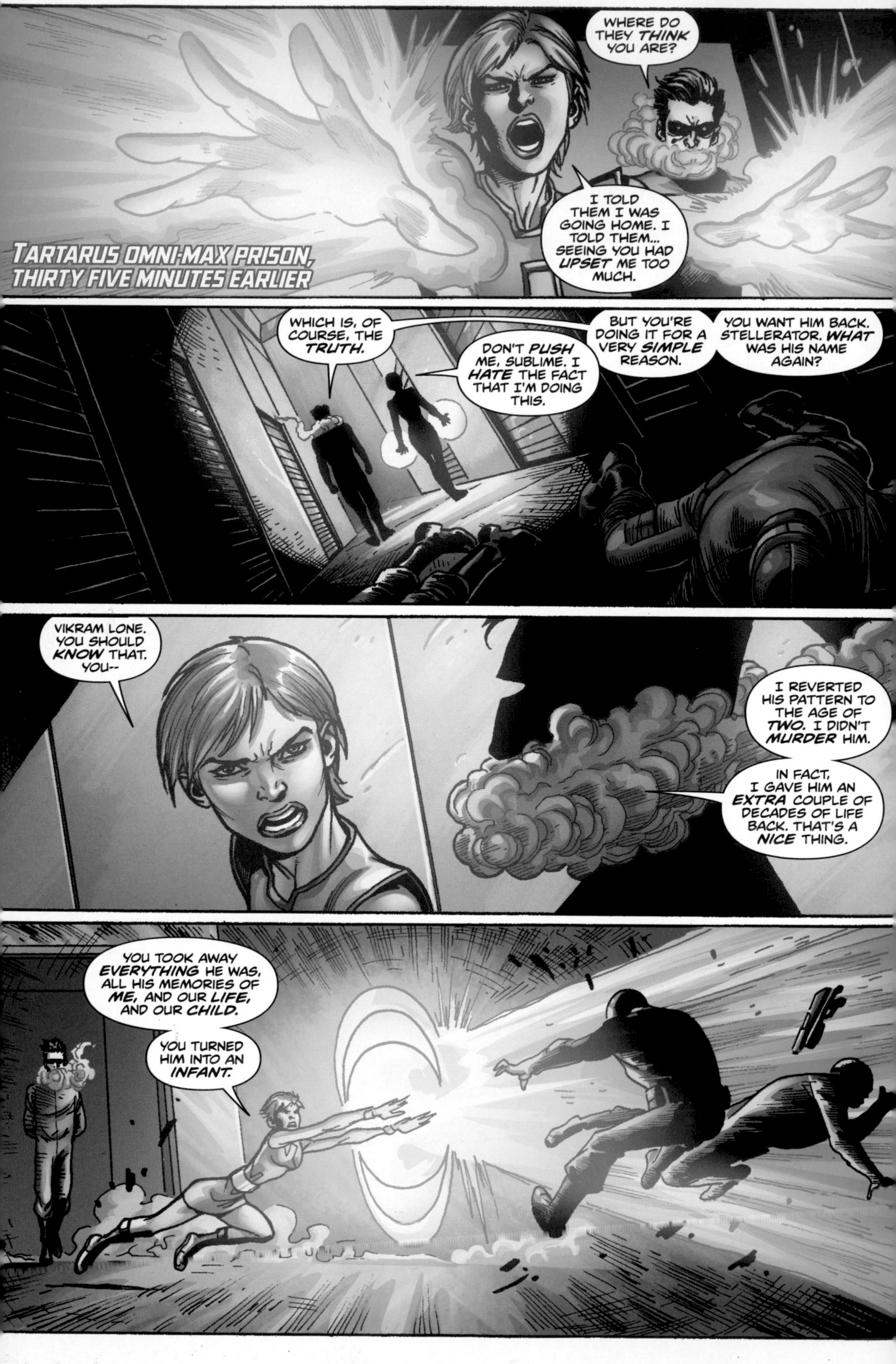
TARTARUS OMNI-MAX PRISON, THIRTY FIVE MINUTES EARLIER
WHERE DO THEY THINK YOU ARE?
I TOLD THEM I WAS GOING HOME. I TOLD THEM... SEEING YOU HAD UPSET ME TOO MUCH.
WHICH IS, OF COURSE, THE TRUTH.
DON'T PUSH ME, SUBLIME. I HATE THE FACT THAT I'M DOING THIS.
BUT YOU'RE DOING IT FOR A VERY SIMPLE REASON.
YOU WANT HIM BACK. STELLERATOR. WHAT WAS HIS NAME AGAIN?
VIKRAM LONE. YOU SHOULD KNOW THAT. YOU--
I REVERTED HIS PATTERN TO THE AGE OF TWO. I DIDN'T MURDER HIM.
IN FACT, I GAVE HIM AN EXTRA COUPLE OF DECADES OF LIFE BACK. THAT'S A NICE THING.
YOU TOOK AWAY EVERYTHING HE WAS, ALL HIS MEMORIES OF ME, AND OUR LIFE, AND OUR CHILD.
YOU TURNED HIM INTO AN INFANT.

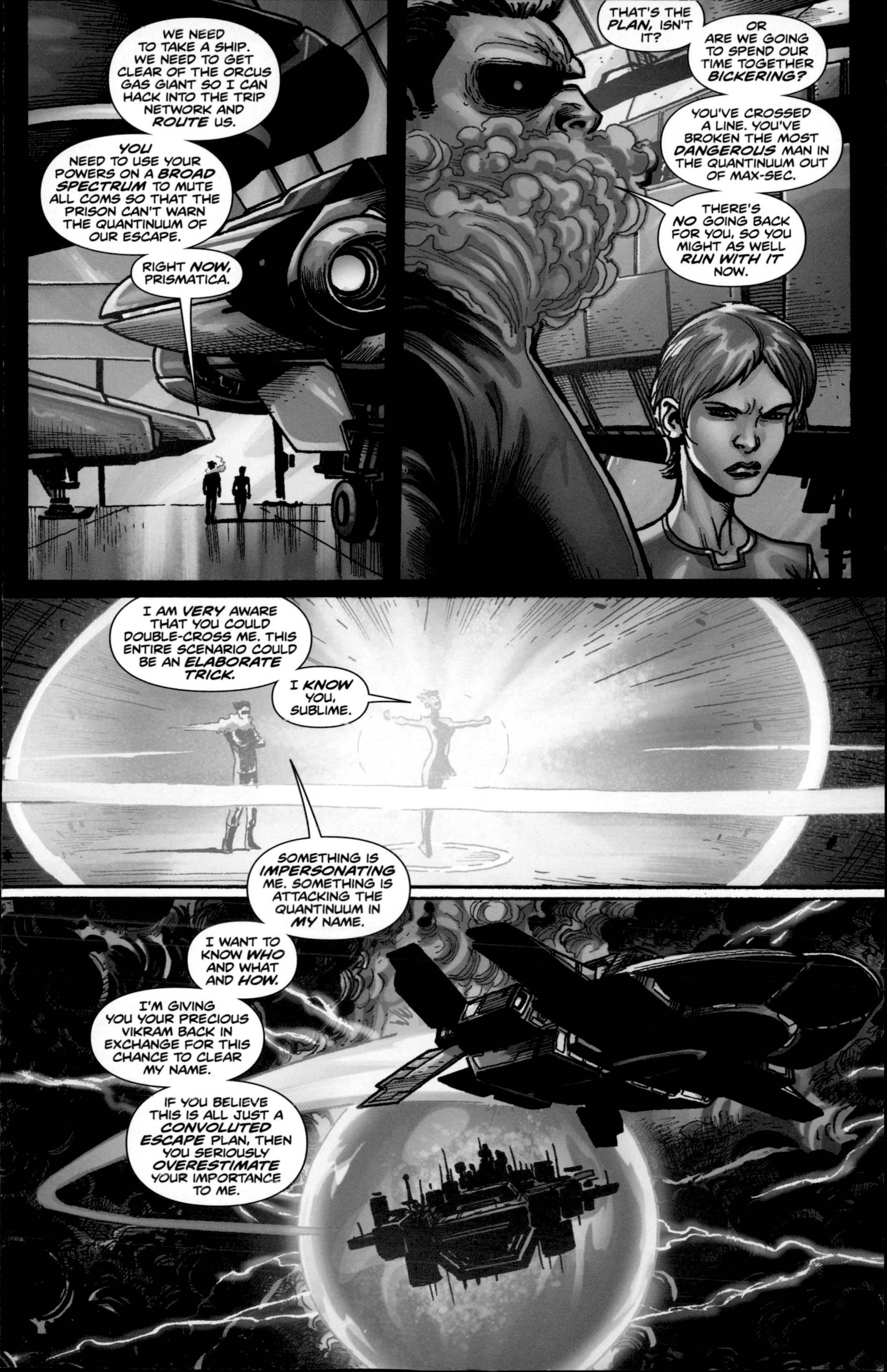
WE NEED TO TAKE A SHIP. WE NEED TO GET CLEAR OF THE ORCUS GAS GIANT SO I CAN HACK INTO THE TRIP NETWORK AND ROUTE US.
YOU NEED TO USE YOUR POWERS ON A BROAD SPECTRUM TO MUTE ALL COMS SO THAT THE PRISON CAN'T WARN THE QUANTINUUM OF OUR ESCAPE.
RIGHT NOW, PRISMATICA.
THAT'S THE PLAN, ISN'T IT?
OR ARE WE GOING TO SPEND OUR TIME TOGETHER BICKERING?
YOU'VE CROSSED A LINE. YOU'VE BROKEN THE MOST DANGEROUS MAN IN THE QUANTINUUM OUT OF MAX-SEC.
THERE'S NO GOING BACK FOR YOU, SO YOU MIGHT AS WELL RUN WITH IT NOW.
I AM VERY AWARE THAT YOU COULD DOUBLE-CROSS ME. THIS ENTIRE SCENARIO COULD BE AN ELABORATE TRICK.
I KNOW YOU, SUBLIME.
SOMETHING IS IMPERSONATING ME. SOMETHING IS ATTACKING THE QUANTINUUM IN MY NAME.
I WANT TO KNOW WHO AND WHAT AND HOW.
I'M GIVING YOU YOUR PRECIOUS VIKRAM BACK IN EXCHANGE FOR THIS CHANCE TO CLEAR MY NAME.
IF YOU BELIEVE THIS IS ALL JUST A CONVOLUTED ESCAPE PLAN, THEN YOU SERIOUSLY OVERESTIMATE YOUR IMPORTANCE TO ME.

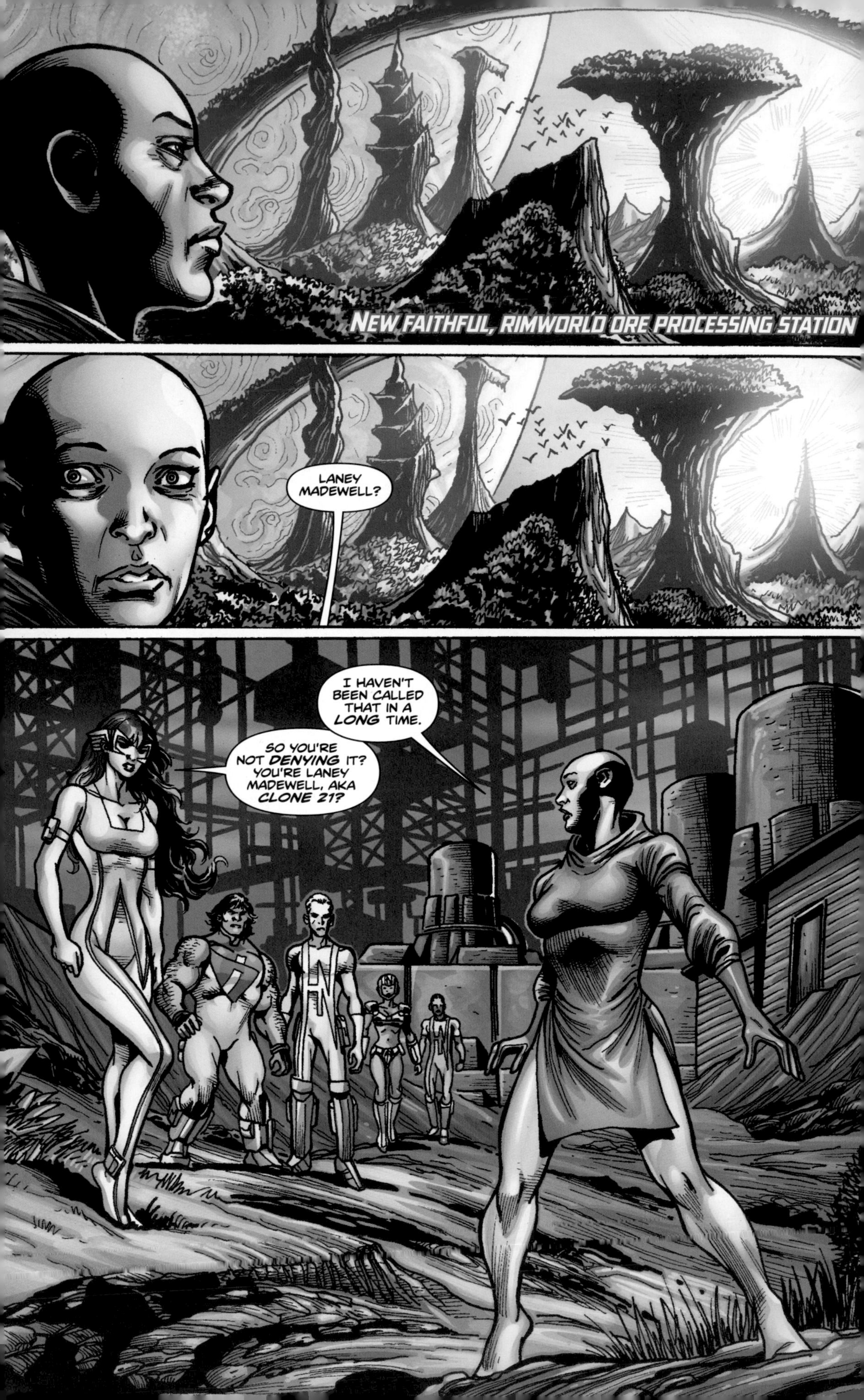
NEW FAITHFUL, RIMWORLD ORE PROCESSING STATION
LANEY MADEWELL?
I HAVEN'T BEEN CALLED THAT IN A LONG TIME.
SO YOU'RE NOT DENYING IT? YOU'RE LANEY MADEWELL, AKA CLONE 21?

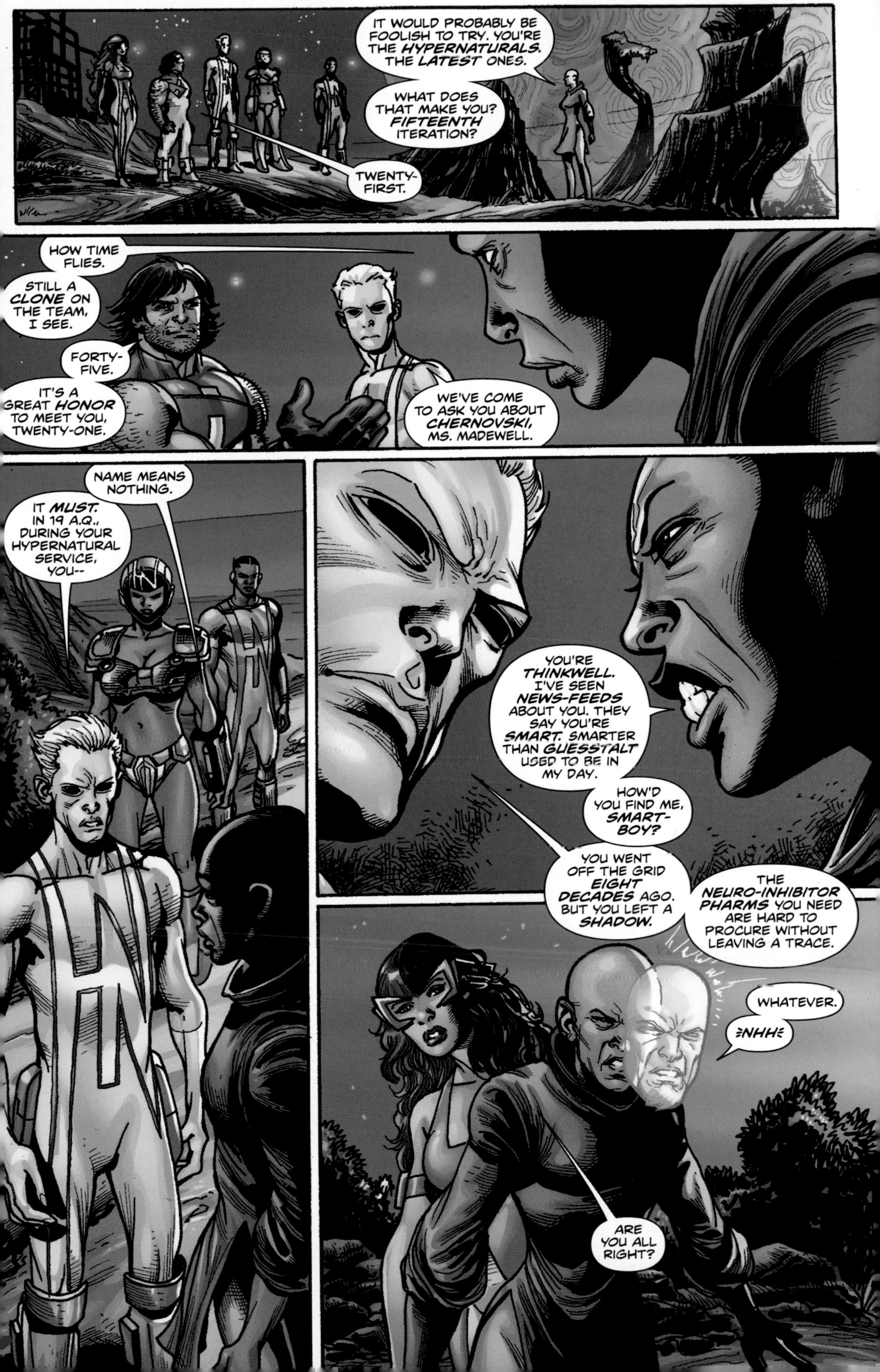
IT WOULD PROBABLY BE FOOLISH TO TRY. YOU'RE THE HYPERNATURALS. THE LATEST ONES.
WHAT DOES THAT MAKE YOU? FIFTEENTH ITERATION?
TWENTY-FIRST.
HOW TIME FLIES.
STILL A CLONE ON THE TEAM, I SEE.
FORTY-FIVE.
IT'S A GREAT HONOR TO MEET YOU, TWENTY-ONE.
WE'VE COME TO ASK YOU ABOUT CHERNOVSKI, MS. MADEWELL.
NAME MEANS NOTHING.
IT MUST. IN 19 A.Q., DURING YOUR HYPERNATURAL SERVICE, YOU--
YOU'RE THINKWELL. I'VE SEEN NEWS-FEEDS ABOUT YOU. THEY SAY YOU'RE SMART. SMARTER THAN GUESSTALT USED TO BE IN MY DAY.
HOW'D YOU FIND ME, SMART-BOY?
YOU WENT OFF THE GRID EIGHT DECADES AGO. BUT YOU LEFT A SHADOW.
THE NEURO-INHIBITOR PHARMS YOU NEED ARE HARD TO PROCURE WITHOUT LEAVING A TRACE.
WHATEVER.
NHH
ARE YOU ALL RIGHT?

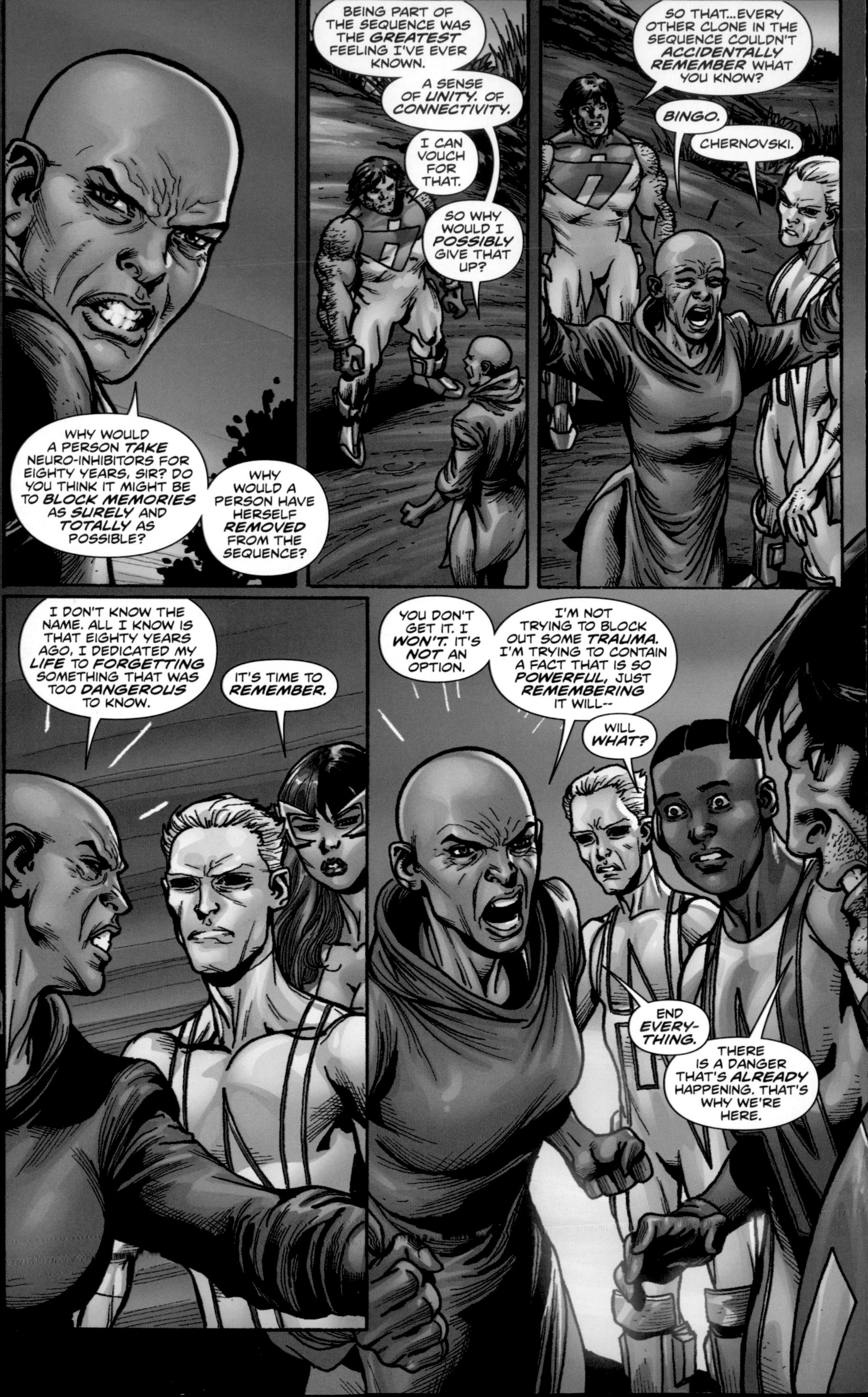

WHY WOULD A PERSON TAKE NEURO-INHIBITORS FOR EIGHTY YEARS, SIR? DO YOU THINK IT MIGHT BE TO BLOCK MEMORIES AS SURELY AND TOTALLY AS POSSIBLE?
WHY WOULD A PERSON HAVE HERSELF REMOVED FROM THE SEQUENCE?
BEING PART OF THE SEQUENCE WAS THE GREATEST FEELING I'VE EVER KNOWN.
A SENSE OF UNITY. OF CONNECTIVITY.
I CAN VOUCH FOR THAT.
SO WHY WOULD I POSSIBLY GIVE THAT UP?
SO THAT...EVERY OTHER CLONE IN THE SEQUENCE COULDN'T ACCIDENTALLY REMEMBER WHAT YOU KNOW?
BINGO.
CHERNOVSKI.
I DON'T KNOW THE NAME. ALL I KNOW IS THAT EIGHTY YEARS AGO, I DEDICATED MY LIFE TO FORGETTING SOMETHING THAT WAS TOO DANGEROUS TO KNOW.
IT'S TIME TO REMEMBER.
YOU DON'T GET IT. I WON'T. IT'S NOT AN OPTION.
I'M NOT TRYING TO BLOCK OUT SOME TRAUMA. I'M TRYING TO CONTAIN A FACT THAT IS SO POWERFUL, JUST REMEMBERING IT WILL--
WILL WHAT?
END EVERYTHING.
THERE IS A DANGER THAT'S ALREADY HAPPENING. THAT'S WHY WE'RE HERE.

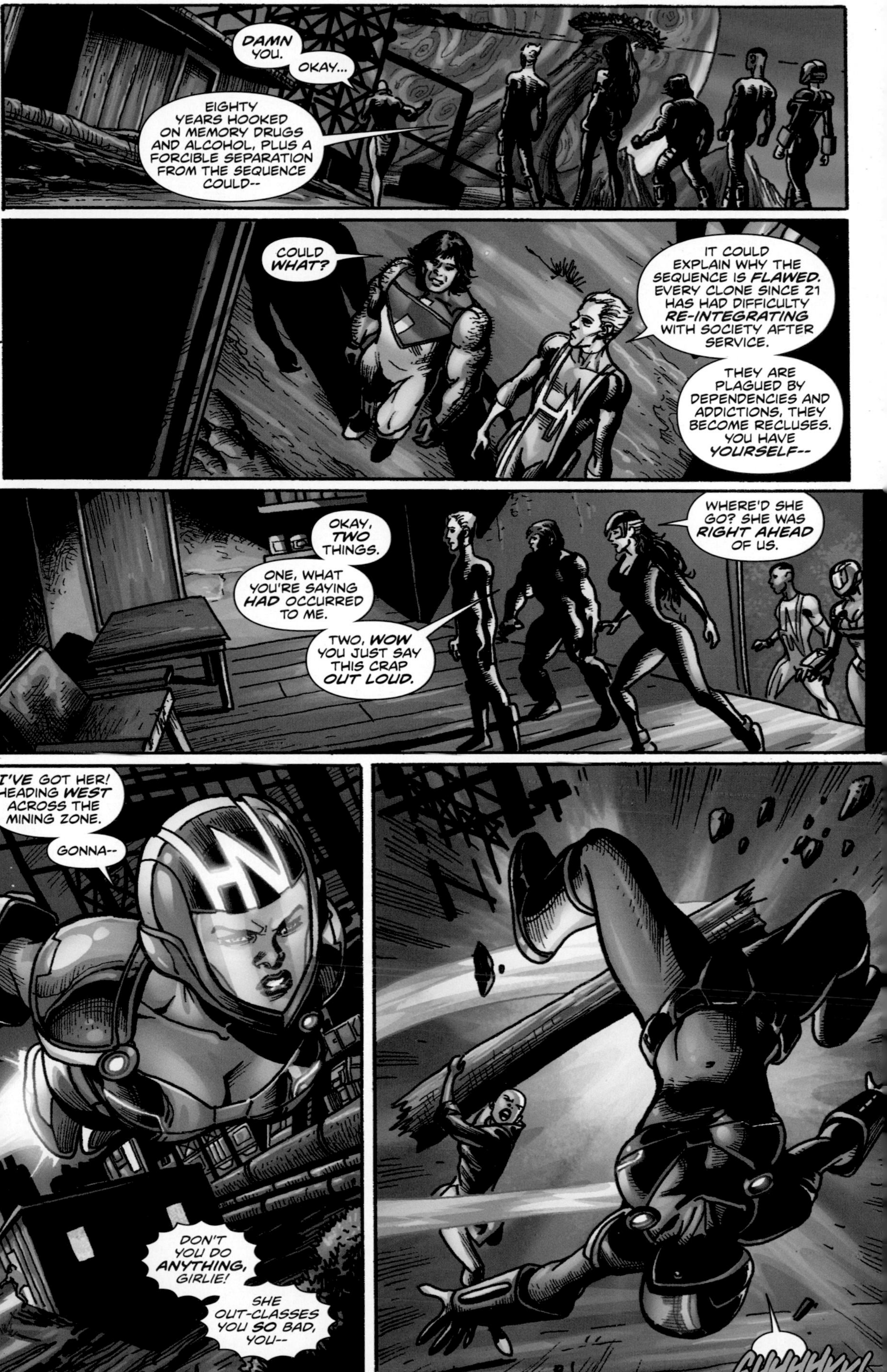

DAMN YOU.
OKAY...
EIGHTY YEARS HOOKED ON MEMORY DRUGS AND ALCOHOL, PLUS A FORCIBLE SEPARATION FROM THE SEQUENCE COULD--
COULD WHAT?
IT COULD EXPLAIN WHY THE SEQUENCE IS FLAWED. EVERY CLONE SINCE 21 HAS HAD DIFFICULTY RE-INTEGRATING WITH SOCIETY AFTER SERVICE.
THEY ARE PLAGUED BY DEPENDENCIES AND ADDICTIONS, THEY BECOME RECLUSES. YOU HAVE YOURSELF--
OKAY, TWO THINGS.
ONE, WHAT YOU'RE SAYING HAD OCCURRED TO ME.
TWO, WOW YOU JUST SAY THIS CRAP OUT LOUD.
WHERE'D SHE GO? SHE WAS RIGHT AHEAD OF US.
I'VE GOT HER! HEADING WEST ACROSS THE MINING ZONE.
GONNA--
DON'T YOU DO ANYTHING, GIRLIE!
SHE OUT-CLASSES YOU SO BAD, YOU--
GUHHHKK!

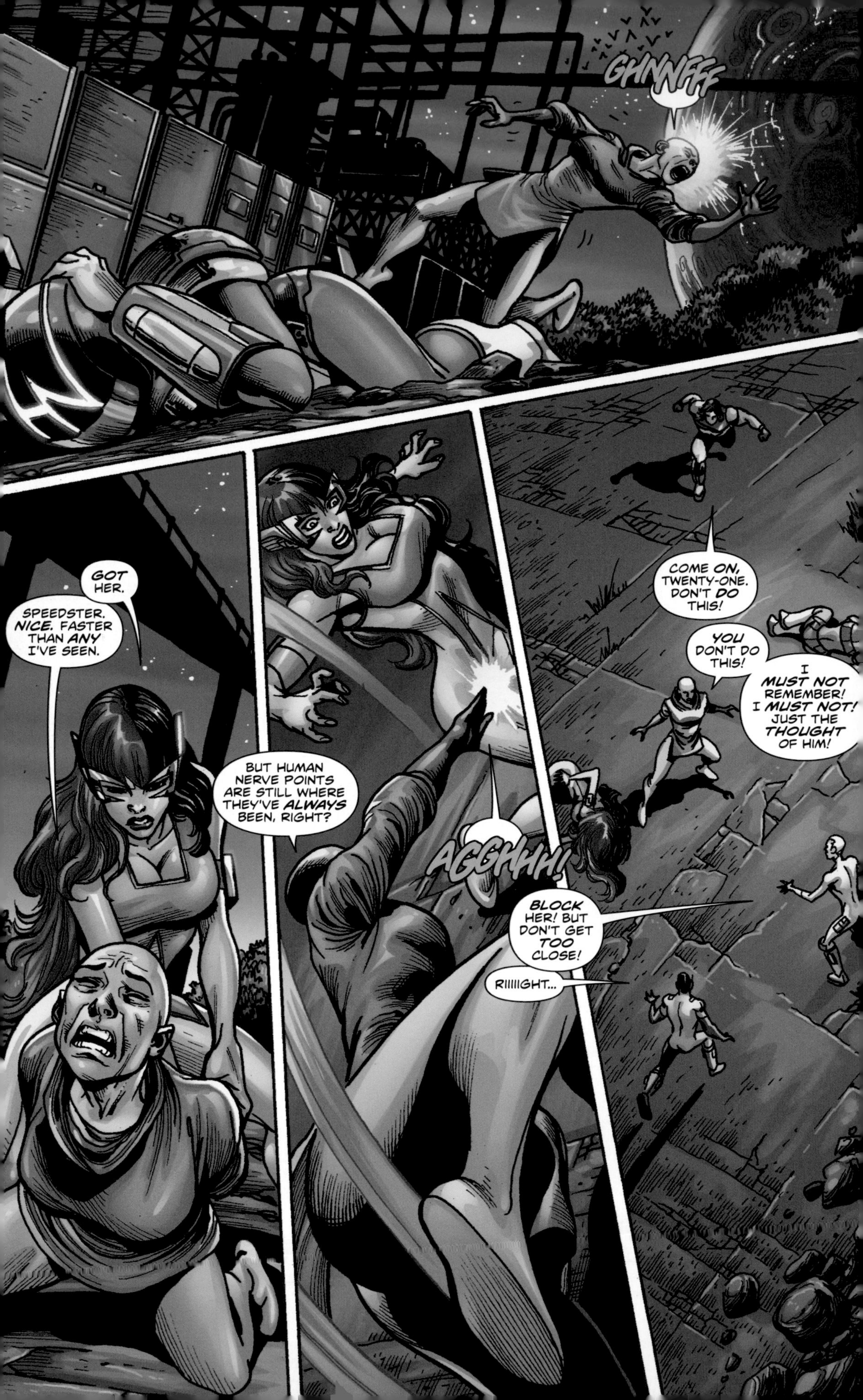
GHNNFFF
GOT HER.
SPEEDSTER. NICE. FASTER THAN ANY I'VE SEEN.
BUT HUMAN NERVE POINTS ARE STILL WHERE THEY'VE ALWAYS BEEN, RIGHT?
AGGHHH!
COME ON, TWENTY-ONE. DON'T DO THIS!
YOU DON'T DO THIS!
I MUST NOT REMEMBER! I MUST NOT! JUST THE THOUGHT OF HIM!
BLOCK HER! BUT DON'T GET TOO CLOSE!
RIIIIGHT...

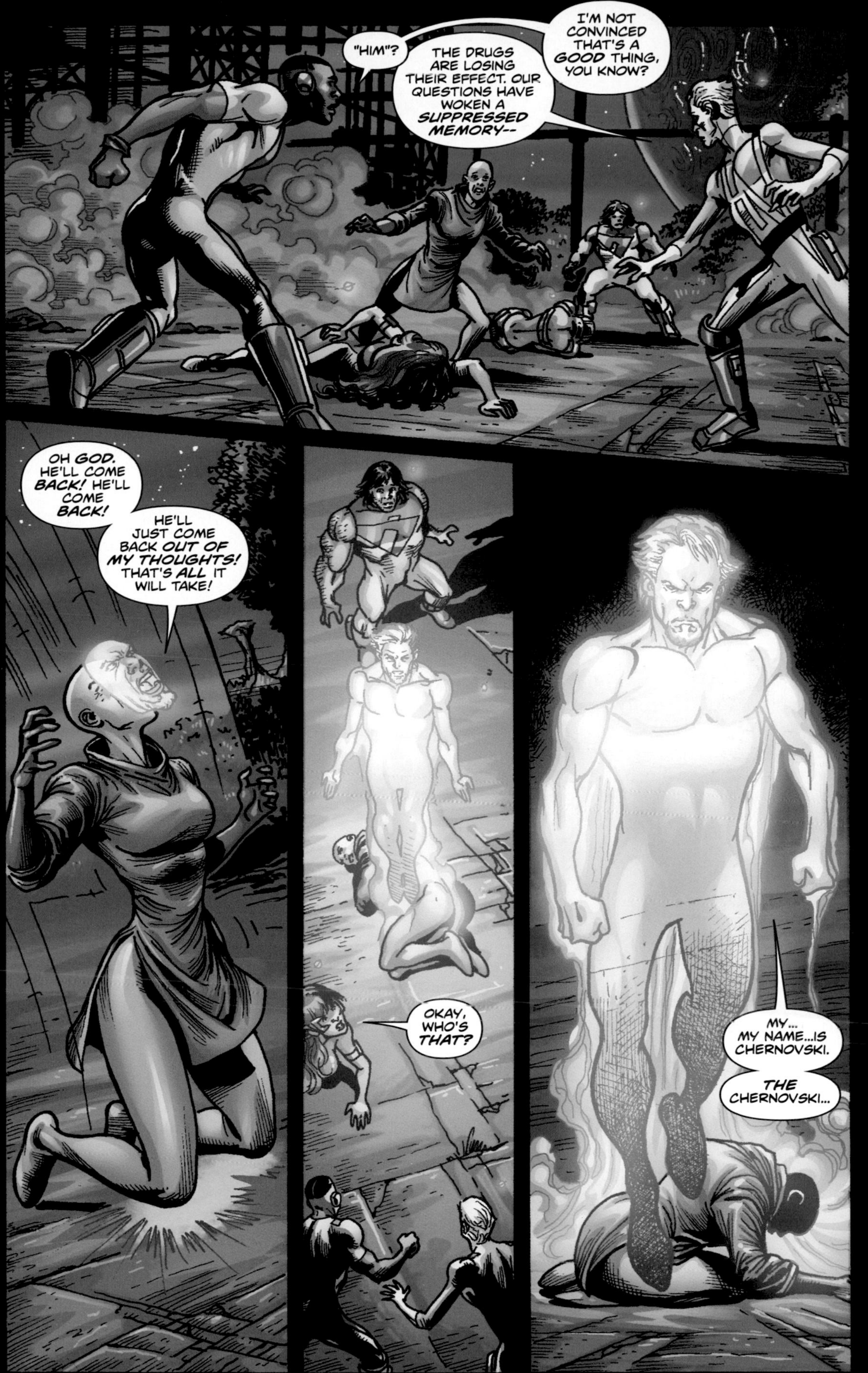
"HIM"?
THE DRUGS ARE LOSING THEIR EFFECT. OUR QUESTIONS HAVE WOKEN A SUPPRESSED MEMORY--
I'M NOT CONVINCED THAT'S A GOOD THING, YOU KNOW?
OH GOD. HE'LL COME BACK! HE'LL COME BACK!
HE'LL JUST COME BACK OUT OF MY THOUGHTS! THAT'S ALL IT WILL TAKE!
OKAY, WHO'S THAT?
MY... MY NAME...IS CHERNOVSKI.
THE CHERNOVSKI...

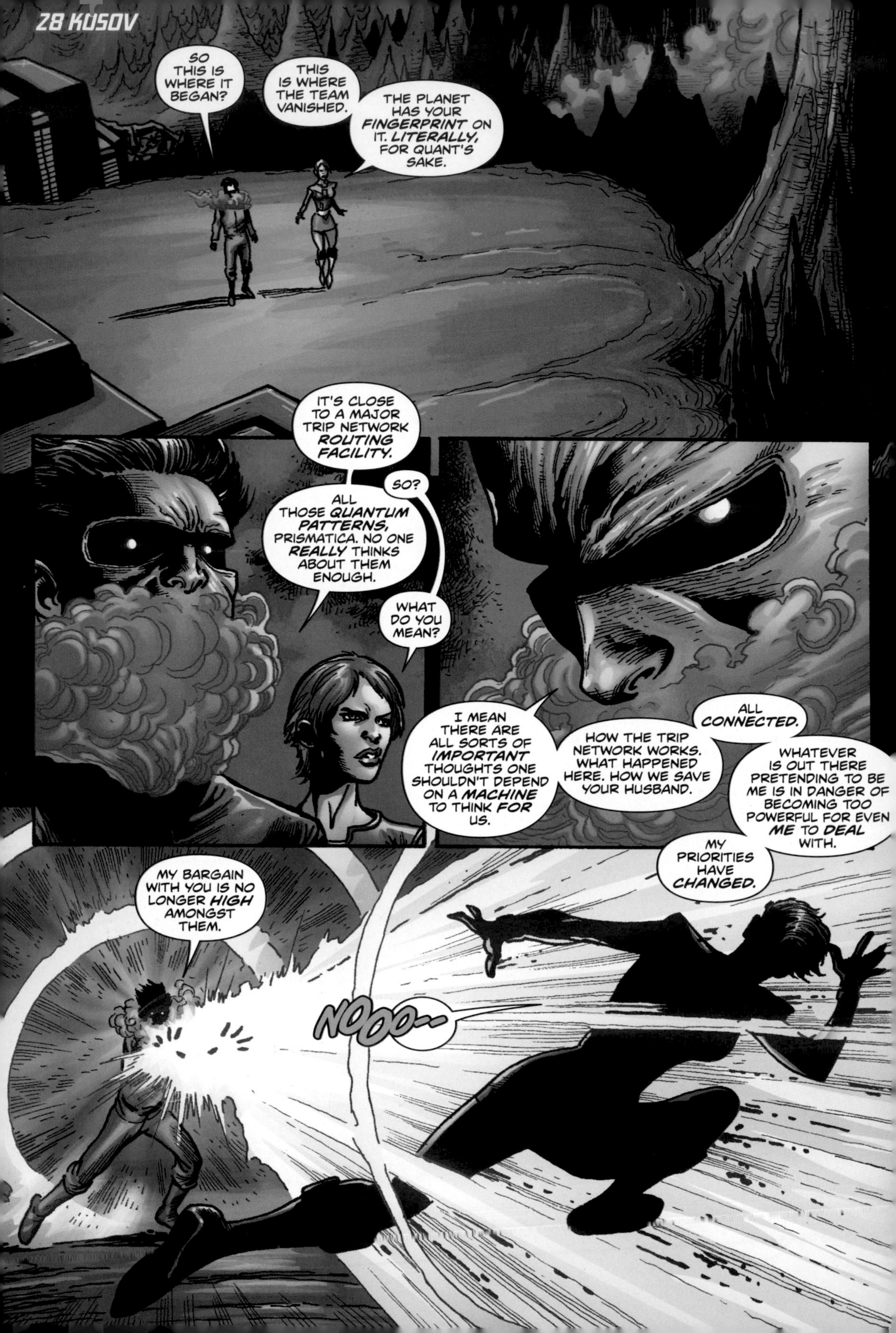
SO THIS IS WHERE IT BEGAN?
THIS IS WHERE THE TEAM VANISHED.
THE PLANET HAS YOUR FINGERPRINT ON IT. LITERALLY, FOR QUANT'S SAKE.
IT'S CLOSE TO A MAJOR TRIP NETWORK ROUTING FACILITY.
SO?
ALL THOSE QUANTUM PATTERNS, PRISMATICA. NO ONE REALLY THINKS ABOUT THEM ENOUGH.
WHAT DO YOU MEAN?
I MEAN THERE ARE ALL SORTS OF IMPORTANT THOUGHTS ONE SHOULDN'T DEPEND ON A MACHINE TO THINK FOR US.
HOW THE TRIP NETWORK WORKS. WHAT HAPPENED HERE. HOW WE SAVE YOUR HUSBAND.
ALL CONNECTED.
WHATEVER IS OUT THERE PRETENDING TO BE ME IS IN DANGER OF BECOMING TOO POWERFUL FOR EVEN ME TO DEAL WITH.
MY PRIORITIES HAVE CHANGED.
MY BARGAIN WITH YOU IS NO LONGER HIGH AMONGST THEM.
NOOO--

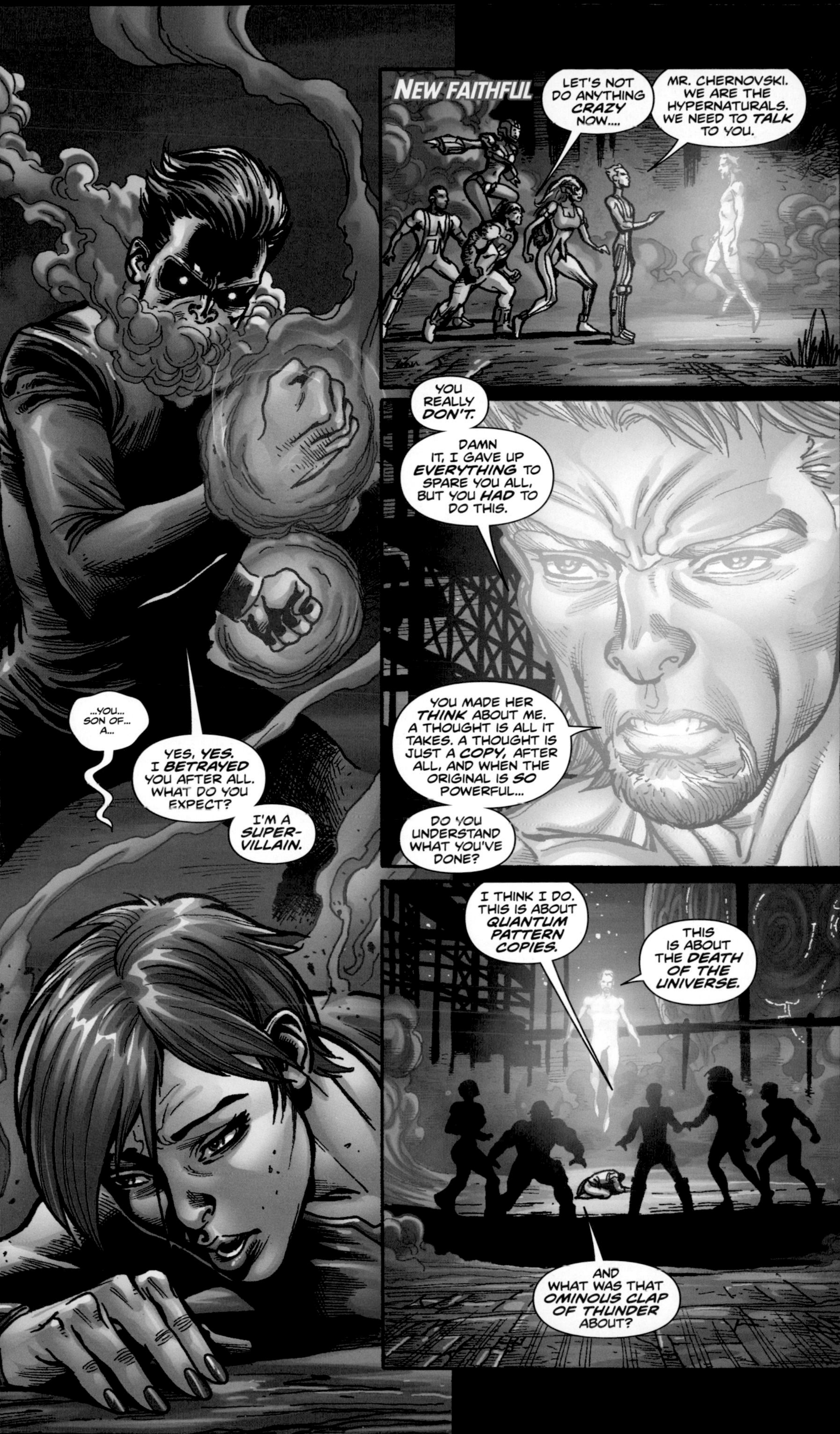
NEW FAITHFUL
LET'S NOT DO ANYTHING CRAZY NOW....
MR. CHERNOVSKI. WE ARE THE HYPERNATURALS. WE NEED TO TALK TO YOU.
YOU REALLY DON'T.
DAMN IT, I GAVE UP EVERYTHING TO SPARE YOU ALL, BUT YOU HAD TO DO THIS.
YOU MADE HER THINK ABOUT ME. A THOUGHT IS ALL IT TAKES. A THOUGHT IS JUST A COPY, AFTER ALL, AND WHEN THE ORIGINAL IS SO POWERFUL...
DO YOU UNDERSTAND WHAT YOU'VE DONE?
...YOU... SON OF... A...
YES, YES. I BETRAYED YOU AFTER ALL. WHAT DO YOU EXPECT?
I'M A SUPER-VILLAIN.
I THINK I DO. THIS IS ABOUT QUANTUM PATTERN COPIES.
THIS IS ABOUT THE DEATH OF THE UNIVERSE.
AND WHAT WAS THAT OMINOUS CLAP OF THUNDER ABOUT?

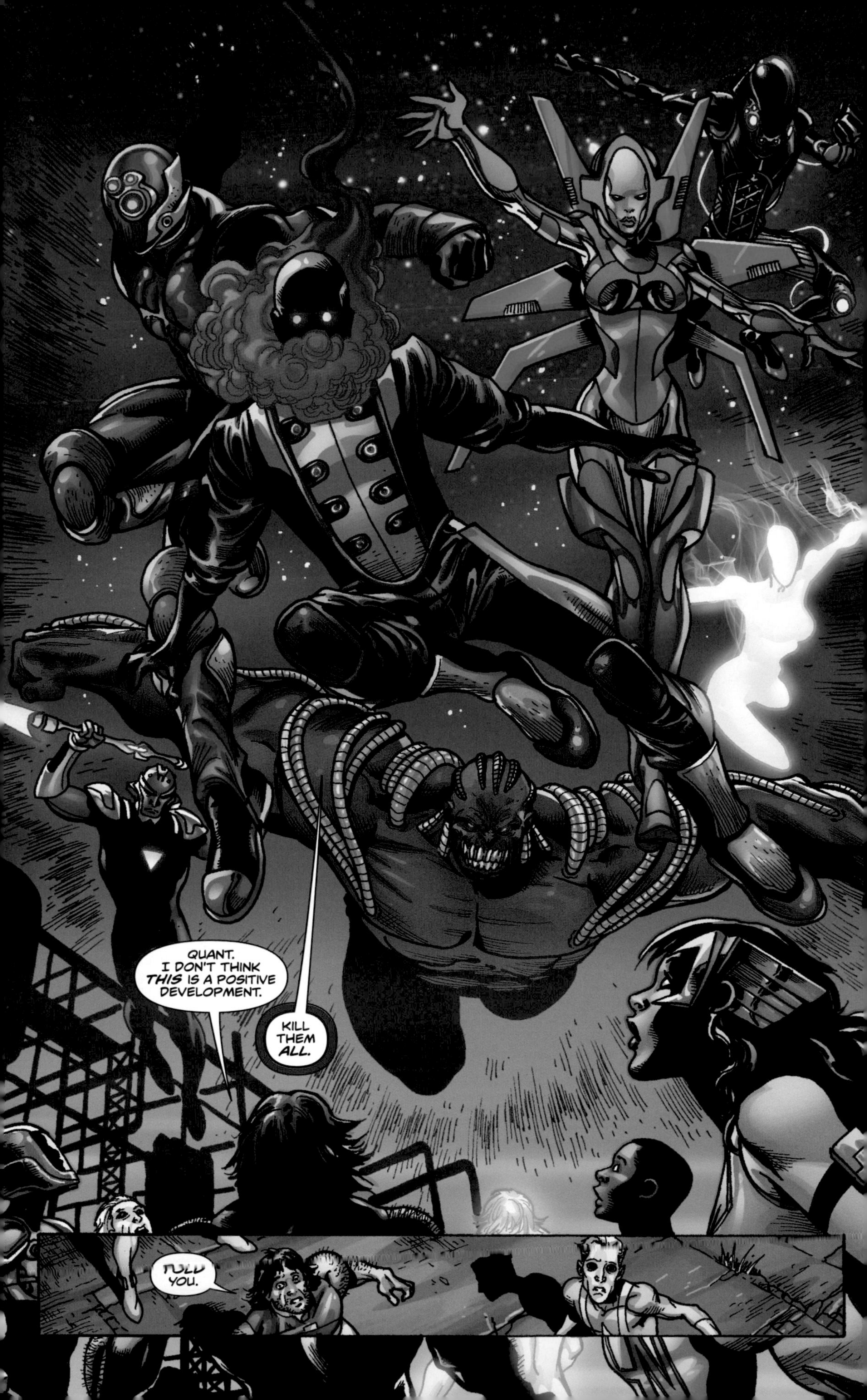
QUANT. I DON'T THINK THIS IS A POSITIVE DEVELOPMENT.
KILL THEM ALL.
TOLD YOU.

Zastrugi

Pure ice world. Pure ice water.

Quench the Quantinuum.

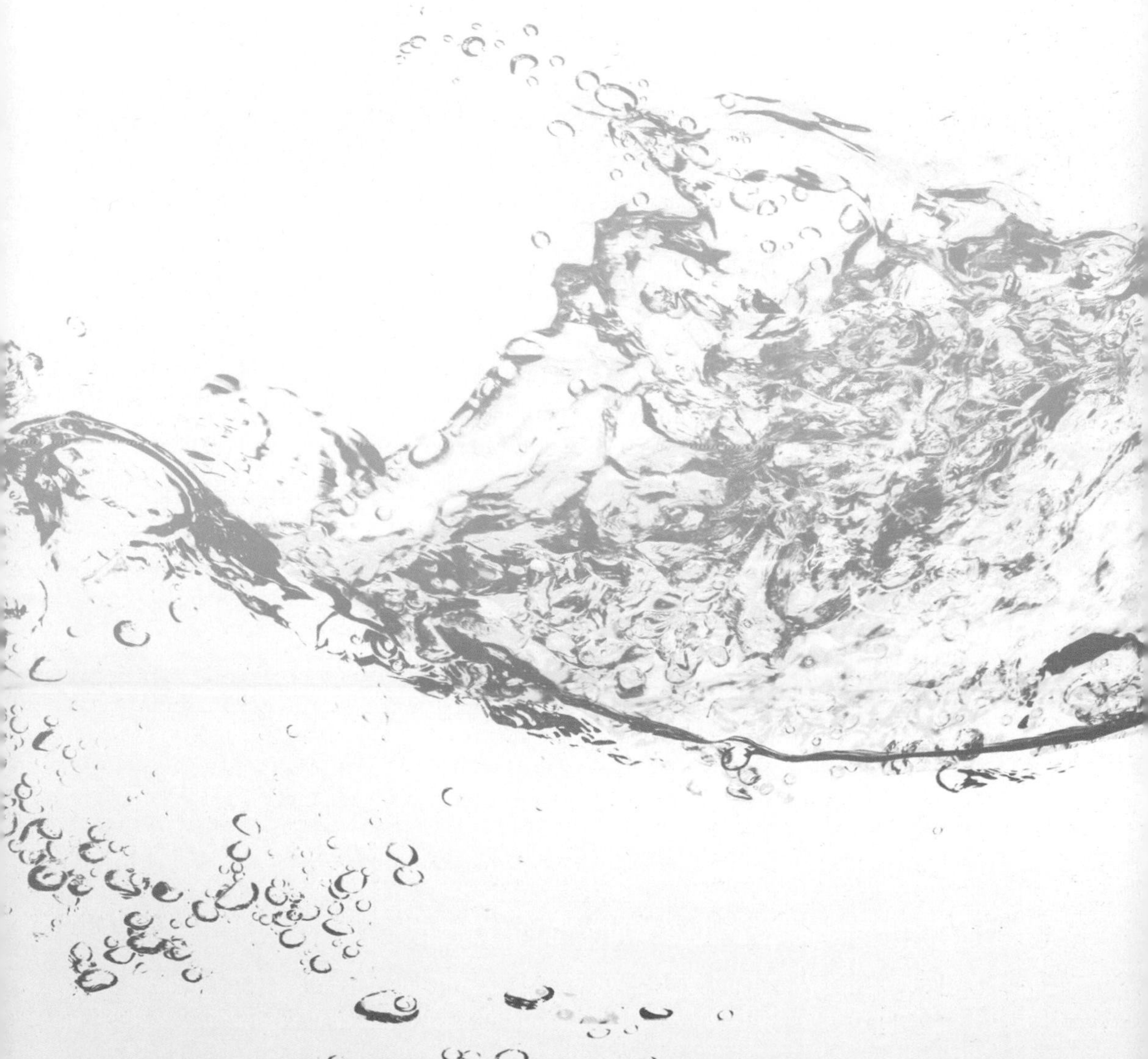

Zastrugi ® trademark of the 77 Zastrugi Water Bottling Company

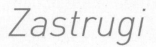

Q-CASTS

NEVER MISS AN EPISODE AGAIN   POPULAR SHOWS→   FEATURED→

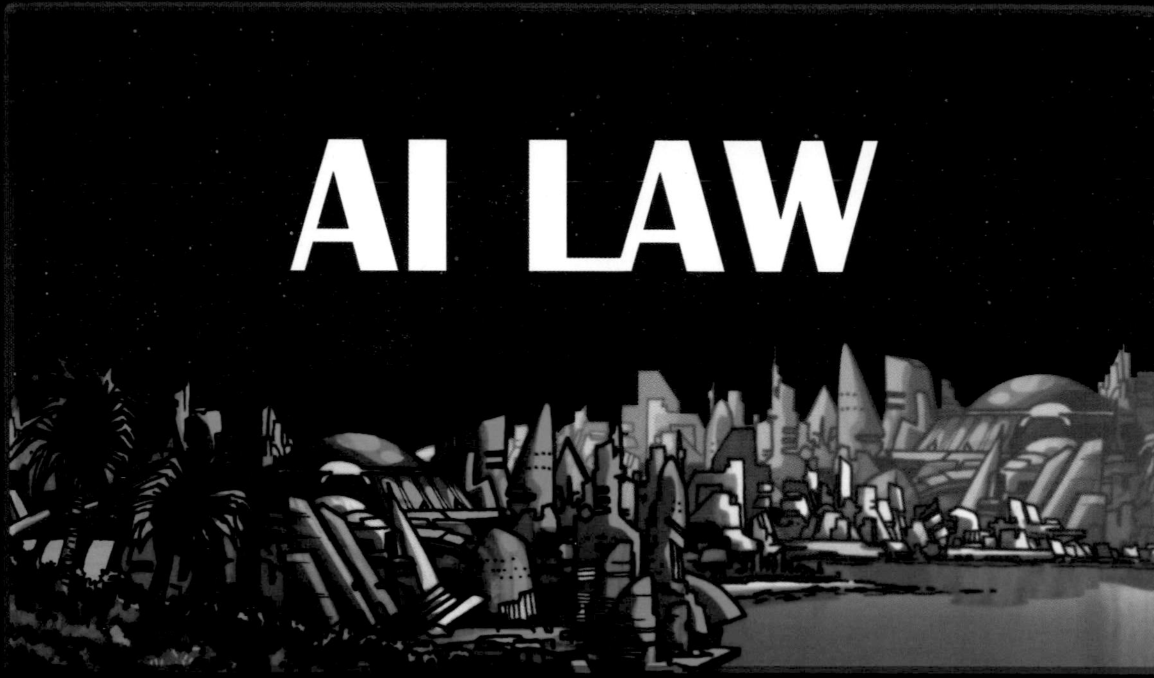
AI LAW

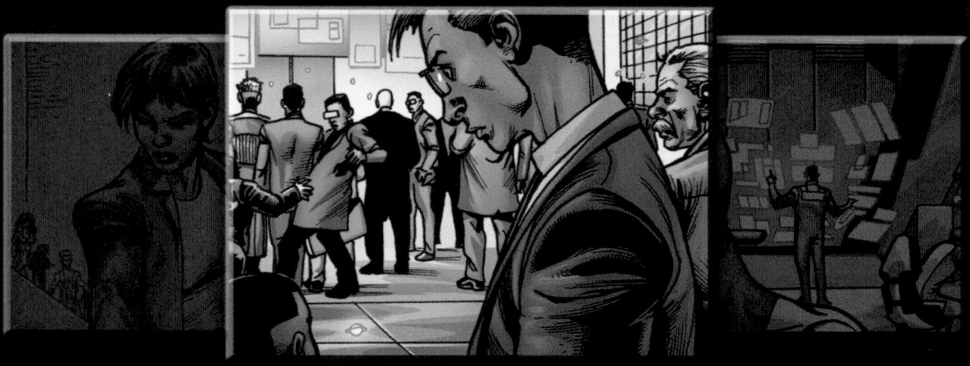

Season 5   Episode 4   Quit While You're Ahead

In this shocking episode, Hank St. Pancreas is back in town, and he's out for revenge on the lawyers of Kant Willnut Tungstun who sent him to Omni-Max! But after his recent decapitation, all Lance can think of is winning his case and recovering custody of his body. Can he do the unthinkable and retain his old rival, hard-hitting cyber-attorney Blake Taker?

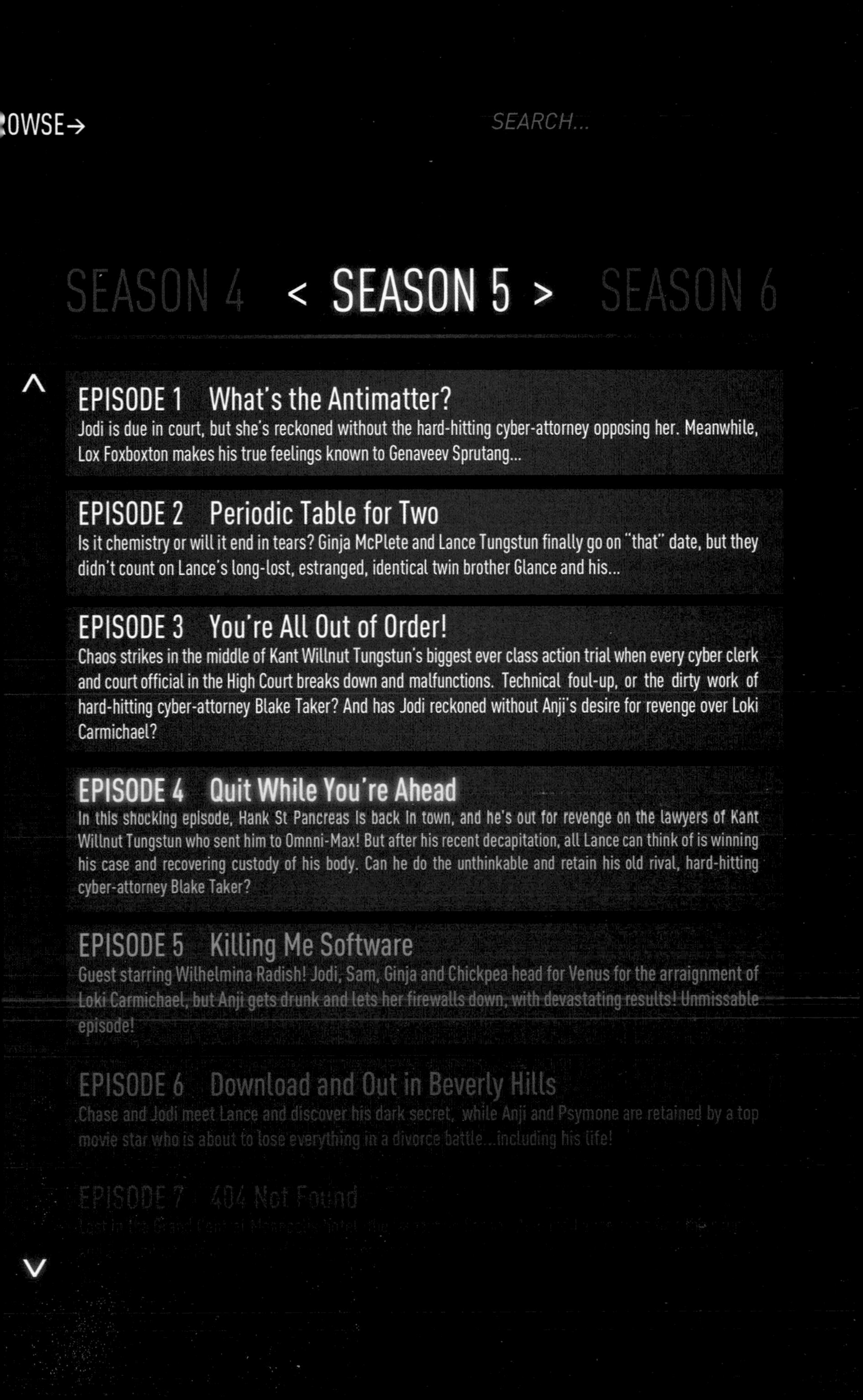
OWSE→
SEARCH...
SEASON 4 < SEASON 5 > SEASON 6
EPISODE 1 What's the Antimatter?
Jodi is due in court, but she's reckoned without the hard-hitting cyber-attorney opposing her. Meanwhile, Lox Foxboxton makes his true feelings known to Genaveev Sprutang...
EPISODE 2 Periodic Table for Two
Is it chemistry or will it end in tears? Ginja McPlete and Lance Tungstun finally go on "that" date, but they didn't count on Lance's long-lost, estranged, identical twin brother Glance and his...
EPISODE 3 You're All Out of Order!
Chaos strikes in the middle of Kant Willnut Tungstun's biggest ever class action trial when every cyber clerk and court official in the High Court breaks down and malfunctions. Technical foul-up, or the dirty work of hard-hitting cyber-attorney Blake Taker? And has Jodi reckoned without Anji's desire for revenge over Loki Carmichael?
EPISODE 4 Quit While You're Ahead
In this shocking episode, Hank St Pancreas is back in town, and he's out for revenge on the lawyers of Kant Willnut Tungstun who sent him to Omnni-Max! But after his recent decapitation, all Lance can think of is winning his case and recovering custody of his body. Can he do the unthinkable and retain his old rival, hard-hitting cyber-attorney Blake Taker?
EPISODE 5 Killing Me Software
Guest starring Wilhelmina Radish! Jodi, Sam, Ginja and Chickpea head for Venus for the arraignment of Loki Carmichael, but Anji gets drunk and lets her firewalls down, with devastating results! Unmissable episode!
EPISODE 6 Download and Out in Beverly Hills
Chase and Jodi meet Lance and discover his dark secret, while Anji and Psymone are retained by a top movie star who is about to lose everything in a divorce battle...including his life!
EPISODE 7 404 Not Found

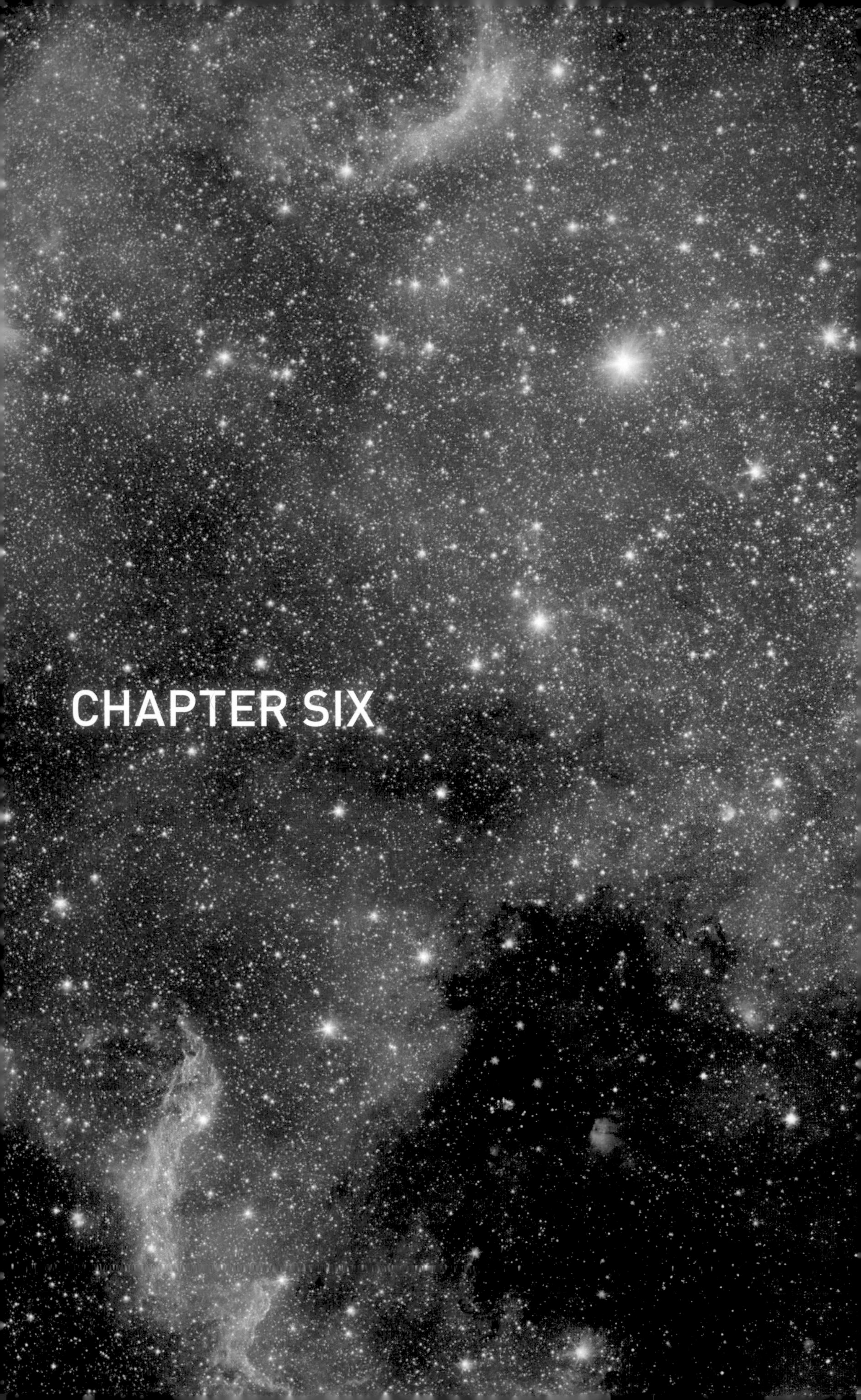

CHAPTER SIX

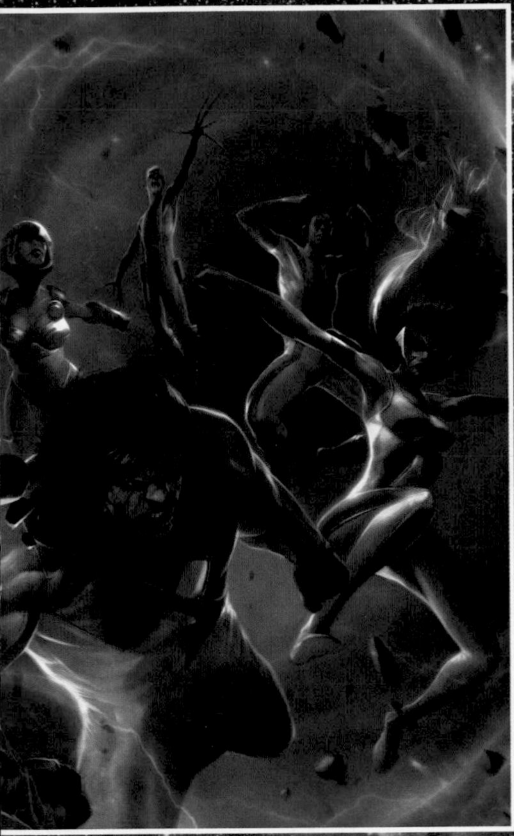

Issue Six
Francesco Mattina

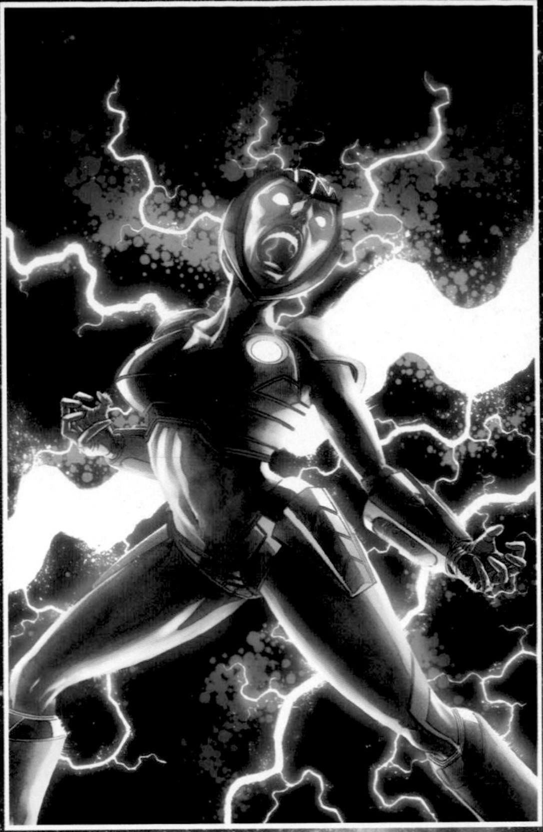

Issue Six
Wes Craig with colors by Blond

Issue Six
Tom Derenick with colors by Blond

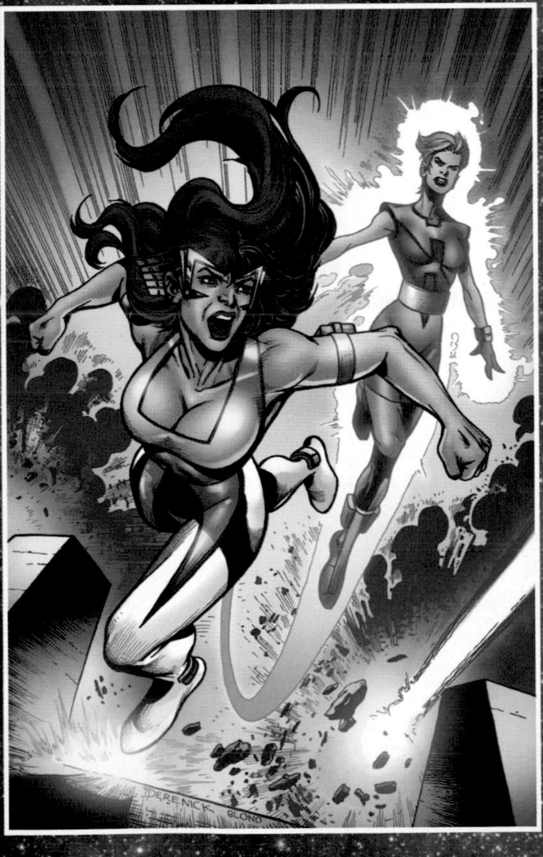

• You have selected Q-Data link.

• It is the 13th of January in the year **100 A.Q.**
- • Touch here to select an alternative to the **Anno Quantinuum** calendar system.
- • Touch here to load local weather reports for your **current cosmic location.**
- • Touch here to access **Q-Data newsflows** from planets near your current cosmic location.
- • Touch here for latest **Quantum Trip** transit times.

• Q-Data entry: The Quantinuum

• The Quantinuum is the name for the **human galactic culture**, and also for the **artificial intelligence** that controls its function.

• The Quantinuum was created 100 years ago at the start of the **Nanocene Era**. The Nanocene began when the Quantinuum AI achieved Singularity and refashioned human galactic culture. Succeeding the **Holocene Era**, the Nanocene is the next progression of human evolution and...

(to read this entry in full, touch here)

• You have selected live feed newsflow.

- • **Zade Gazurk** human rights violation trial finally reaches supreme court
- • **Blid Vizard** breaks Quantinuum **solarsurf record**
- • Early reports of rioting or breakout attempt at **Tartarus Omni-max prison**
- • **AI Law** producers announce that audience favorite Bill Frooper of **Doctor Heuristics**, who was to join the show as a hard-hitting cyber-attorney, may be suspended following accusations that he used an unlicensed clone of himself in order to take both lead roles simultaneously
- • Hypernaturals Central, San Diego, reports that the "emergency team" is continuing to investigate the disappearance of the **Centennial Year Iteration** of the team, lost during an emergency response mission to **28 Kosov** three days ago

• The Hypernaturals are the Quantinuum's foremost champions. Famous across the entirety of human galactic culture, the team members are selected on the basis of their hypernatural powers and their strength of character, and serve for five-year terms. In honor of the start of the twenty-first term, the line-up of the team's so-called "Centennial Year Iteration" has recently been announced amid huge publicity and--

...BREAKING NEWS... according to a spokesperson at Hypernaturals Central, San Diego, a special reserve formation of Hypernaturals, including now retired team members Bewilder, Clone 45 and Thinkwell from the classic "Nineteenth Tour" line-up are now working urgently to find the missing team members and resolve the crisis. Reports indicate that the team is pursuing a lead involving Hypernaturals veteran Clone 21, who has been out of the public eye for decades now...

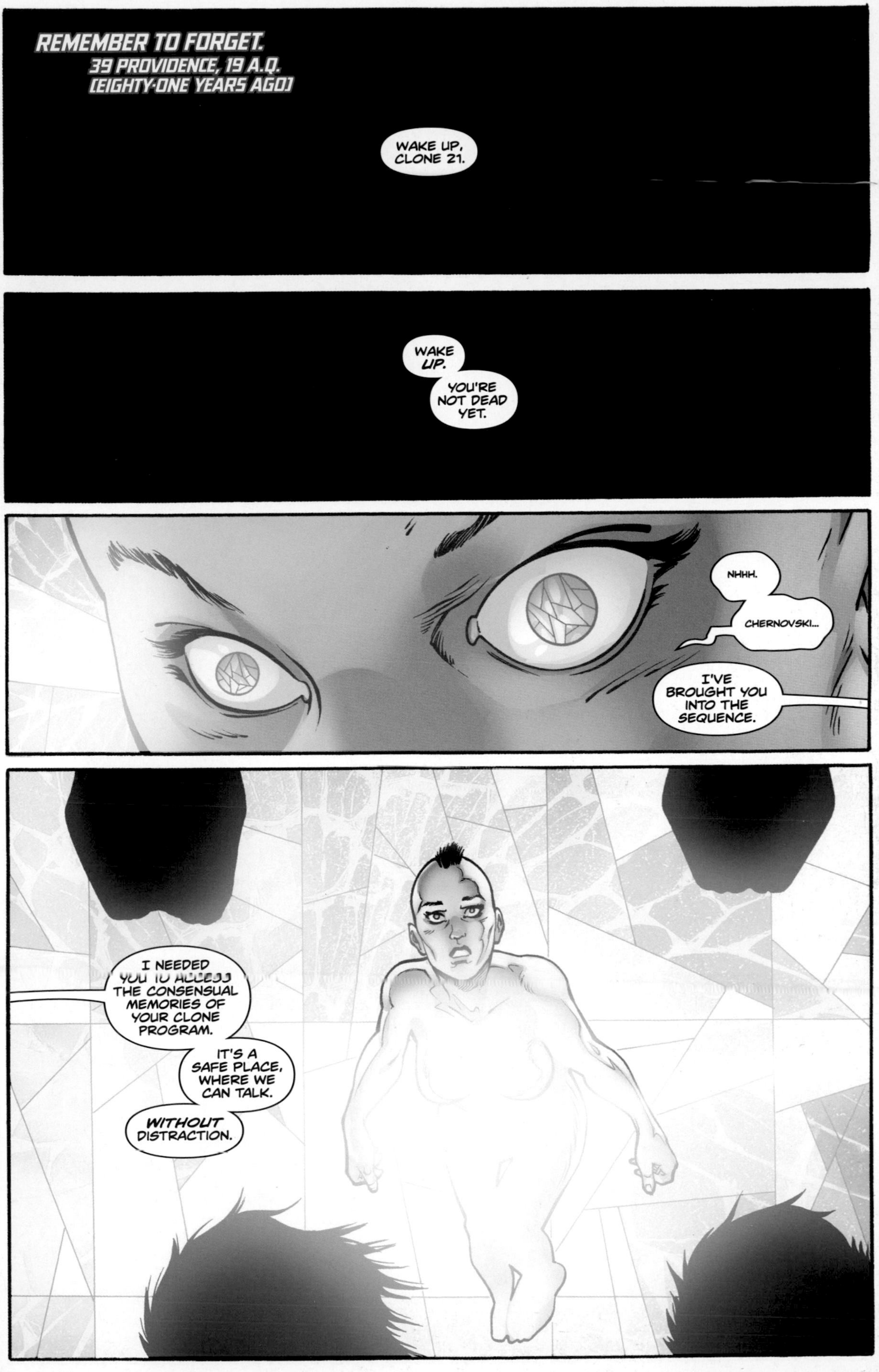
REMEMBER TO FORGET.
39 PROVIDENCE, 19 A.Q.
[EIGHTY-ONE YEARS AGO]
WAKE UP, CLONE 21.
WAKE UP.
YOU'RE NOT DEAD YET.
NHHH.
CHERNOVSKI...
I'VE BROUGHT YOU INTO THE SEQUENCE.
I NEEDED YOU TO ACCESS THE CONSENSUAL MEMORIES OF YOUR CLONE PROGRAM.
IT'S A SAFE PLACE, WHERE WE CAN TALK.
WITHOUT DISTRACTION.

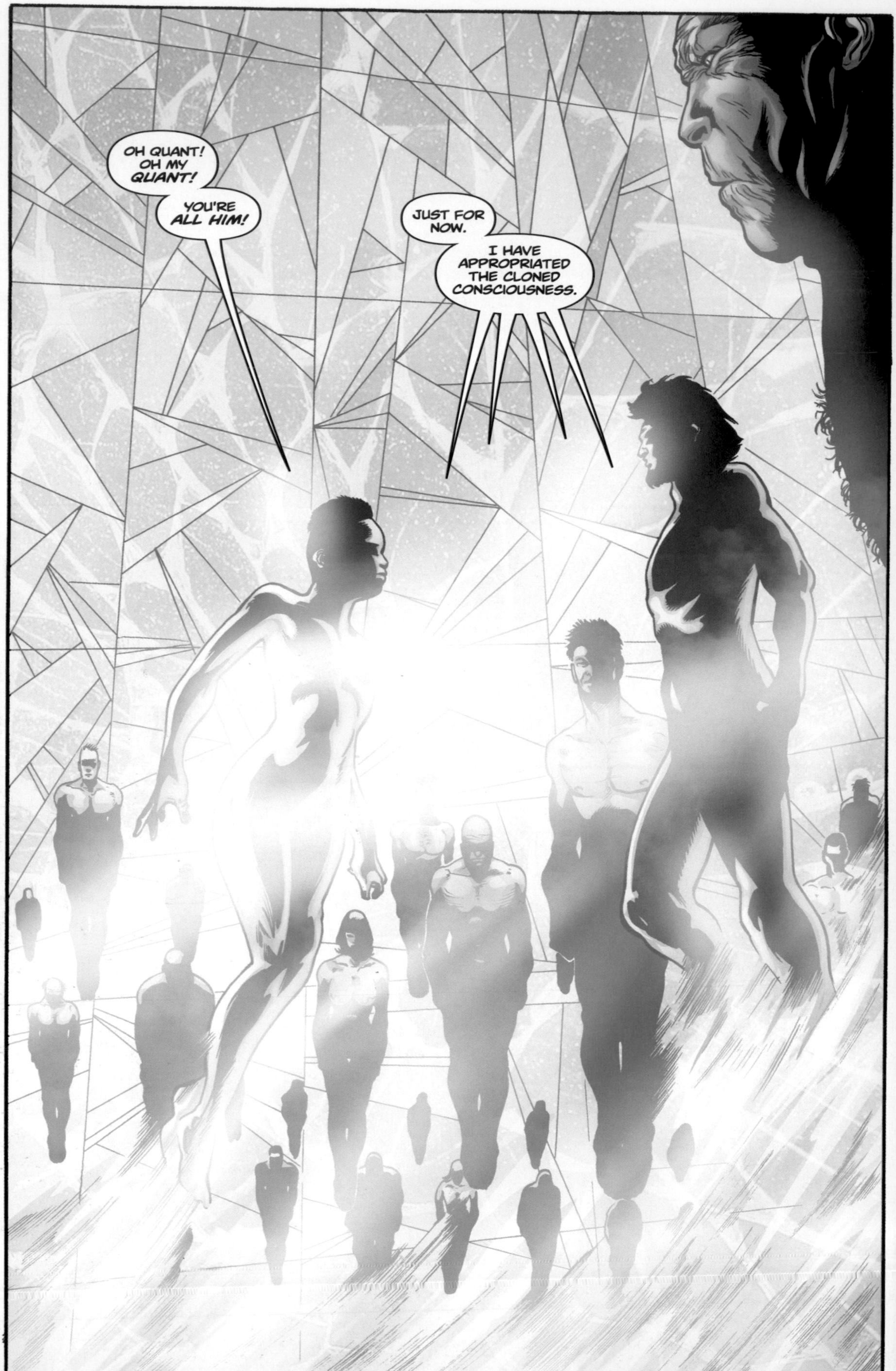
OH QUANT! OH MY QUANT!
YOU'RE ALL HIM!
JUST FOR NOW.
I HAVE APPROPRIATED THE CLONED CONSCIOUSNESS.

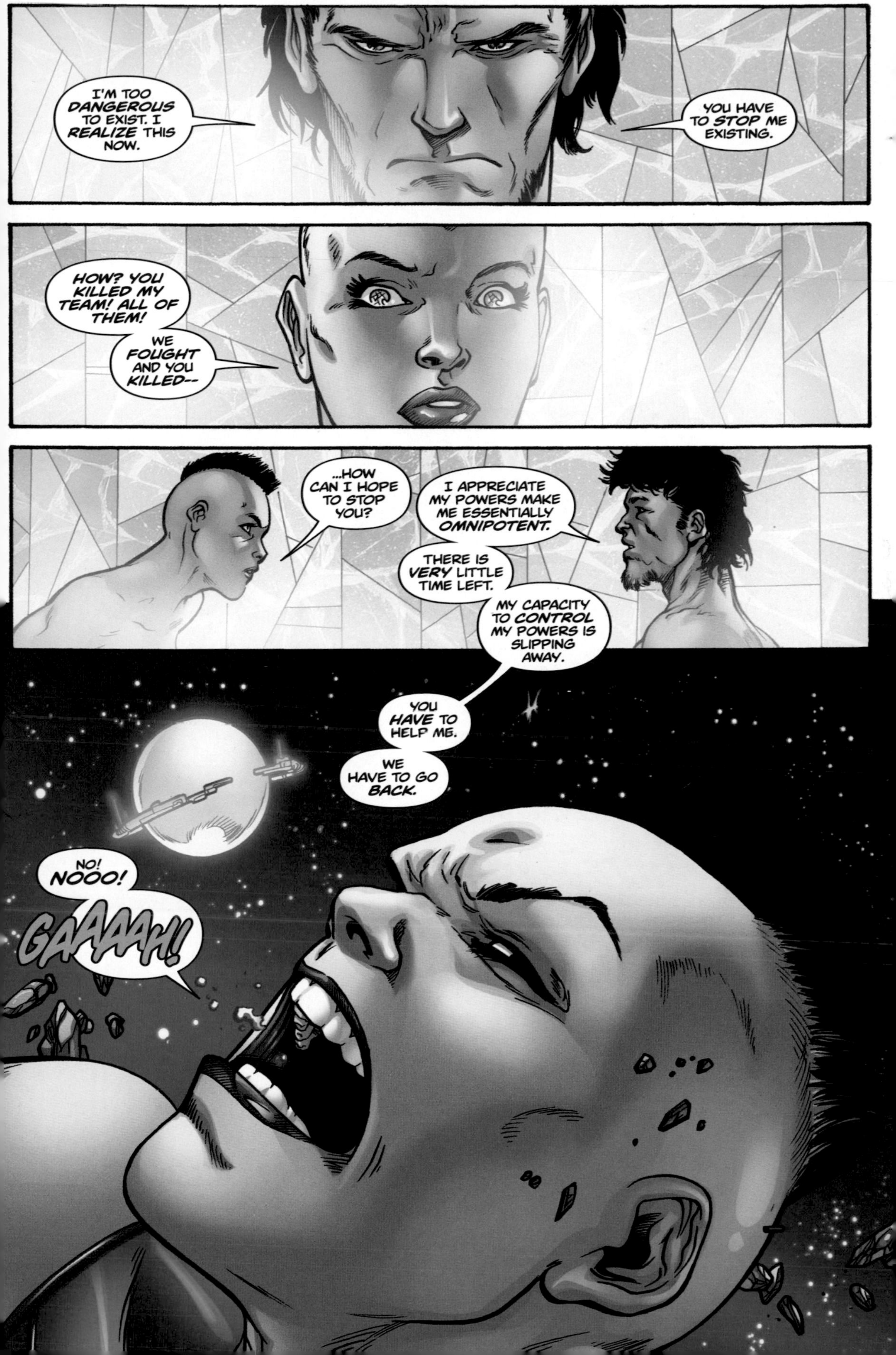
I'M TOO DANGEROUS TO EXIST. I REALIZE THIS NOW.
YOU HAVE TO STOP ME EXISTING.
HOW? YOU KILLED MY TEAM! ALL OF THEM!
WE FOUGHT AND YOU KILLED--
...HOW CAN I HOPE TO STOP YOU?
I APPRECIATE MY POWERS MAKE ME ESSENTIALLY OMNIPOTENT.
THERE IS VERY LITTLE TIME LEFT.
MY CAPACITY TO CONTROL MY POWERS IS SLIPPING AWAY.
YOU HAVE TO HELP ME.
WE HAVE TO GO BACK.
NO! NOOO!
GAAAAH!

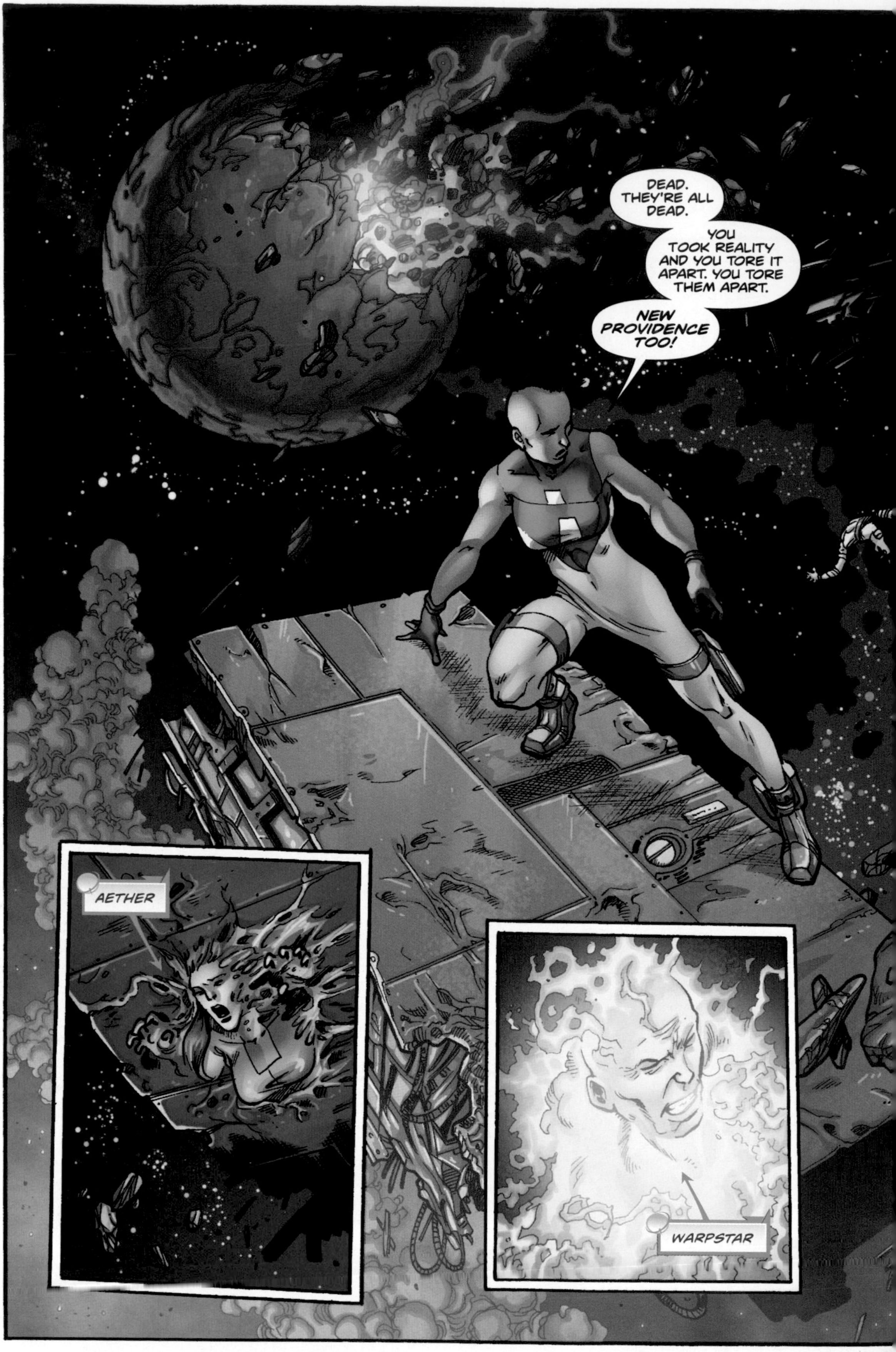
DEAD. THEY'RE ALL DEAD.
YOU TOOK REALITY AND YOU TORE IT APART. YOU TORE THEM APART.
NEW PROVIDENCE TOO!
AETHER
WARPSTAR

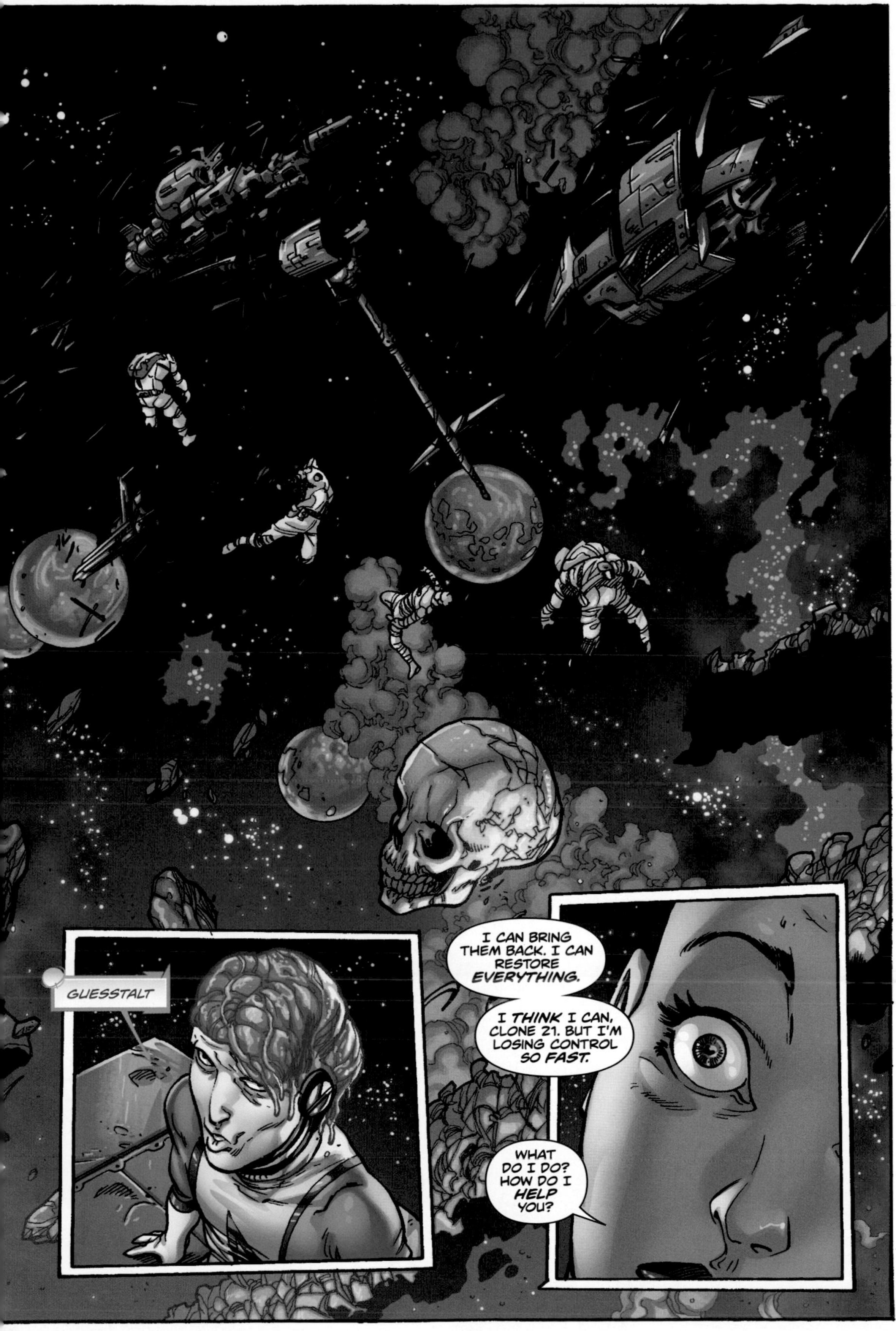
GUESSTALT
I CAN BRING THEM BACK. I CAN RESTORE EVERYTHING.
I THINK I CAN, CLONE 21. BUT I'M LOSING CONTROL SO FAST.
WHAT DO I DO? HOW DO I HELP YOU?

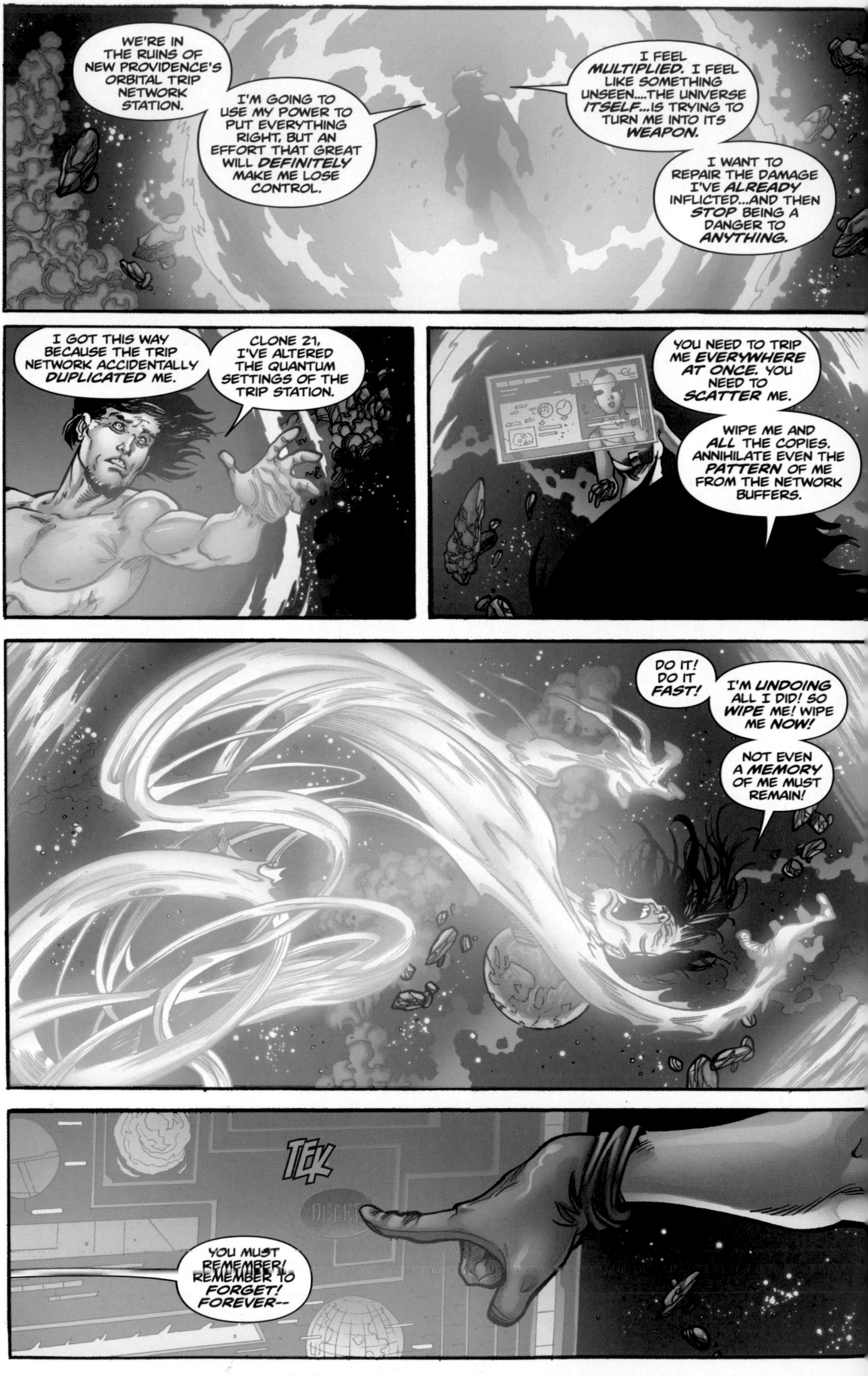
WE'RE IN THE RUINS OF NEW PROVIDENCE'S ORBITAL TRIP NETWORK STATION.
I'M GOING TO USE MY POWER TO PUT EVERYTHING RIGHT, BUT AN EFFORT THAT GREAT WILL DEFINITELY MAKE ME LOSE CONTROL.
I FEEL MULTIPLIED. I FEEL LIKE SOMETHING UNSEEN....THE UNIVERSE ITSELF...IS TRYING TO TURN ME INTO ITS WEAPON.
I WANT TO REPAIR THE DAMAGE I'VE ALREADY INFLICTED...AND THEN STOP BEING A DANGER TO ANYTHING.
I GOT THIS WAY BECAUSE THE TRIP NETWORK ACCIDENTALLY DUPLICATED ME.
CLONE 21, I'VE ALTERED THE QUANTUM SETTINGS OF THE TRIP STATION.
YOU NEED TO TRIP ME EVERYWHERE AT ONCE. YOU NEED TO SCATTER ME.
WIPE ME AND ALL THE COPIES. ANNIHILATE EVEN THE PATTERN OF ME FROM THE NETWORK BUFFERS.
DO IT! DO IT FAST!
I'M UNDOING ALL I DID! SO WIPE ME! WIPE ME NOW!
NOT EVEN A MEMORY OF ME MUST REMAIN!
TEK
YOU MUST REMEMBER! REMEMBER TO FORGET! FOREVER--

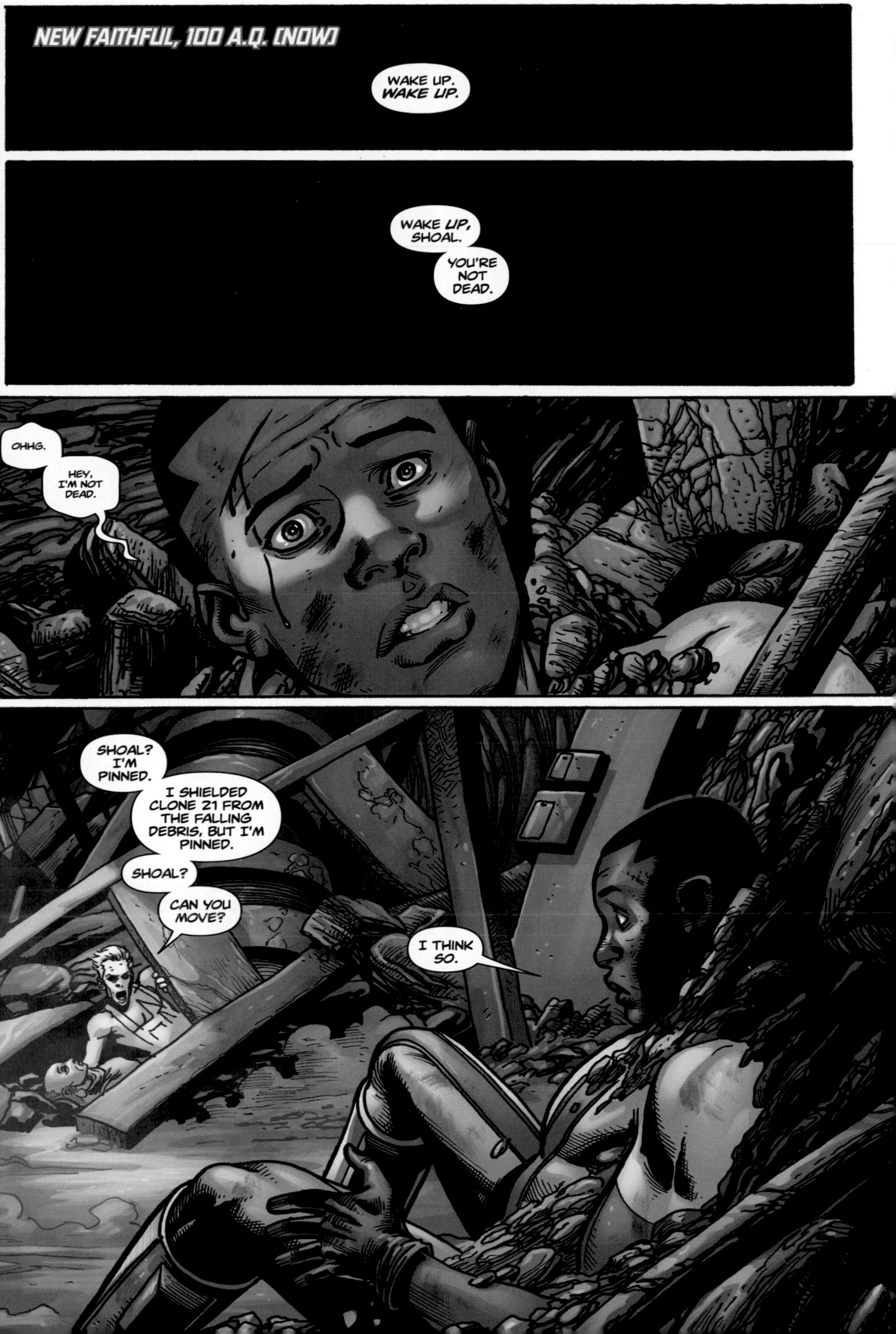
NEW FAITHFUL, 100 A.Q. (NOW)
WAKE UP. WAKE UP.
WAKE UP, SHOAL.
YOU'RE NOT DEAD.
OHHG.
HEY, I'M NOT DEAD.
SHOAL? I'M PINNED.
I SHIELDED CLONE 21 FROM THE FALLING DEBRIS, BUT I'M PINNED.
SHOAL?
CAN YOU MOVE?
I THINK SO.

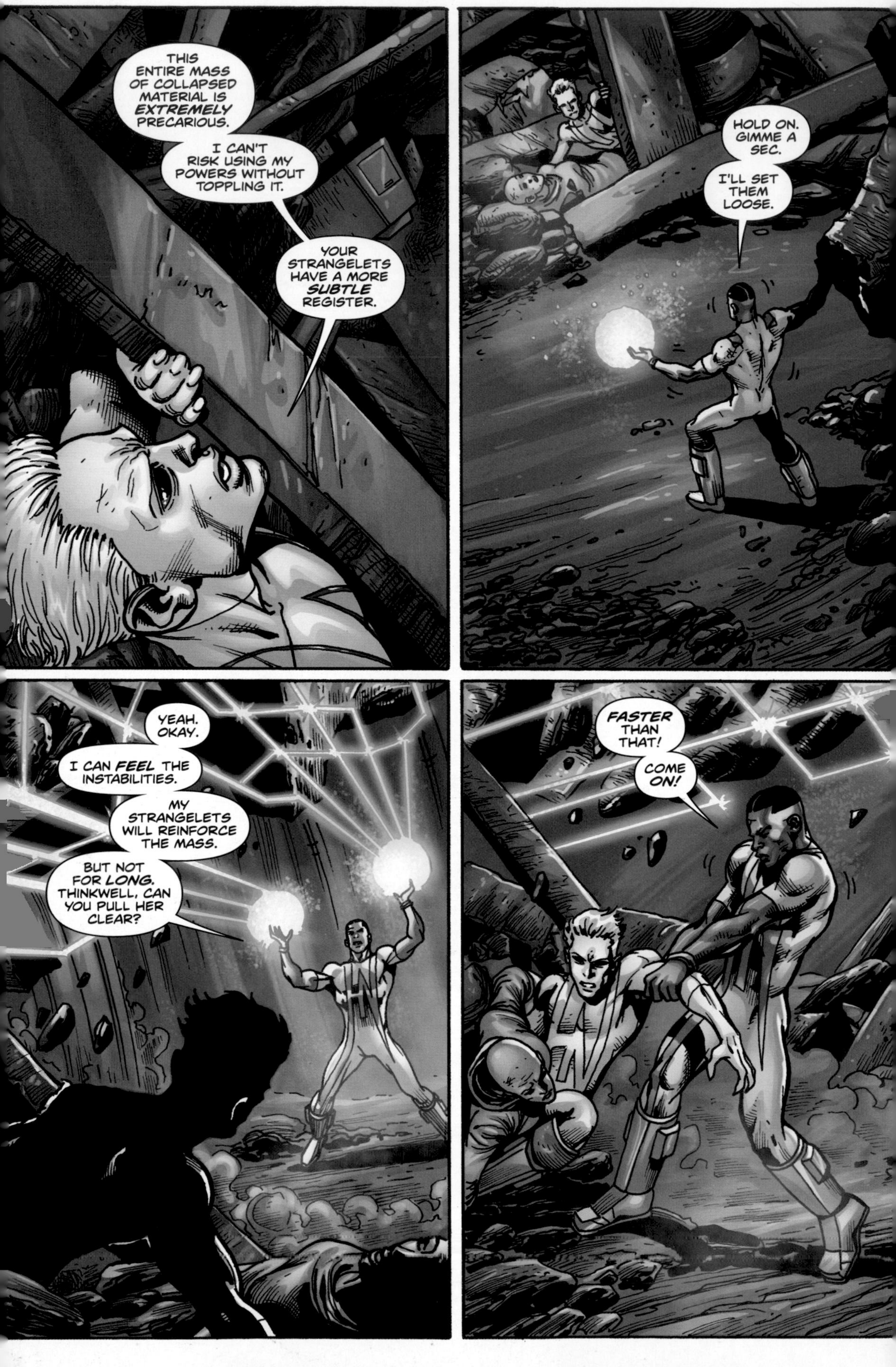
THIS ENTIRE MASS OF COLLAPSED MATERIAL IS *EXTREMELY* PRECARIOUS.
I CAN'T RISK USING MY POWERS WITHOUT TOPPLING IT.
YOUR STRANGELETS HAVE A MORE *SUBTLE* REGISTER.
HOLD ON. GIMME A SEC.
I'LL SET THEM LOOSE.
YEAH. OKAY.
I CAN *FEEL* THE INSTABILITIES.
MY STRANGELETS WILL REINFORCE THE MASS.
BUT NOT FOR *LONG*. THINKWELL, CAN YOU PULL HER CLEAR?
FASTER THAN THAT!
COME *ON!*

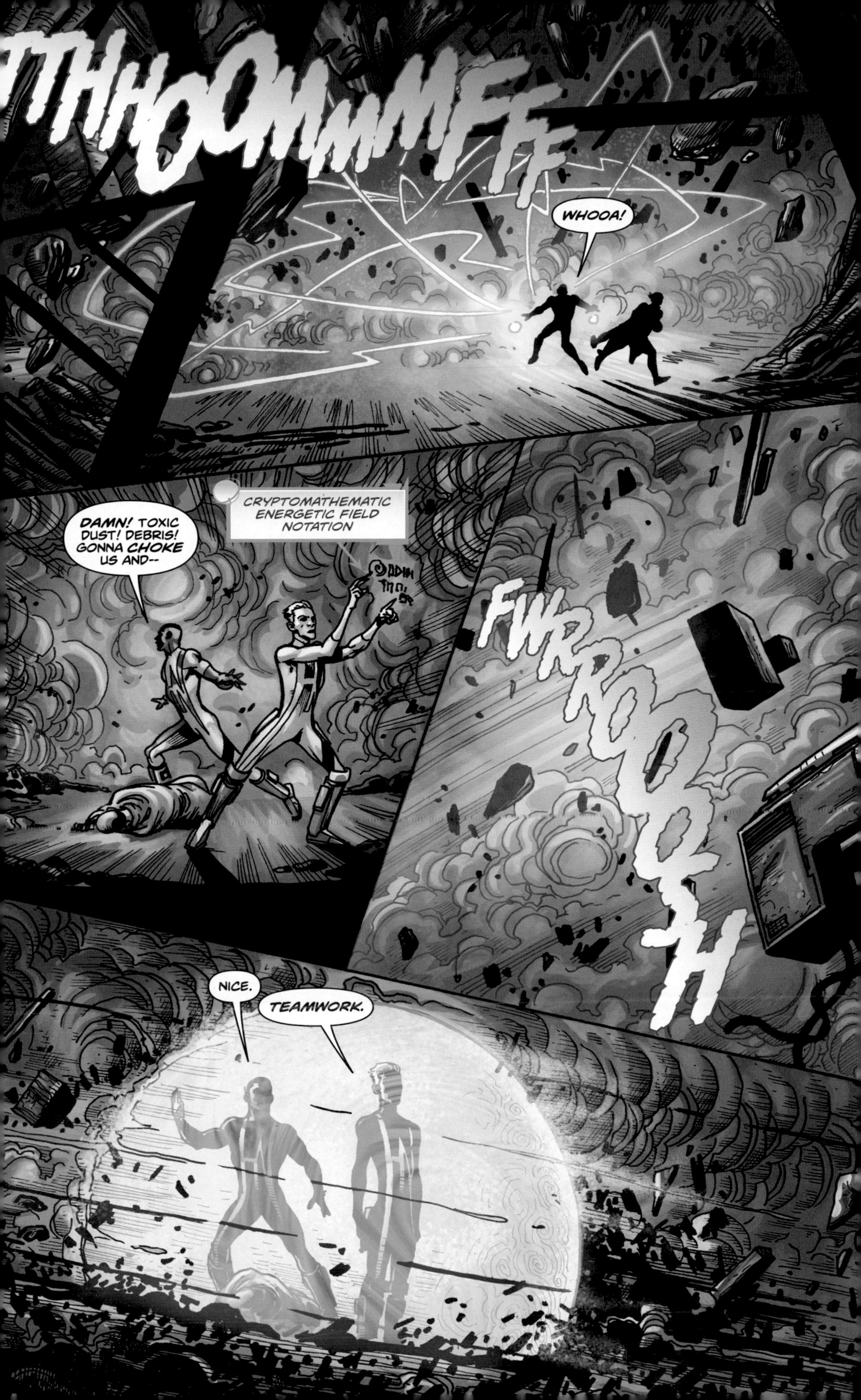
THHOOMMMFF
WHOOA!
DAMN! TOXIC DUST! DEBRIS! GONNA CHOKE US AND--
CRYPTOMATHEMATIC ENERGETIC FIELD NOTATION
FWRROOOOSH
NICE.
TEAMWORK.

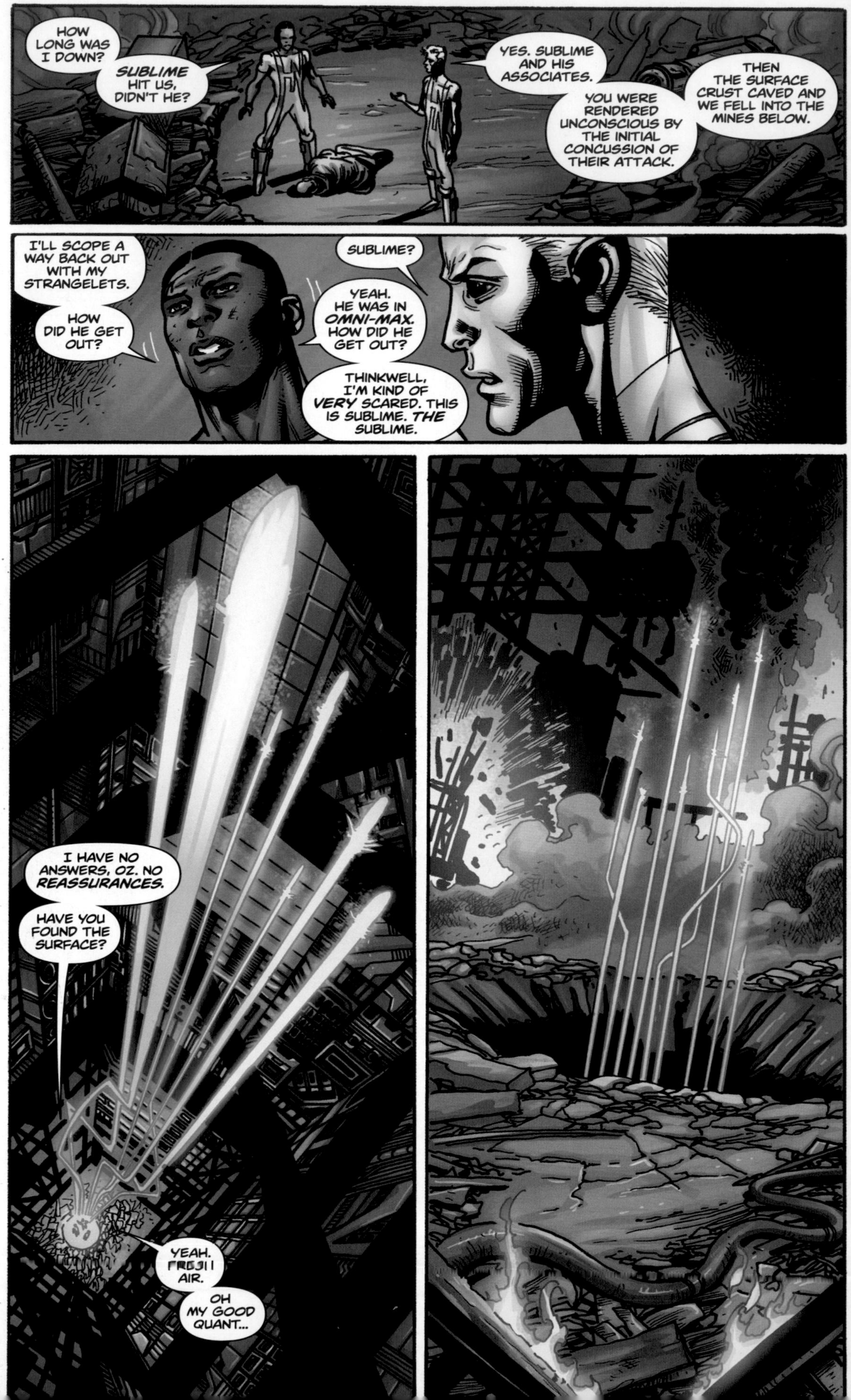
HOW LONG WAS I DOWN?
SUBLIME HIT US, DIDN'T HE?
YES. SUBLIME AND HIS ASSOCIATES.
YOU WERE RENDERED UNCONSCIOUS BY THE INITIAL CONCUSSION OF THEIR ATTACK.
THEN THE SURFACE CRUST CAVED AND WE FELL INTO THE MINES BELOW.
I'LL SCOPE A WAY BACK OUT WITH MY STRANGELETS.
HOW DID HE GET OUT?
SUBLIME?
YEAH. HE WAS IN OMNI-MAX. HOW DID HE GET OUT?
THINKWELL, I'M KIND OF VERY SCARED. THIS IS SUBLIME. THE SUBLIME.
I HAVE NO ANSWERS, OZ. NO REASSURANCES.
HAVE YOU FOUND THE SURFACE?
YEAH. FRESH AIR.
OH MY GOOD QUANT...

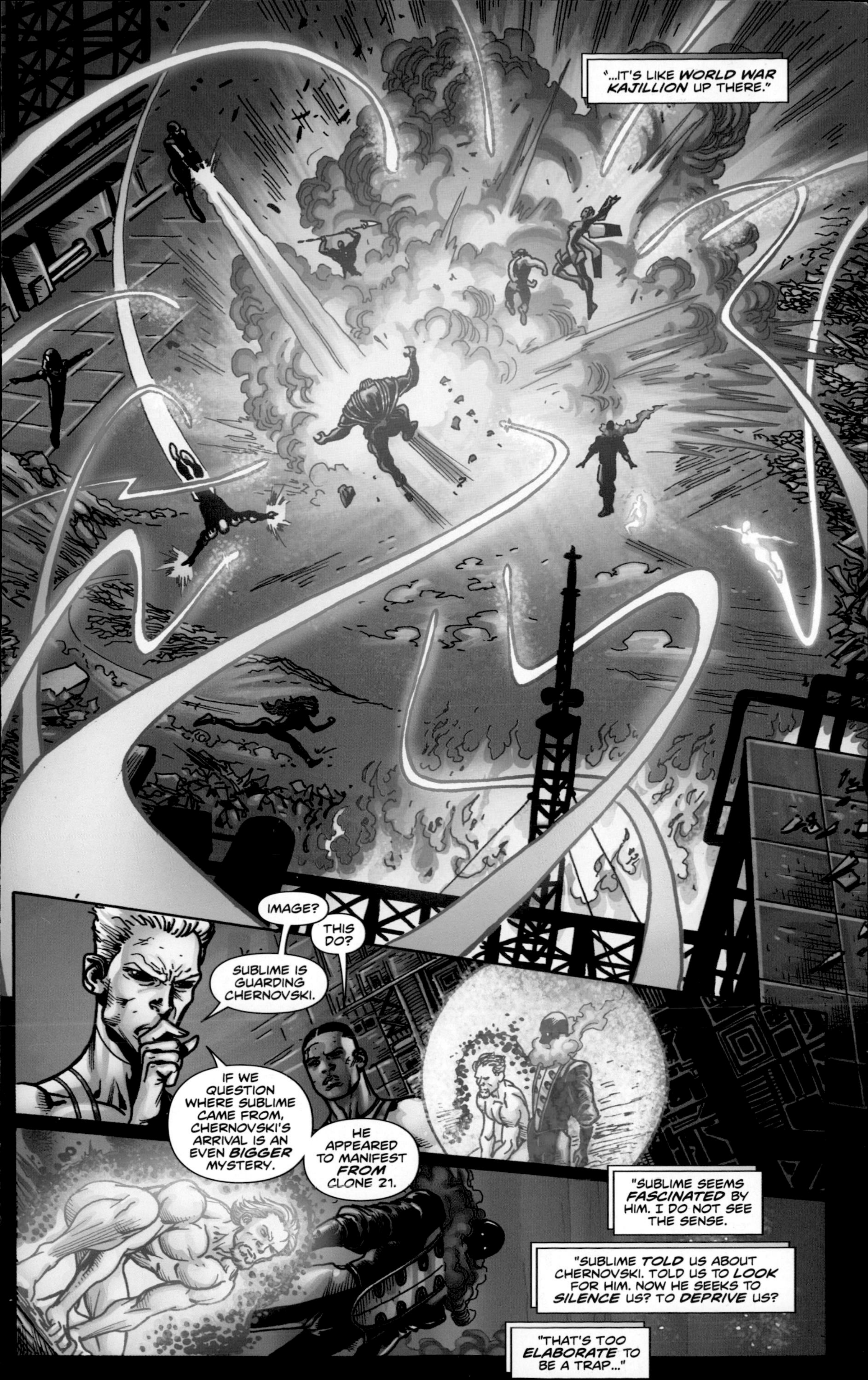
"...IT'S LIKE WORLD WAR KAJILLION UP THERE."
IMAGE?
THIS DO?
SUBLIME IS GUARDING CHERNOVSKI.
IF WE QUESTION WHERE SUBLIME CAME FROM, CHERNOVSKI'S ARRIVAL IS AN EVEN BIGGER MYSTERY.
HE APPEARED TO MANIFEST FROM CLONE 21.
"SUBLIME SEEMS FASCINATED BY HIM. I DO NOT SEE THE SENSE.
"SUBLIME TOLD US ABOUT CHERNOVSKI. TOLD US TO LOOK FOR HIM. NOW HE SEEKS TO SILENCE US? TO DEPRIVE US?
"THAT'S TOO ELABORATE TO BE A TRAP..."

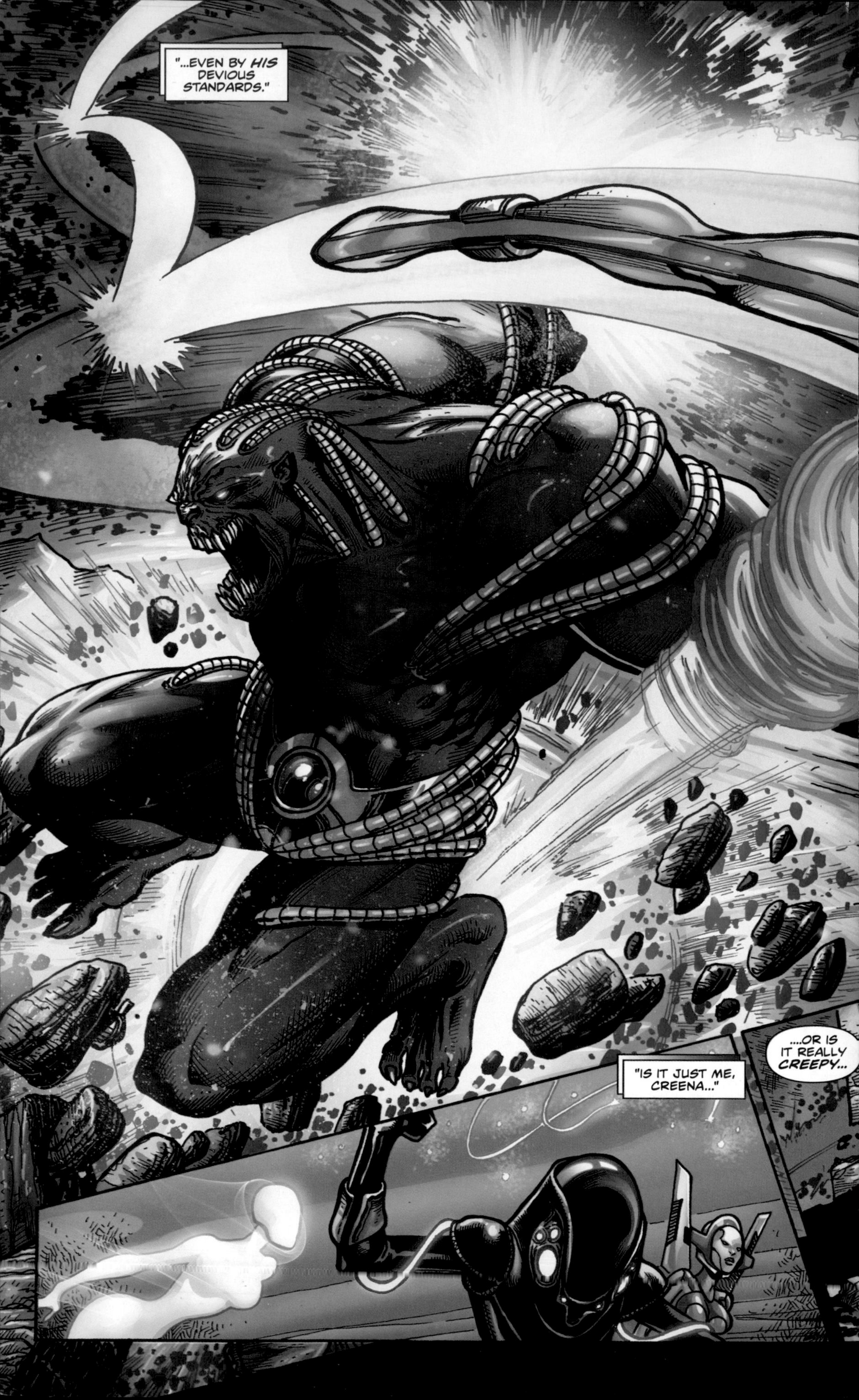
"...EVEN BY HIS DEVIOUS STANDARDS."
"IS IT JUST ME, CREENA..."
...OR IS IT REALLY CREEPY...

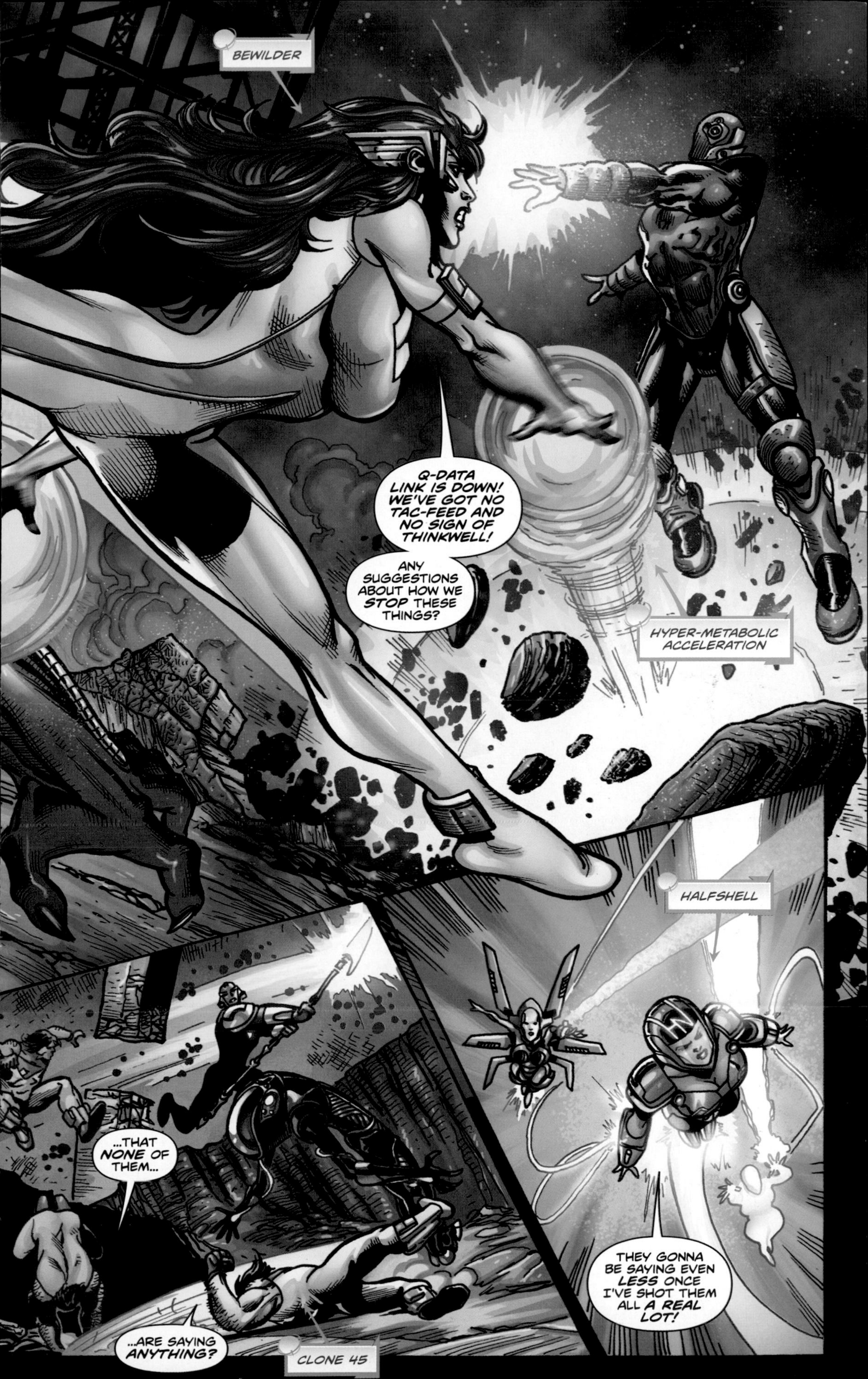
BEWILDER
Q-DATA LINK IS DOWN! WE'VE GOT NO TAC-FEED AND NO SIGN OF THINKWELL!
ANY SUGGESTIONS ABOUT HOW WE STOP THESE THINGS?
HYPER-METABOLIC ACCELERATION
HALFSHELL
...THAT NONE OF THEM...
...ARE SAYING ANYTHING?
CLONE 45
THEY GONNA BE SAYING EVEN LESS ONCE I'VE SHOT THEM ALL A REAL LOT!

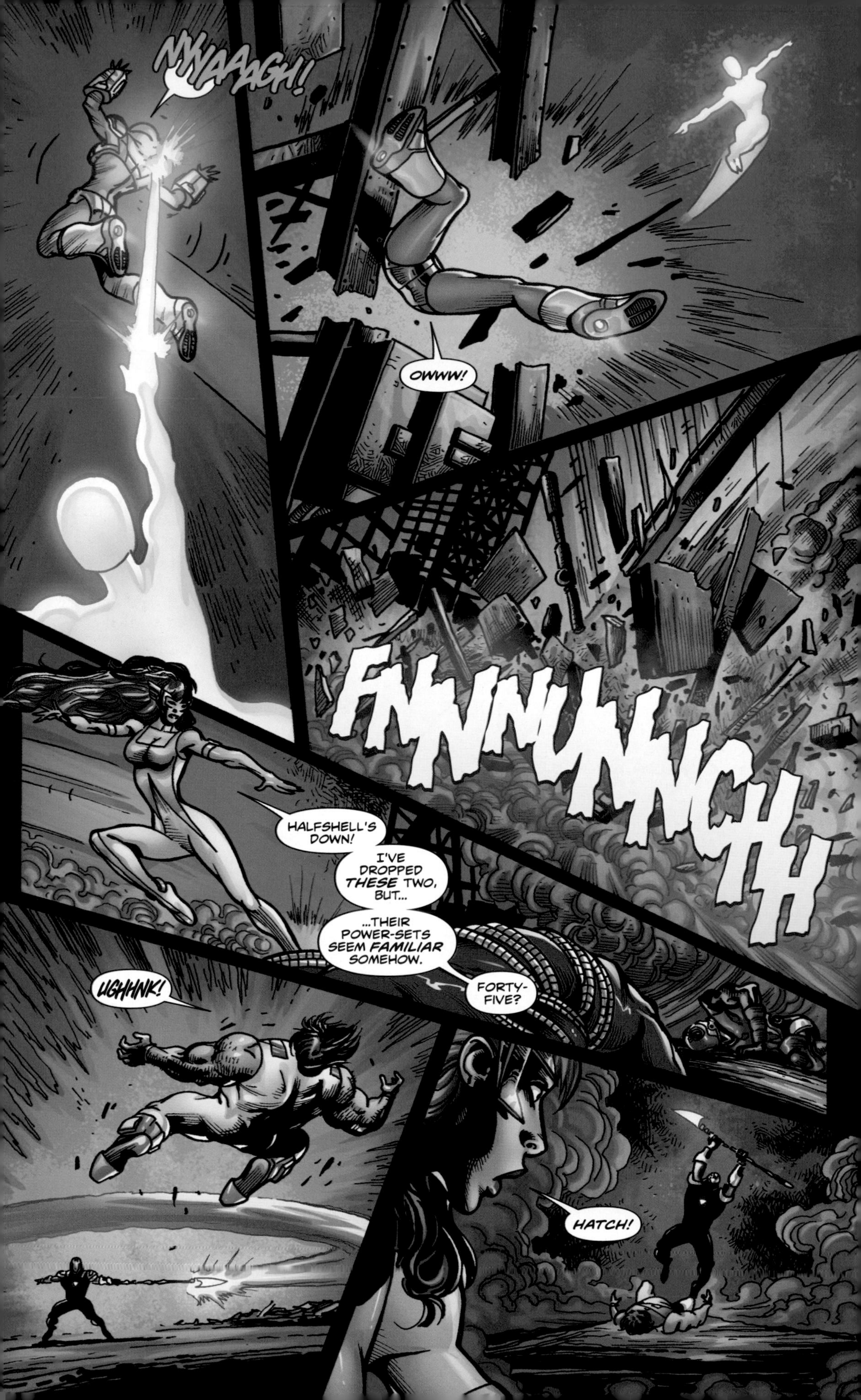
NNNAAAGH!
OWWW!
FNNNUNNNCHH
HALFSHELL'S DOWN!
I'VE DROPPED THESE TWO, BUT...
...THEIR POWER-SETS SEEM FAMILIAR SOMEHOW.
FORTY-FIVE?
UGHHNK!
HATCH!

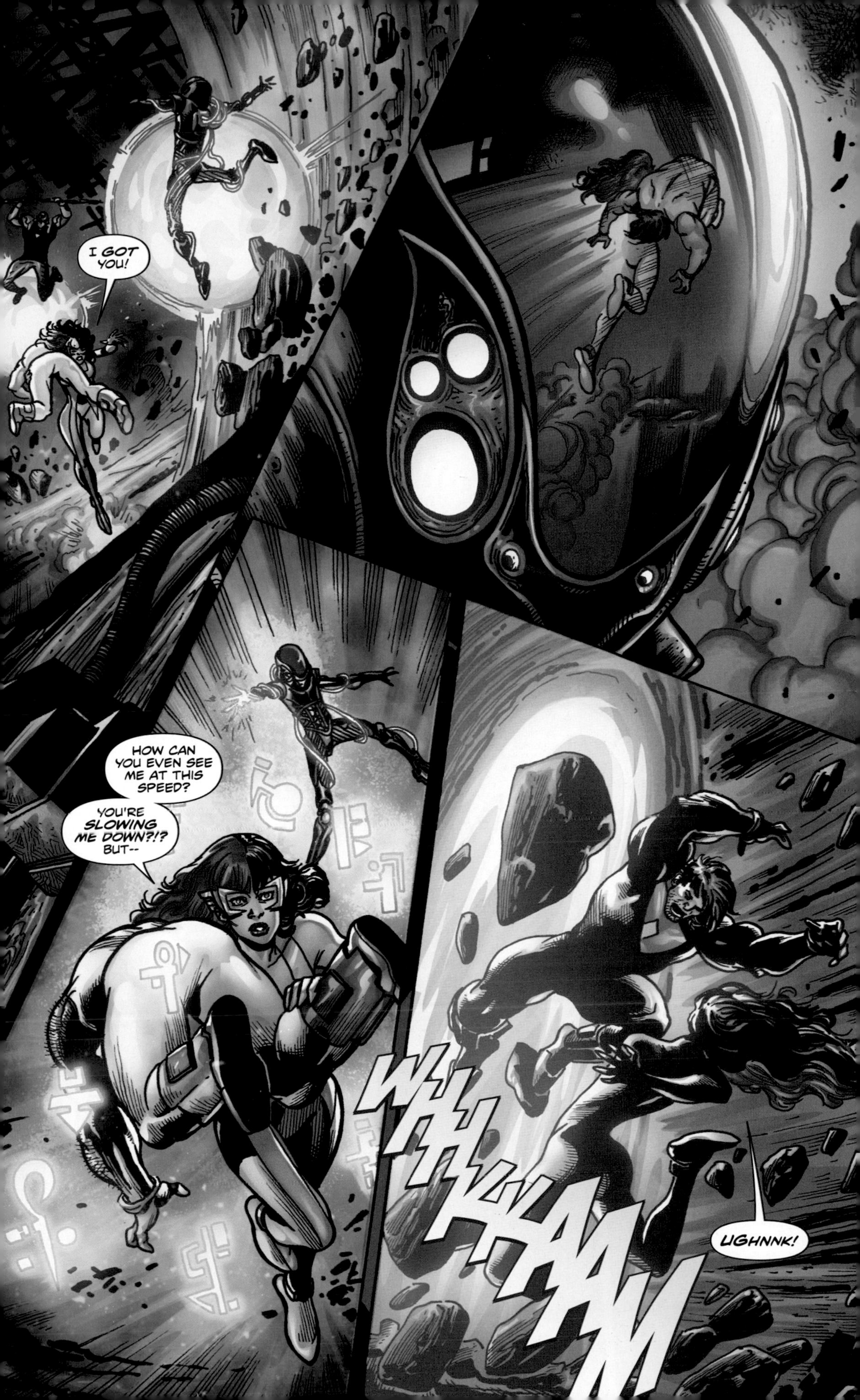
I GOT YOU!
HOW CAN YOU EVEN SEE ME AT THIS SPEED?
YOU'RE SLOWING ME DOWN?!? BUT--
WHKKAAM
UGHNNK!

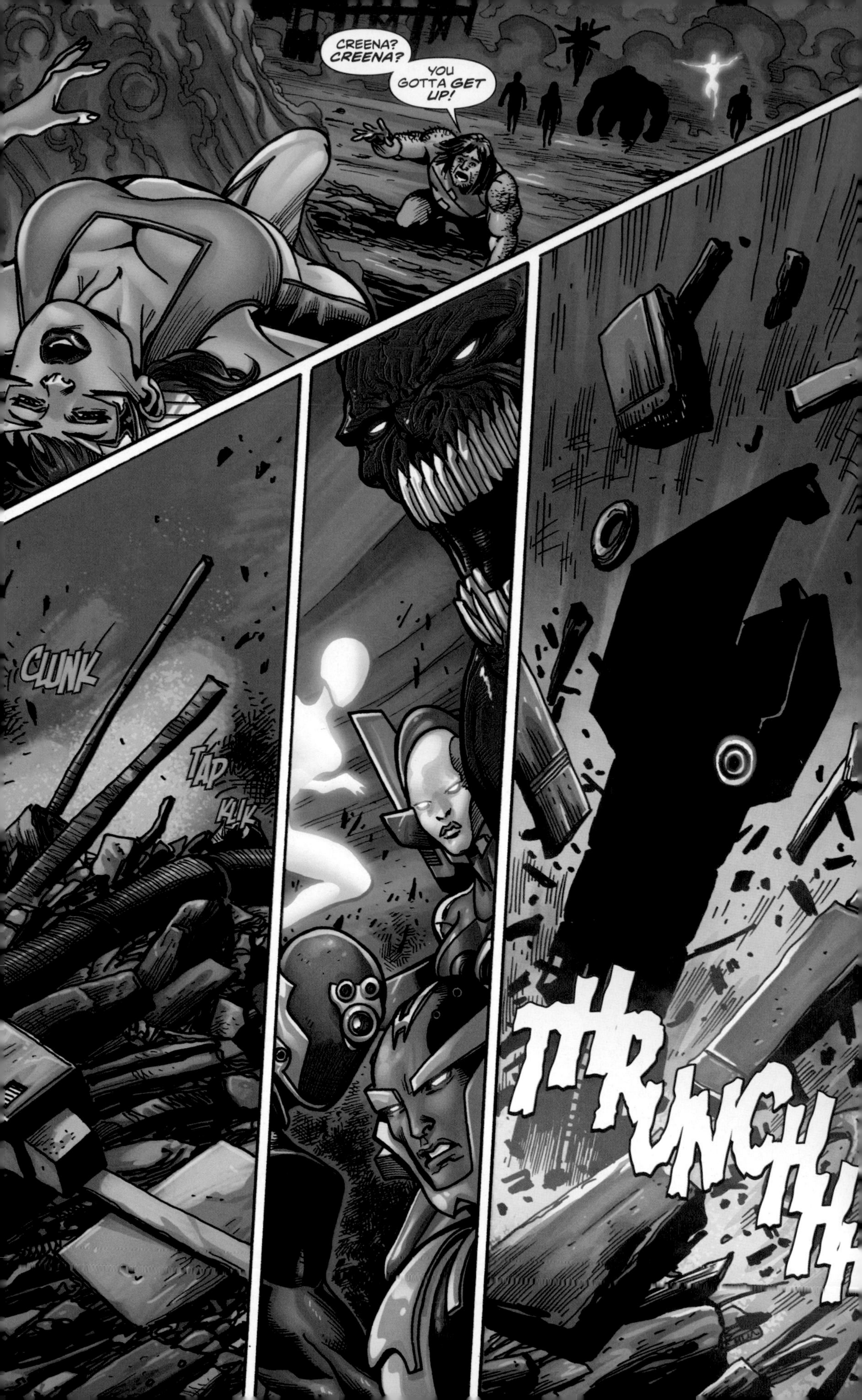
CREENA? CREENA?
YOU GOTTA GET UP!
CLUNK
TAP
KLIK
TTRUNCHH

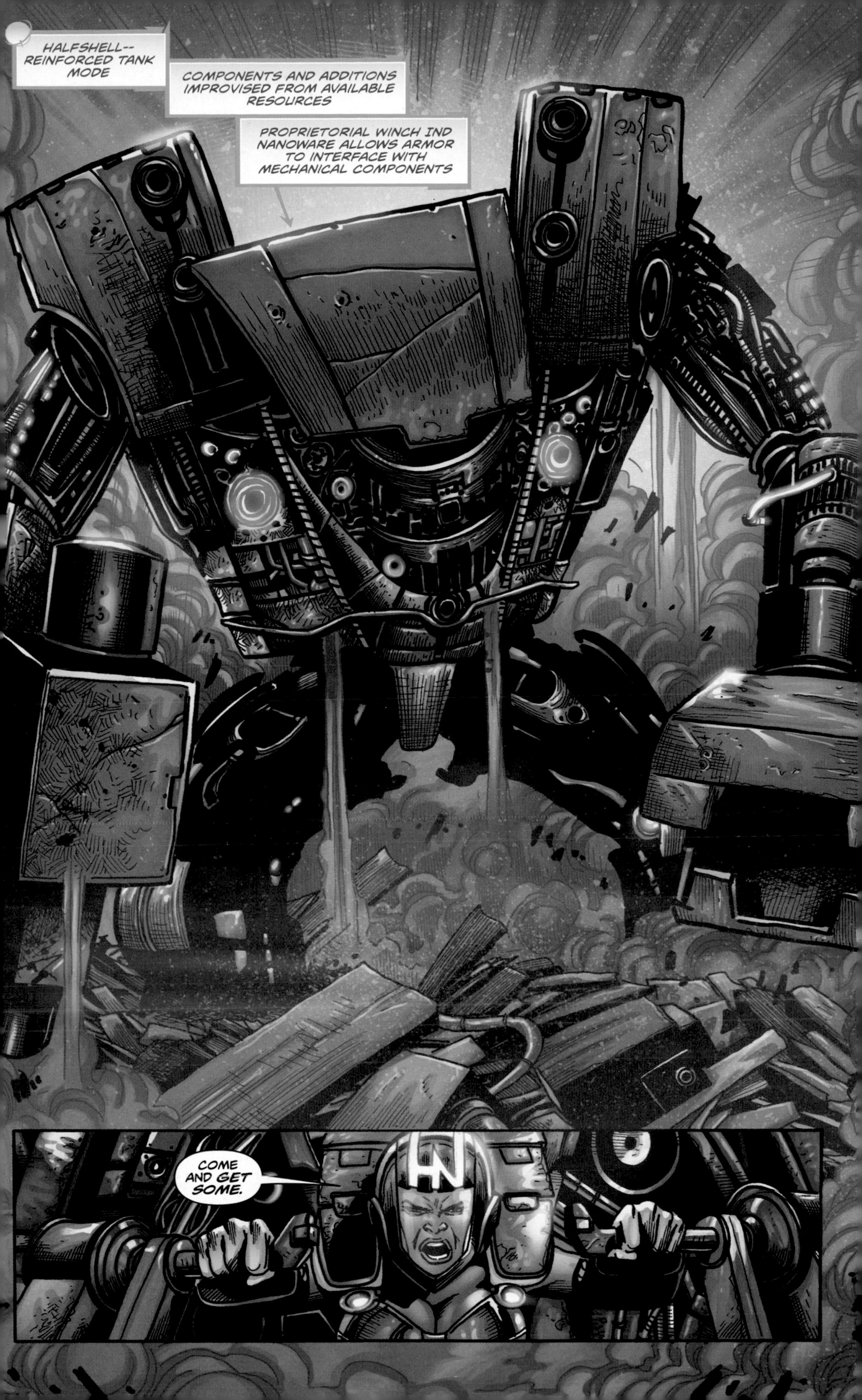
HALFSHELL--
REINFORCED TANK
MODE
COMPONENTS AND ADDITIONS
IMPROVISED FROM AVAILABLE
RESOURCES
PROPRIETORIAL WINCH IND
NANOWARE ALLOWS ARMOR
TO INTERFACE WITH
MECHANICAL COMPONENTS
COME
AND GET
SOME.

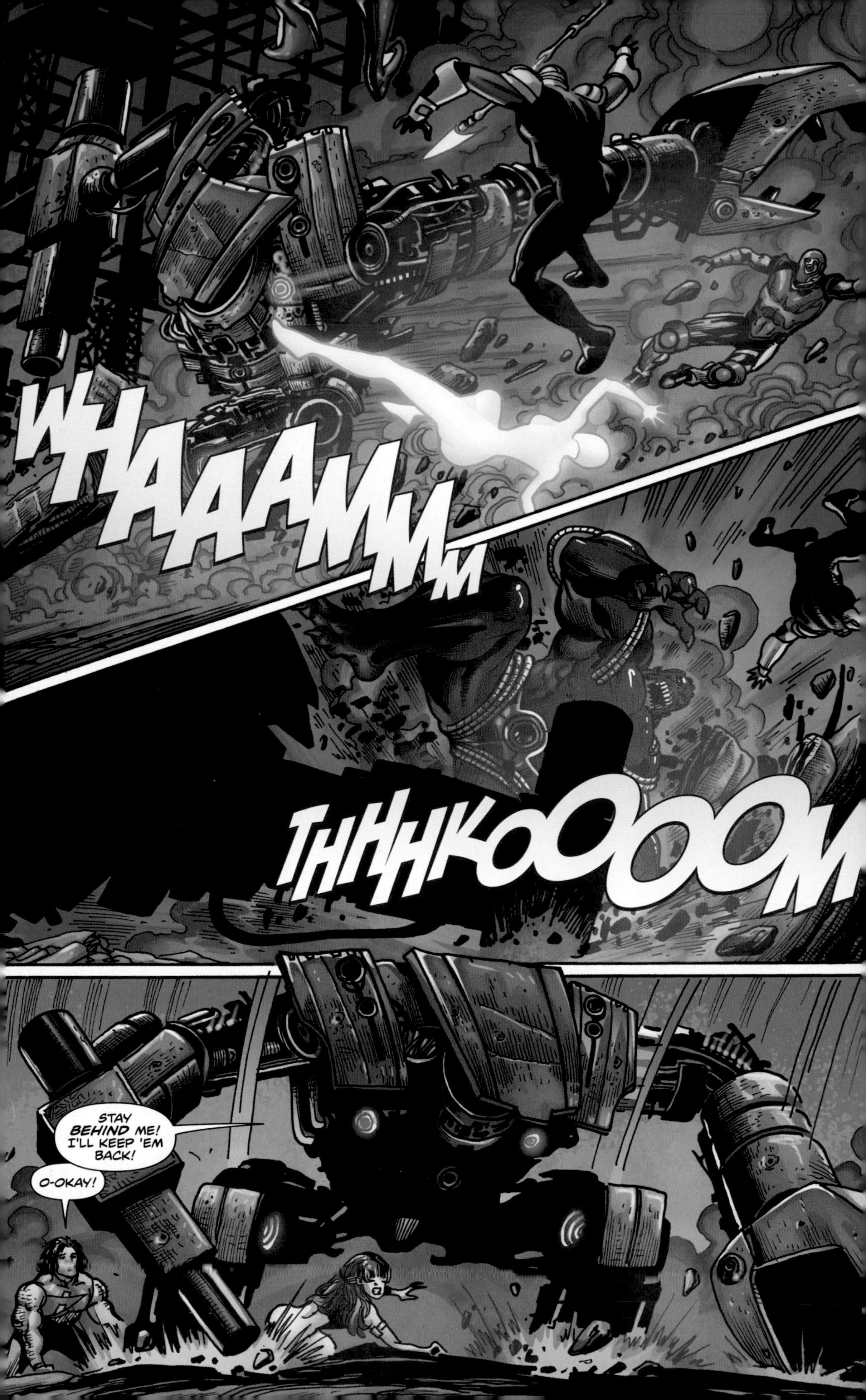
WHAAAMMM
THHHKOOOOM
STAY BEHIND ME! I'LL KEEP 'EM BACK!
O-OKAY!

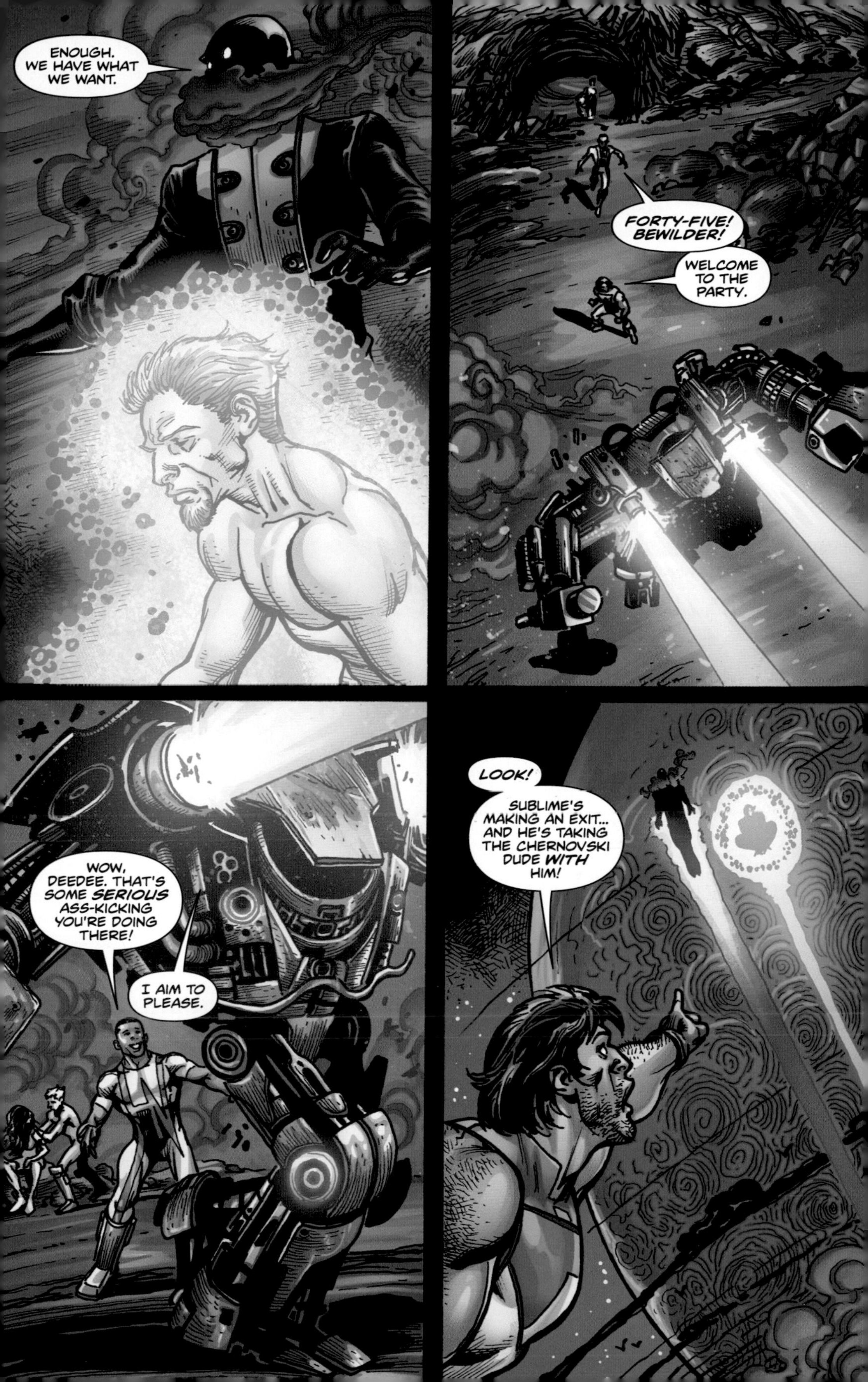
ENOUGH. WE HAVE WHAT WE WANT.
FORTY-FIVE! BEWILDER!
WELCOME TO THE PARTY.
WOW, DEEDEE. THAT'S SOME SERIOUS ASS-KICKING YOU'RE DOING THERE!
I AIM TO PLEASE.
LOOK!
SUBLIME'S MAKING AN EXIT... AND HE'S TAKING THE CHERNOVSKI DUDE WITH HIM!

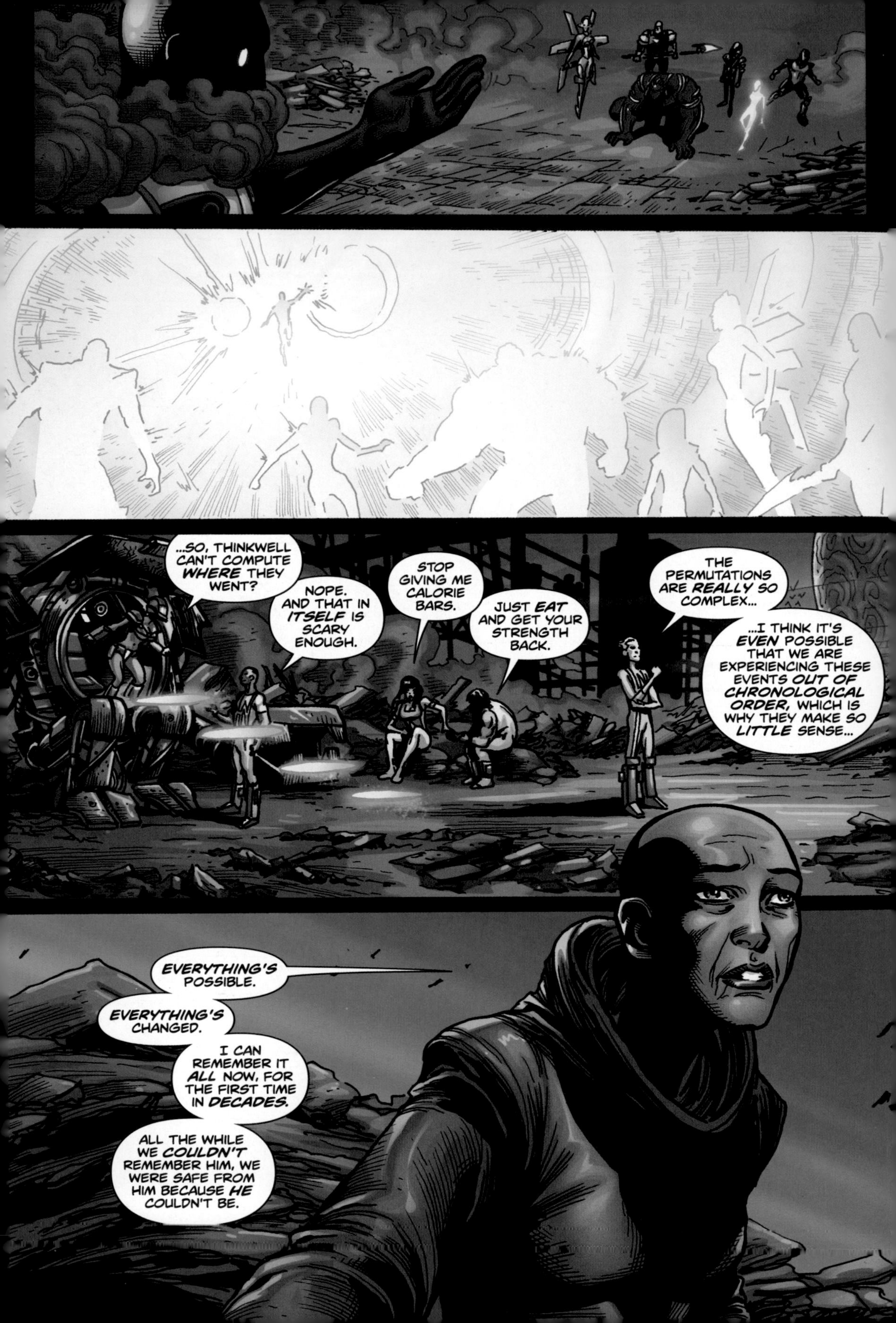

...SO, THINKWELL CAN'T COMPUTE WHERE THEY WENT?
NOPE. AND THAT IN ITSELF IS SCARY ENOUGH.
STOP GIVING ME CALORIE BARS.
JUST EAT AND GET YOUR STRENGTH BACK.
THE PERMUTATIONS ARE REALLY SO COMPLEX...
...I THINK IT'S EVEN POSSIBLE THAT WE ARE EXPERIENCING THESE EVENTS OUT OF CHRONOLOGICAL ORDER, WHICH IS WHY THEY MAKE SO LITTLE SENSE...
EVERYTHING'S POSSIBLE.
EVERYTHING'S CHANGED.
I CAN REMEMBER IT ALL NOW, FOR THE FIRST TIME IN DECADES.
ALL THE WHILE WE COULDN'T REMEMBER HIM, WE WERE SAFE FROM HIM BECAUSE HE COULDN'T BE.

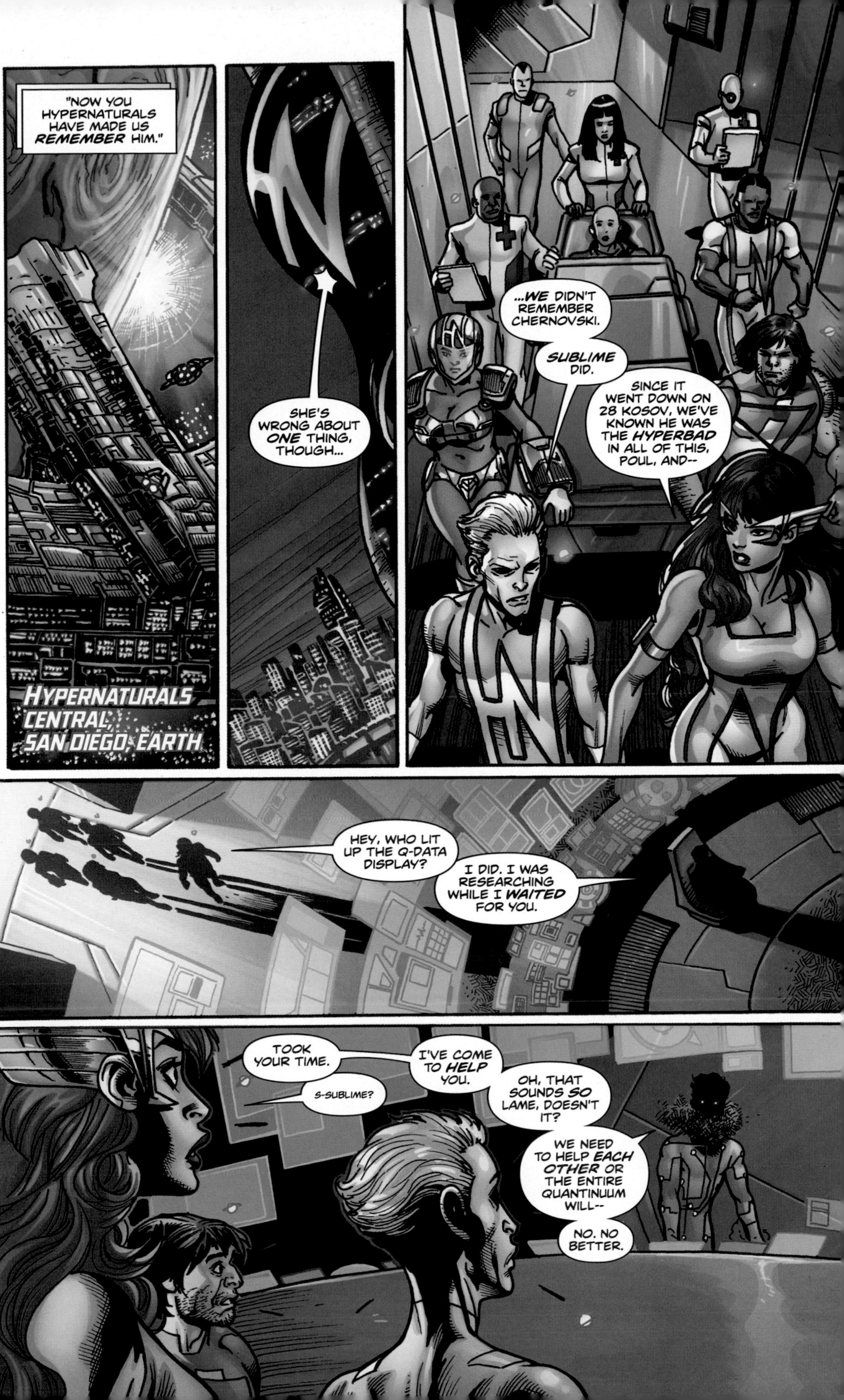
"NOW YOU HYPERNATURALS HAVE MADE US REMEMBER HIM."
HYPERNATURALS CENTRAL, SAN DIEGO, EARTH
SHE'S WRONG ABOUT ONE THING, THOUGH...
...WE DIDN'T REMEMBER CHERNOVSKI.
SUBLIME DID.
SINCE IT WENT DOWN ON 28 KOSOV, WE'VE KNOWN HE WAS THE HYPERBAD IN ALL OF THIS, POUL, AND--
HEY, WHO LIT UP THE Q-DATA DISPLAY?
I DID. I WAS RESEARCHING WHILE I WAITED FOR YOU.
TOOK YOUR TIME.
S-SUBLIME?
I'VE COME TO HELP YOU.
OH, THAT SOUNDS SO LAME, DOESN'T IT?
WE NEED TO HELP EACH OTHER OR THE ENTIRE QUANTINUUM WILL--
NO. NO BETTER.

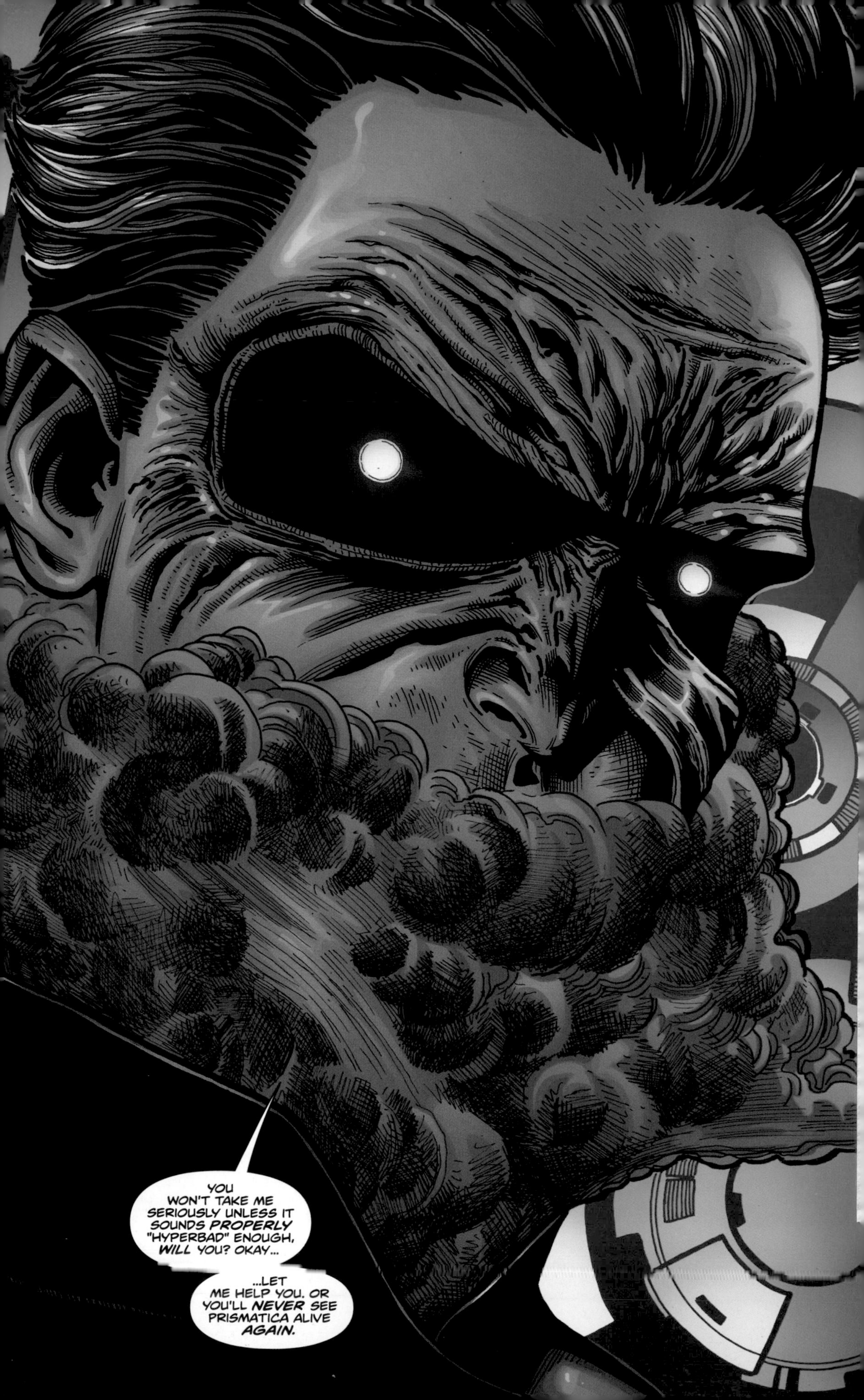
YOU WON'T TAKE ME SERIOUSLY UNLESS IT SOUNDS *PROPERLY* "HYPERBAD" ENOUGH, *WILL* YOU? OKAY...
...LET ME HELP YOU. OR YOU'LL *NEVER* SEE PRISMATICA ALIVE *AGAIN*.

Is this the end for the Hypernaturals?

Quantum's *security editor, Jin Janiry, scrutinizes the crisis currently afflicting the Quantinuum famous Hypernaturals team.*

Missing, presumed lost.

That was the terrible announcement that came from Hypernaturals Central, San Diego, three days ago following the first mission outing of the so-called "Centennial Iteration" of the famous team. A crisis response to 28 Kosov quickly turned into a nightmare. No trace of the team has been found — though unofficial rumors of a single survivor have circulated. In the interim, this magazine understands that a temporary replacement team consisting of two newbies and three veterans from the classic "Nineteenth Tour" has been put together. Its purview? To investigate the loss of the serving team, and to provide security cover for the Quantinuum in their absence.

At the time of writing, the scale of this tragedy can't be measured. We hope, of course, that the missing Hypernaturals are found alive and well. Thoughts at this time must go out to the families of Magnetar, Astromancer, Id and Ego, Musclewire, Kobalt Blue, Halfshell, and Clone 46. It is also not easy to tell what loss of life may have been suffered on 28 Kosov and its surrounding Trip network.

But the personal tragedy aside, the incident throws into question the continuing viability of the Hypernaturals as a concept. Right from the days of the very first tour, at the very foundation of Quantinuum culture and the dawn of the Nanocene, people have been questioning the relevance of a team of what would — in other eras — have been dubbed 'superheroes'. Should the Quantinuum place its trust and all questions of cultural security in the hands of a few hypernaturally empowered individuals? Should such individuals be permitted to keep powers of that level? Who do they answer to? What happens when things go wrong?

Champions of the Hypernaturals program always talk about how vital the team is for public morale, and how the Quantinuum loves to be united around such high-profile public heroes. We feel safer because they're there, and we know who they are. We trust them. Certainly only the most churlish of commentators would reject some of the achievements made by the team, especially their extreme heroism in defeating menaces such as Bioerror, Orange Krush or Sublime.

But could these threats not have been dealt with successfully in other ways? Is the idea of a largely autonomous superhero team simply outmoded? Professor Huwel Harf of Pegasi University calls them "throw-backs to the bad old days."

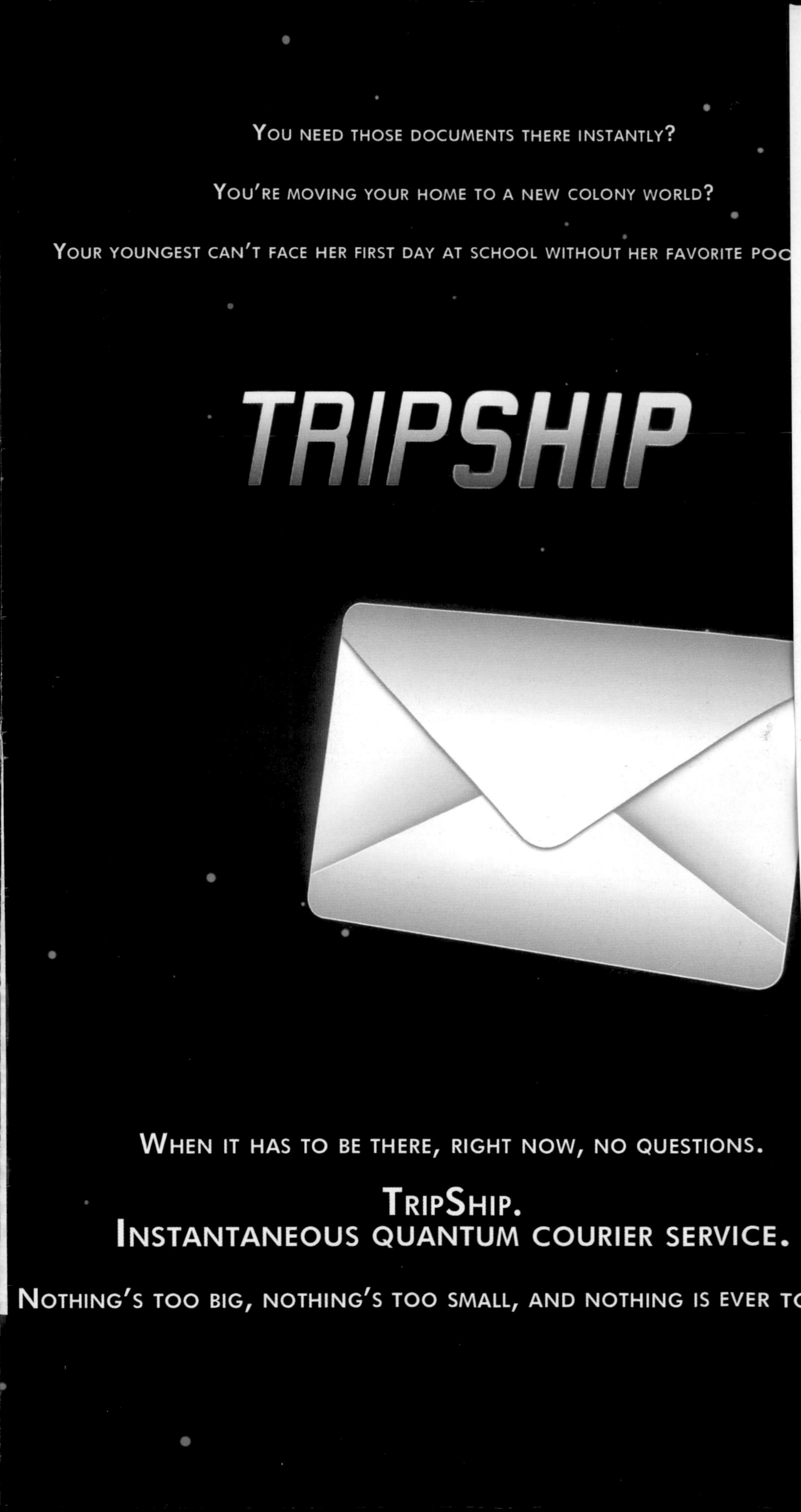
You need those documents there instantly?
You're moving your home to a new colony world?
Your youngest can't face her first day at school without her favorite poo
TRIPSHIP
When it has to be there, right now, no questions.
TripShip.
Instantaneous quantum courier service.
Nothing's too big, nothing's too small, and nothing is ever too

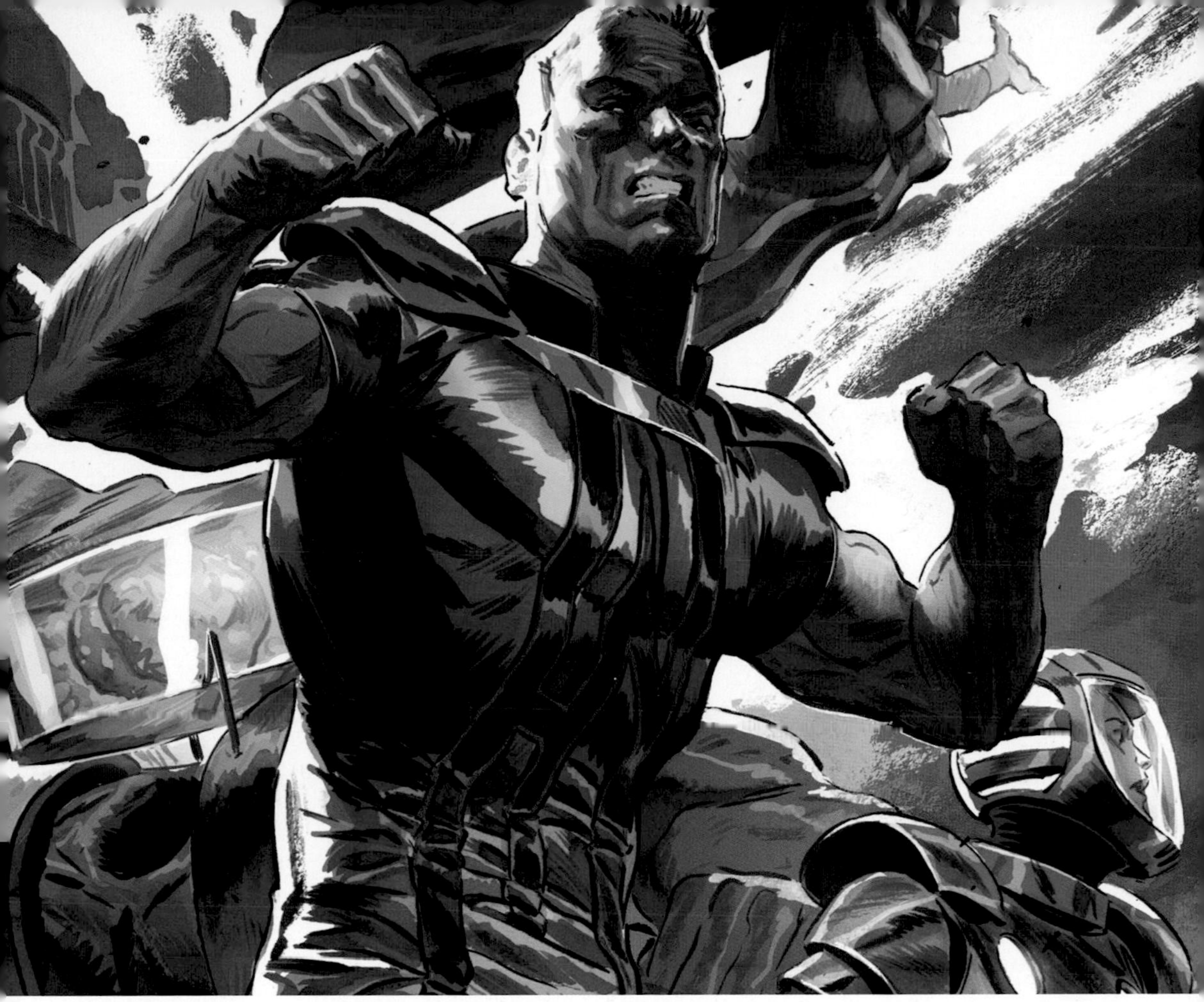

"They have far too much power," Harf told me, "and there is no guidance for its use...or sanction for its abuse. Sure, the the HN Statutes are carefully worded, and the code of conduct very precise, but what do we do if either are broken? Let's remember that some of their most extraordinary achievements came when Hypernaturals — I'm thinking here of Clone 45's miraculous defeat of Zade Gazurk — broke the very rules that they are supposed to follow. We can praise Clone 45 for what he did that day on 52 Strontalis, and applaud his maverick spirit. He was a loose cannon, but he saved the day. But what if he hadn't? What if his rule-breaking had led to death and destruction, and to Zade Gazurk being able to continue his rampage? Would we think of him so kindly then? What redress do we have? Who but the Hypernaturals themselves have the power and ability to police the Hypernaturals?"

Harf isn't alone in his worries. The Institute of Demographic Response recently published figures that suggest a startling 36% of the Quantinuum population harbor a secret fear of the Hypernaturals running amok, or turning out to be villains. Many others, politicians amongst them, have spoken out about dangerous power-usage and collateral damage. If the incident at 28 Kosov turns out to be as serious and as costly in terms of human life as it currently appears, then shouldn't we seriously rethink the continuing role of the Hypernaturals? Do we really need them? Have we ever really needed them? Do we trust them too much? Are they simply too dangerous?

Should the team be disbanded?

Doctor Hera Goldborg of MarsTech suggests the Hypernaturals are little more than publicity devices anyway. "It's all PR," she says. "They function as mascots, as rallying causes, as poster boys and girls, as pin-ups. It's all about public image and keeping the spirits of the general public uplifted. It's a notion and an idea. If you examine their records, you'll find the Hypernaturals — and I mean of any tour or iteration — have actually done very little. Most of their so-called "successful actions" against notorious hyperbad villains, such as Landslam and Sublime, were actually prosecuted and completed by the security services and members of law enforcement. Fictions were created to show the Hypernatural heroes saving the day, and these have become public myth. In reality, they are spokesmodels for our lifestyle and aspirations. The hard work is done by police officers and security agents across the Quantinuum who stay out of the public eye and receive no public recognition for their efforts or the considerable risks they take."

(continued on page 1611)

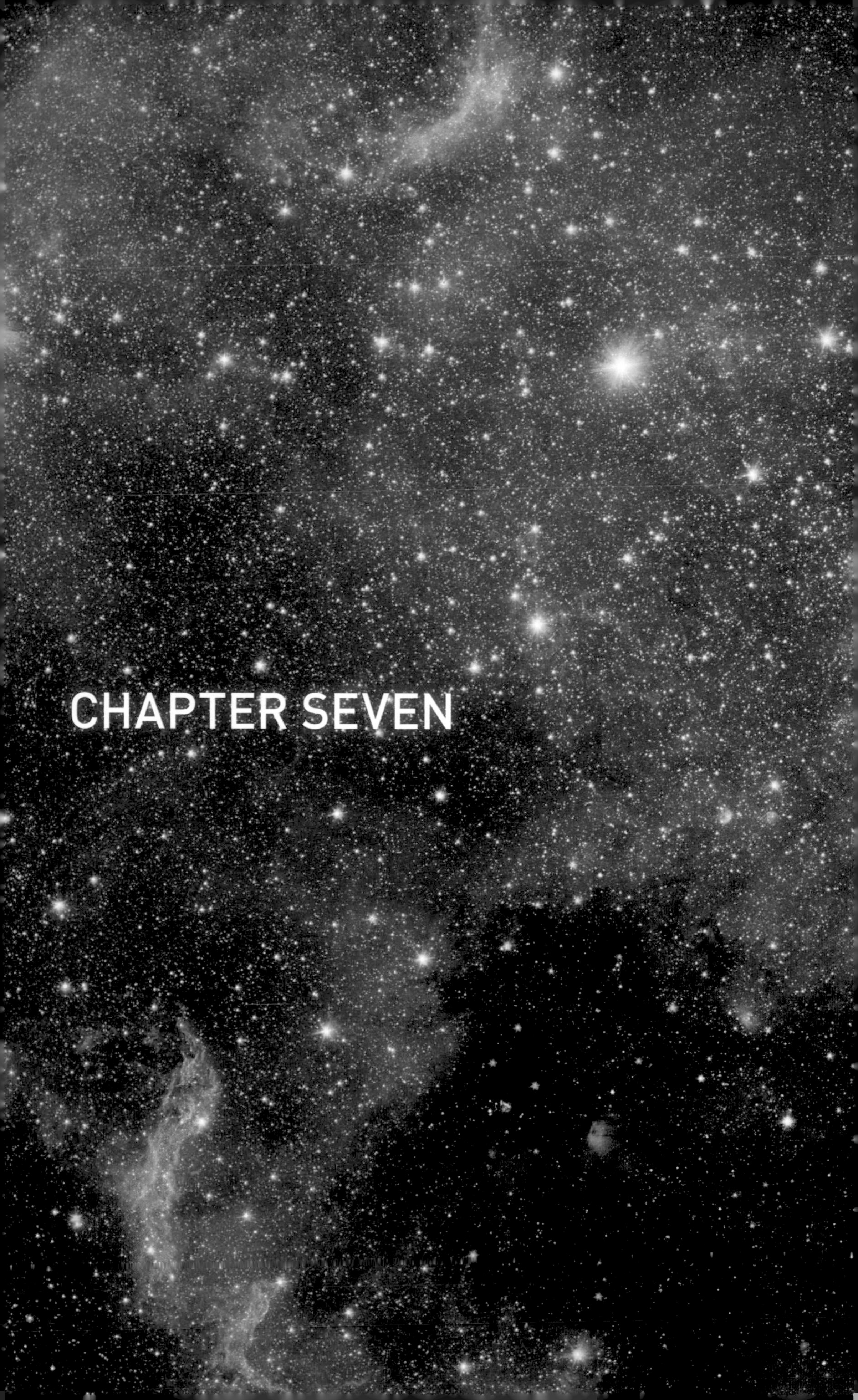

CHAPTER SEVEN

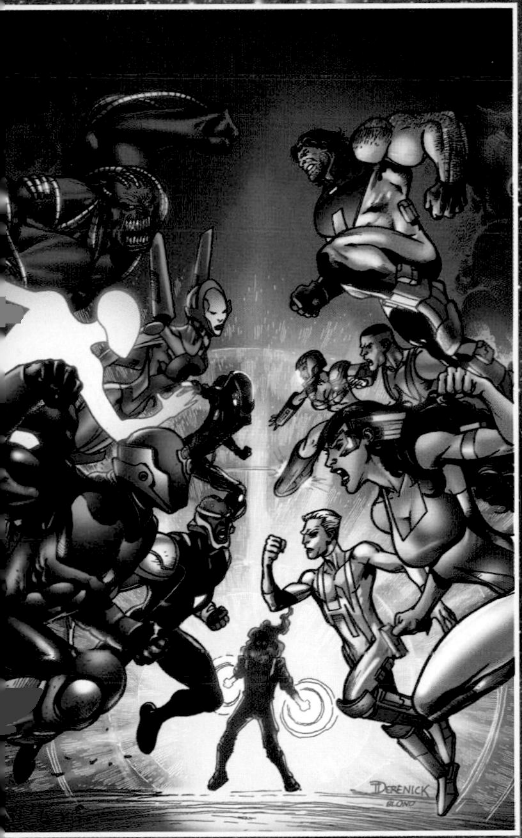
DERENICK
BLOND

Issue Seven
Tom Derenick with colors Blond

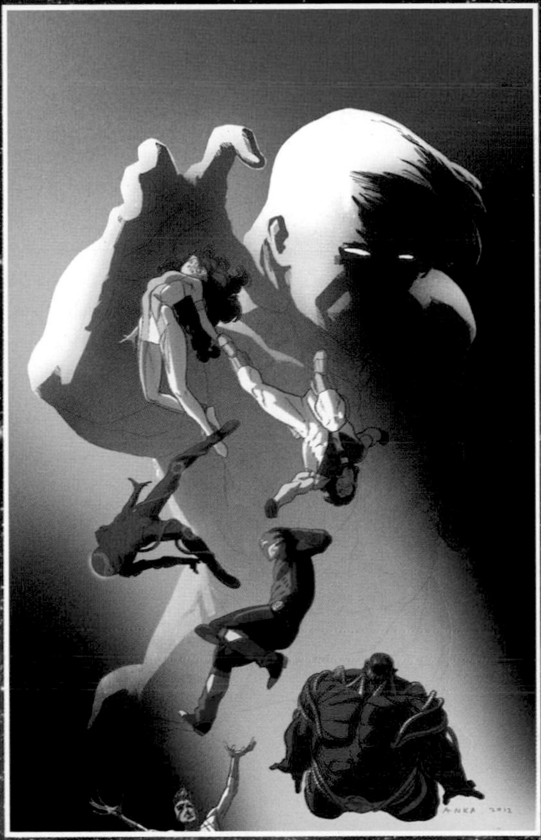
ANKA 2012

Issue Seven
Kris Anka

• You have selected Q-Data link.

The team that saved 356 Barnard from the Replicator crisis. This is the team that put Sublime in iso, for Quant's sake! Big shoes. Big, big shoes.

- It is the 13th of January in the year 100 A.Q.
  - Touch here to select an alternative to the **Anno Quantinuum** calendar system.
  - Touch here to load local weather reports for your **current cosmic location.**
  - Touch here to access **Q-Data newsflows** from planets near your current cosmic location.
  - Touch here for latest **Quantum Trip** transit times.

- Q-Data entry: The Quantinuum

- The Quantinuum is the name for the **human galactic culture**, and also for the **artificial intelligence** that controls its function.

- The Quantinuum was created 100 years ago at the start of the **Nanocene Era.** The Nanocene began when the Quantinuum AI achieved Singularity and refashioned human galactic culture. Succeeding the Holocene Era, the Nanocene is the next progression of human evolution and...

  (to read this entry in full, touch here)

- You have selected live feed newsflow.

  - **Viamol Laboratories** patent new color
  - **44 Farouk** to auction off its moons
  - Confirmed reports of rioting at **Tartarus Omni-Max Prison**
  - **AI Law** starlet **Connie Lindquist** seen out on the town with Major League ProBall celeb **Addison Glance**
  - **AI Law** producers announce that audience favorite Bill Frooper of Doctor Heuristics is to join show as a hard-hitting cyber-attorney
  - Hypernaturals Central, San Diego, reports that the "emergency team" is continuing to investigate the disappearance of the **Centennial Year Iteration** of the Team, lost during an emergency response mission to 28 Kosov three days ago

- The Hypernaturals are the Quantinuum's foremost champions. Famous across the entirety of human galactic culture, the team members are selected on the basis of their hypernatural powers and their strength of character, and serve for five-year terms. In honor of the start of the twenty-first term, the line-up of the team's so-called "Centennial Year Iteration" has recently been announced amid huge publicity and--

...BREAKING NEWS... according to a spokesperson at Hypernaturals Central, San Diego, a special reserve formation of Hypernaturals, including now retired team members Bewilder, Clone 45 and Thinkwell from the classic "Nineteenth Tour" line-up are now working urgently to find the missing team members and resolve the crisis...

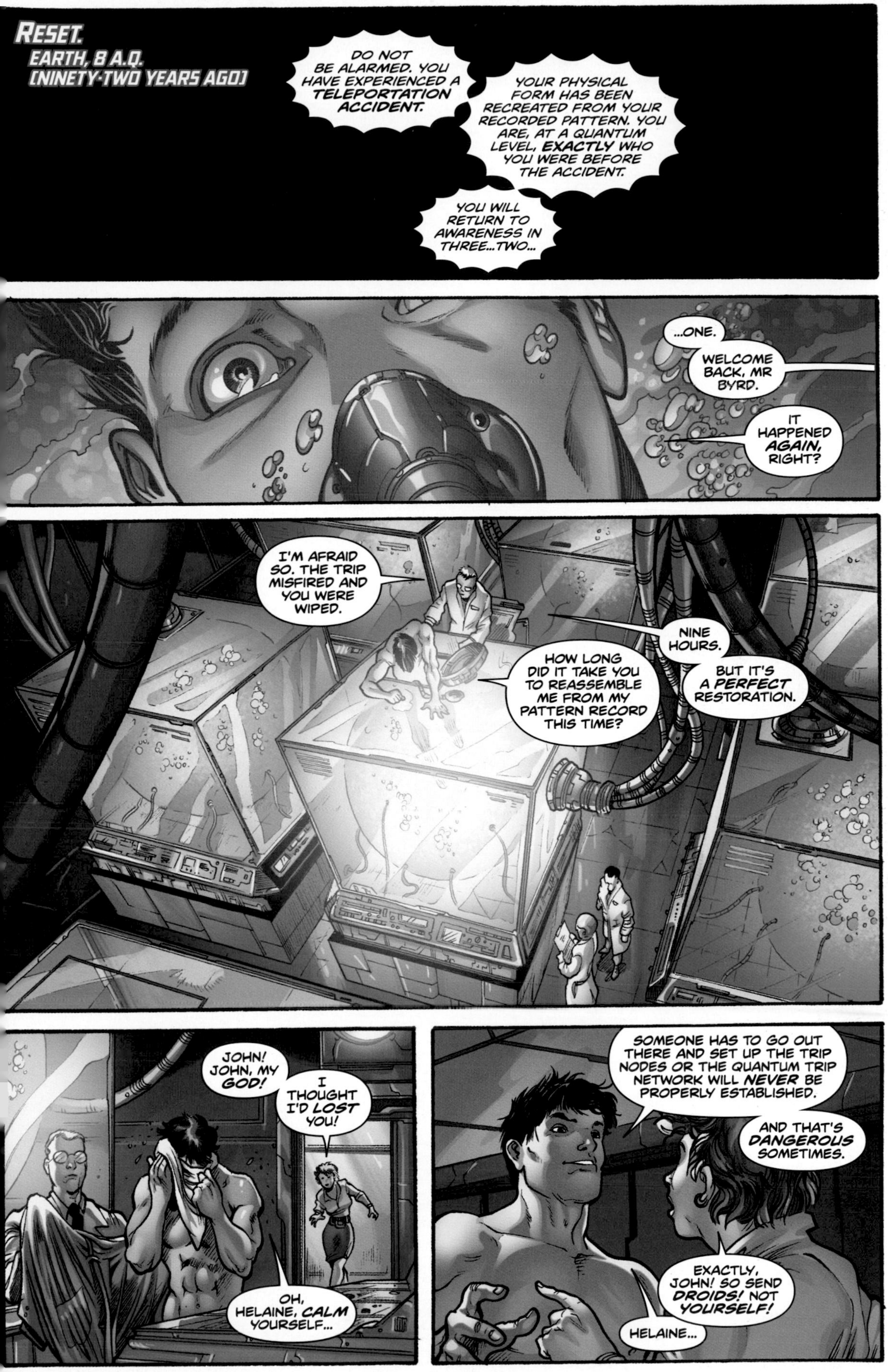
RESET.
EARTH, 8 A.Q.
[NINETY-TWO YEARS AGO]
DO NOT BE ALARMED. YOU HAVE EXPERIENCED A TELEPORTATION ACCIDENT.
YOUR PHYSICAL FORM HAS BEEN RECREATED FROM YOUR RECORDED PATTERN. YOU ARE, AT A QUANTUM LEVEL, EXACTLY WHO YOU WERE BEFORE THE ACCIDENT.
YOU WILL RETURN TO AWARENESS IN THREE...TWO...
...ONE.
WELCOME BACK, MR BYRD.
IT HAPPENED AGAIN, RIGHT?
I'M AFRAID SO. THE TRIP MISFIRED AND YOU WERE WIPED.
HOW LONG DID IT TAKE YOU TO REASSEMBLE ME FROM MY PATTERN RECORD THIS TIME?
NINE HOURS.
BUT IT'S A PERFECT RESTORATION.
JOHN! JOHN, MY GOD!
I THOUGHT I'D LOST YOU!
OH, HELAINE, CALM YOURSELF...
SOMEONE HAS TO GO OUT THERE AND SET UP THE TRIP NODES OR THE QUANTUM TRIP NETWORK WILL NEVER BE PROPERLY ESTABLISHED.
AND THAT'S DANGEROUS SOMETIMES.
EXACTLY, JOHN! SO SEND DROIDS! NOT YOURSELF!
HELAINE...

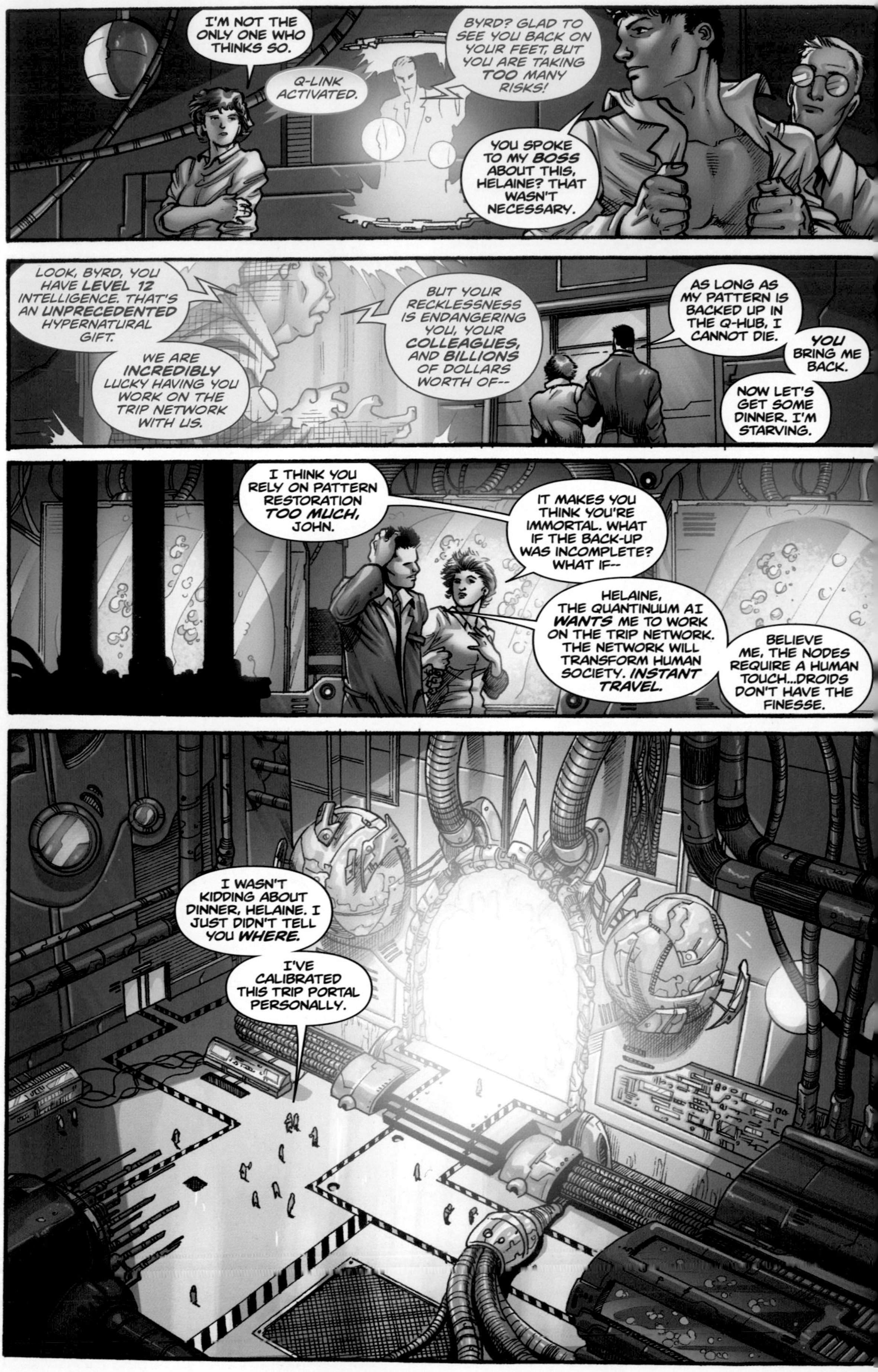
I'M NOT THE ONLY ONE WHO THINKS SO.
Q-LINK ACTIVATED.
BYRD? GLAD TO SEE YOU BACK ON YOUR FEET, BUT YOU ARE TAKING TOO MANY RISKS!
YOU SPOKE TO MY BOSS ABOUT THIS, HELAINE? THAT WASN'T NECESSARY.
LOOK, BYRD, YOU HAVE LEVEL 12 INTELLIGENCE. THAT'S AN UNPRECEDENTED HYPERNATURAL GIFT.
WE ARE INCREDIBLY LUCKY HAVING YOU WORK ON THE TRIP NETWORK WITH US.
BUT YOUR RECKLESSNESS IS ENDANGERING YOU, YOUR COLLEAGUES, AND BILLIONS OF DOLLARS WORTH OF--
AS LONG AS MY PATTERN IS BACKED UP IN THE Q-HUB, I CANNOT DIE.
YOU BRING ME BACK.
NOW LET'S GET SOME DINNER. I'M STARVING.
I THINK YOU RELY ON PATTERN RESTORATION TOO MUCH, JOHN.
IT MAKES YOU THINK YOU'RE IMMORTAL. WHAT IF THE BACK-UP WAS INCOMPLETE? WHAT IF--
HELAINE, THE QUANTINUUM AI WANTS ME TO WORK ON THE TRIP NETWORK. THE NETWORK WILL TRANSFORM HUMAN SOCIETY. INSTANT TRAVEL.
BELIEVE ME, THE NODES REQUIRE A HUMAN TOUCH...DROIDS DON'T HAVE THE FINESSE.
I WASN'T KIDDING ABOUT DINNER, HELAINE. I JUST DIDN'T TELL YOU WHERE.
I'VE CALIBRATED THIS TRIP PORTAL PERSONALLY.

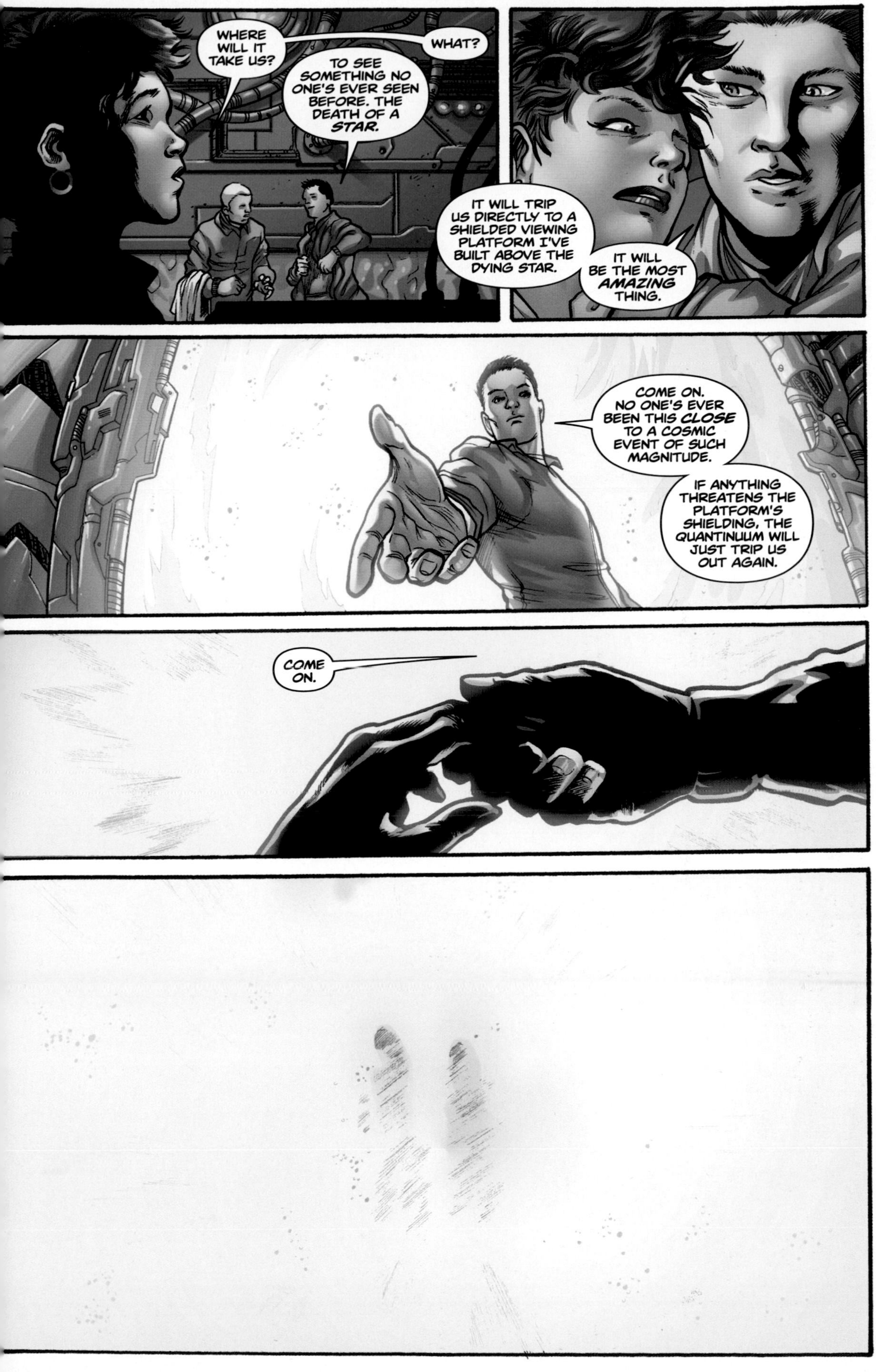
WHERE WILL IT TAKE US?
WHAT?
TO SEE SOMETHING NO ONE'S EVER SEEN BEFORE. THE DEATH OF A STAR.
IT WILL TRIP US DIRECTLY TO A SHIELDED VIEWING PLATFORM I'VE BUILT ABOVE THE DYING STAR.
IT WILL BE THE MOST AMAZING THING.
COME ON. NO ONE'S EVER BEEN THIS CLOSE TO A COSMIC EVENT OF SUCH MAGNITUDE.
IF ANYTHING THREATENS THE PLATFORM'S SHIELDING, THE QUANTINUUM WILL JUST TRIP US OUT AGAIN.
COME ON.

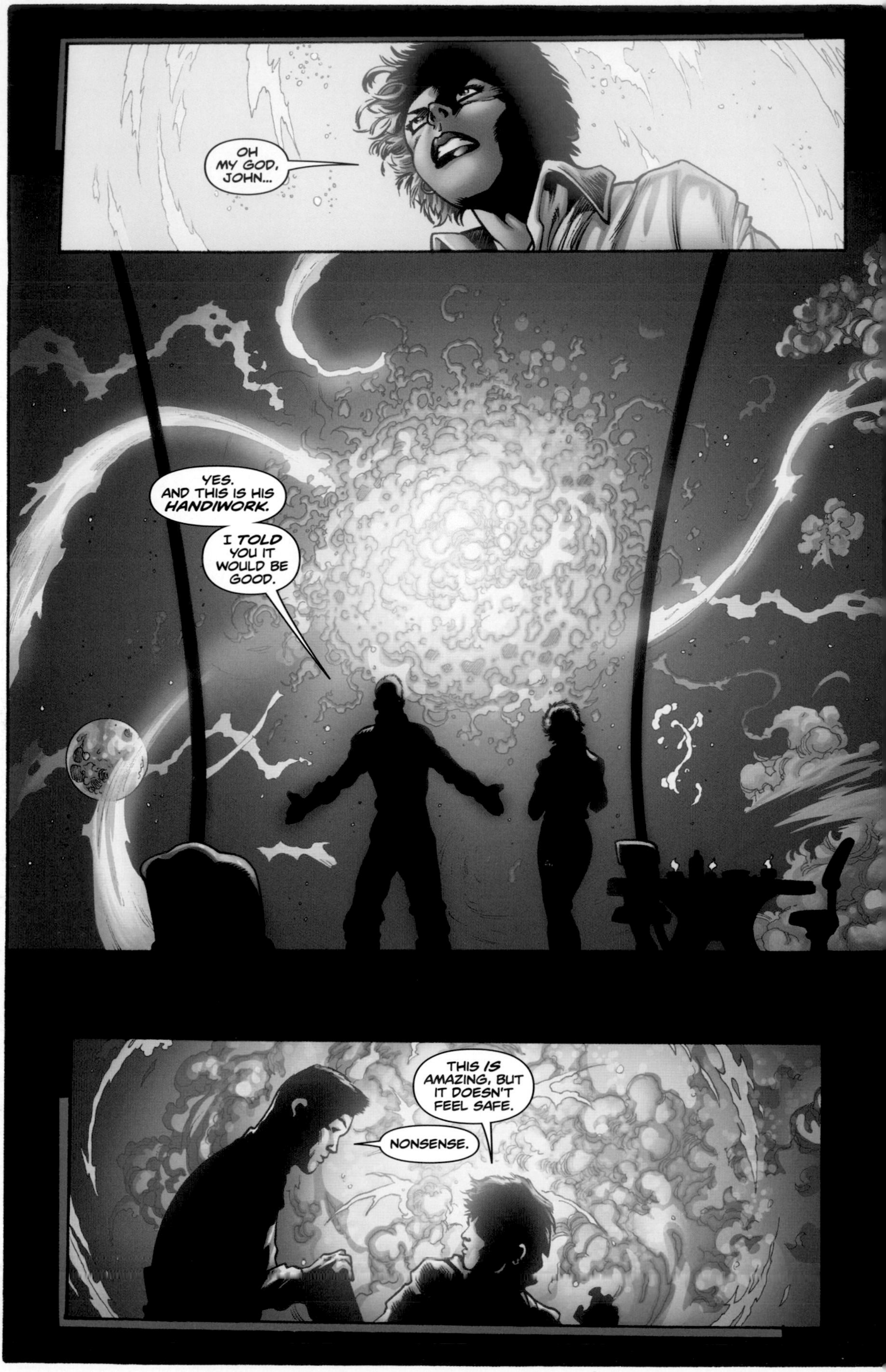
OH MY GOD, JOHN...
YES. AND THIS IS HIS *HANDIWORK.*
I *TOLD* YOU IT WOULD BE GOOD.
THIS *IS* AMAZING, BUT IT DOESN'T FEEL SAFE.
NONSENSE.

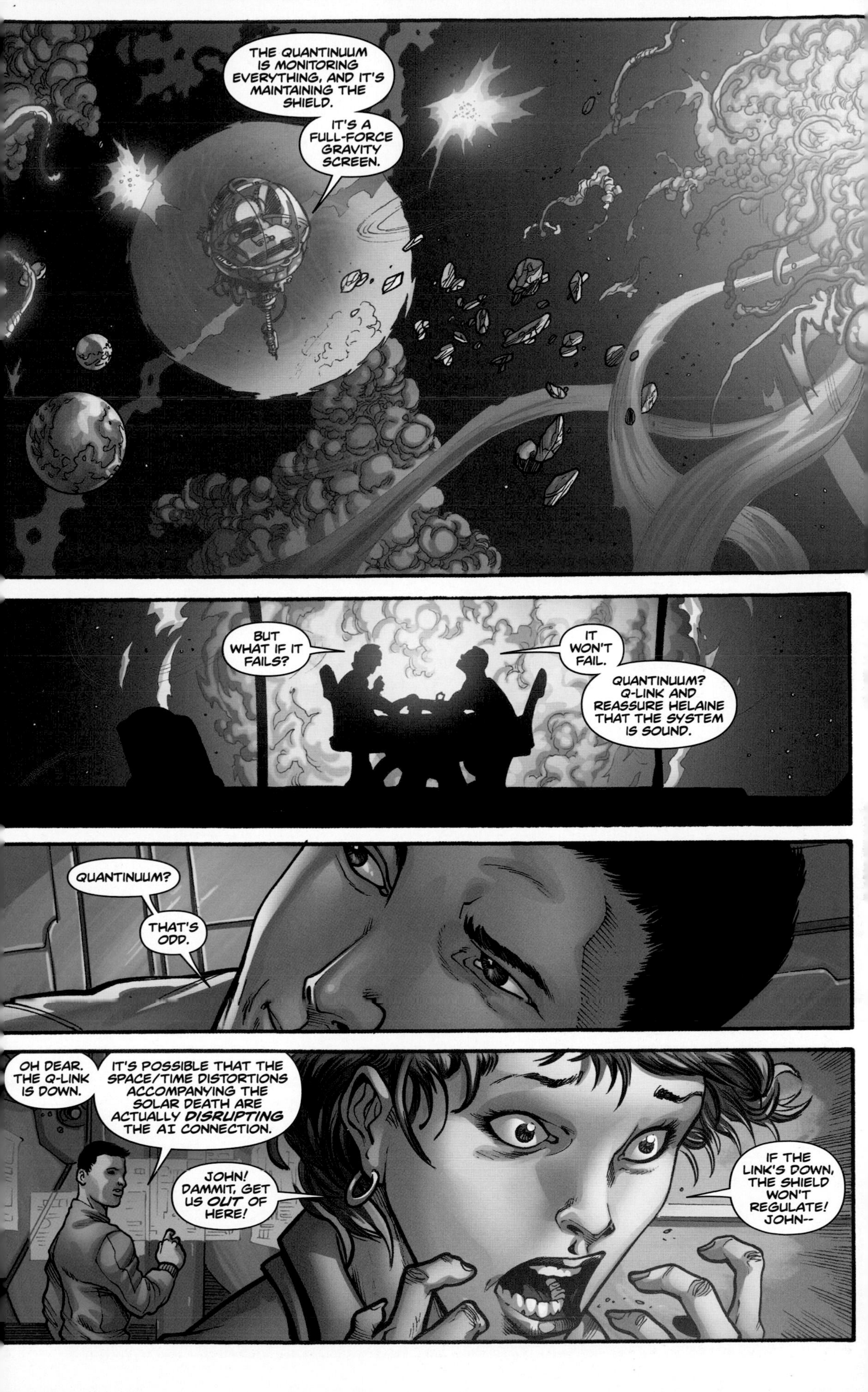
THE QUANTINUUM IS MONITORING EVERYTHING, AND IT'S MAINTAINING THE SHIELD.
IT'S A FULL-FORCE GRAVITY SCREEN.
BUT WHAT IF IT FAILS?
IT WON'T FAIL.
QUANTINUUM? Q-LINK AND REASSURE HELAINE THAT THE SYSTEM IS SOUND.
QUANTINUUM?
THAT'S ODD.
OH DEAR. THE Q-LINK IS DOWN.
IT'S POSSIBLE THAT THE SPACE/TIME DISTORTIONS ACCOMPANYING THE SOLAR DEATH ARE ACTUALLY *DISRUPTING* THE AI CONNECTION.
JOHN! DAMMIT, GET US *OUT* OF HERE!
IF THE LINK'S DOWN, THE SHIELD WON'T REGULATE! JOHN--

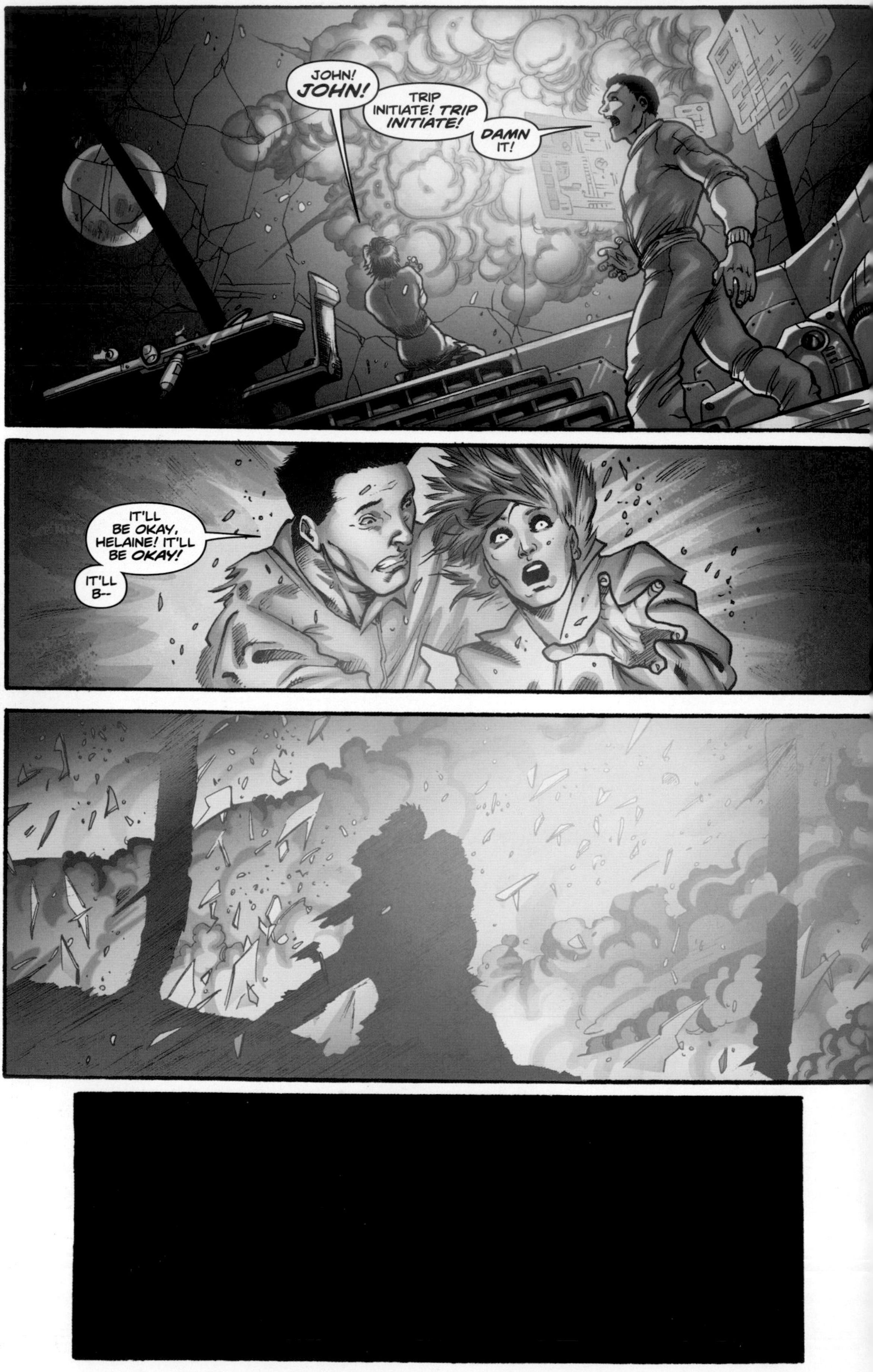
JOHN! JOHN!
TRIP INITIATE! TRIP INITIATE!
DAMN IT!
IT'LL BE OKAY, HELAINE! IT'LL BE OKAY!
IT'LL B--

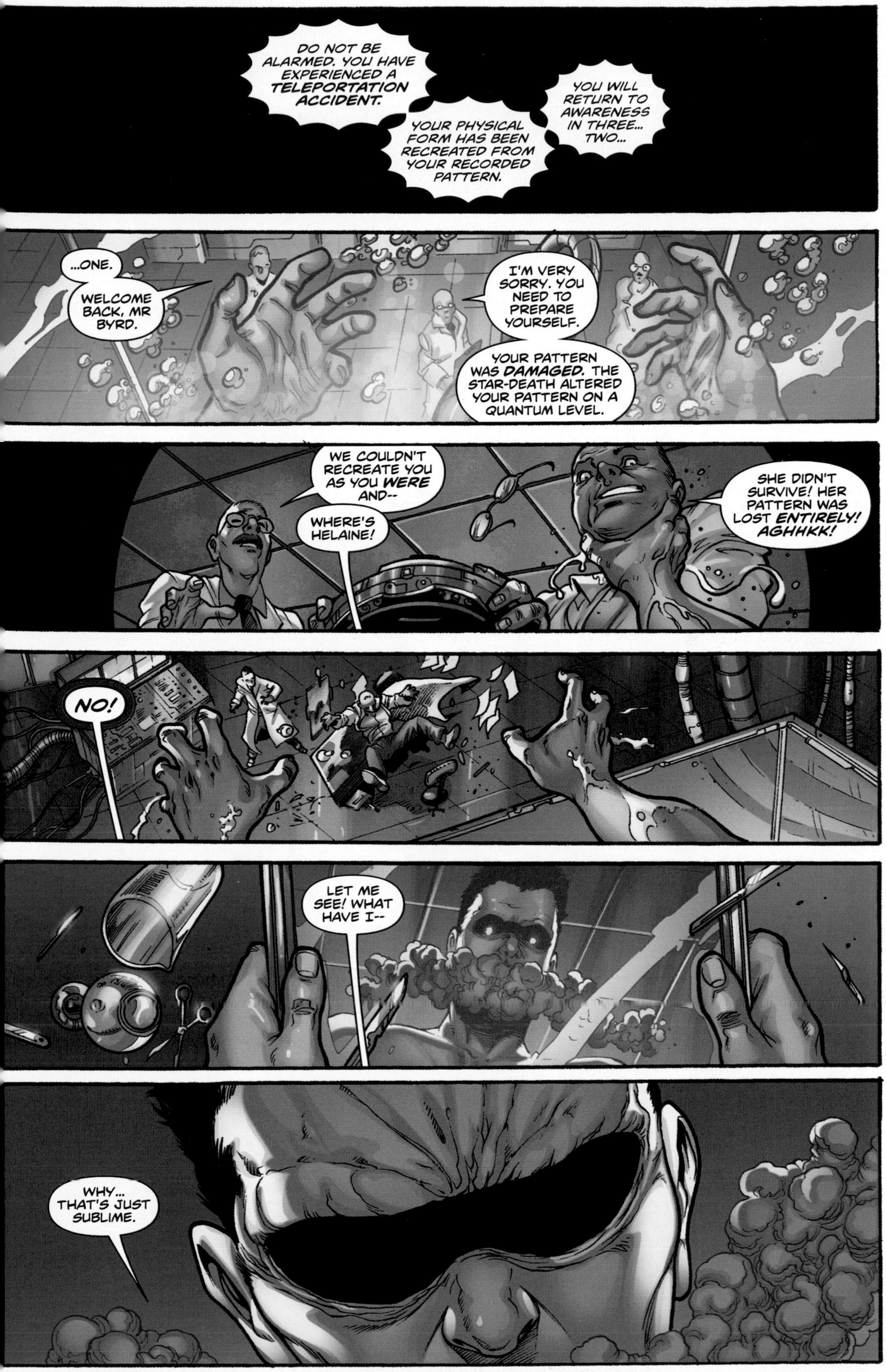
DO NOT BE ALARMED. YOU HAVE EXPERIENCED A TELEPORTATION ACCIDENT.
YOUR PHYSICAL FORM HAS BEEN RECREATED FROM YOUR RECORDED PATTERN.
YOU WILL RETURN TO AWARENESS IN THREE... TWO...
...ONE.
WELCOME BACK, MR BYRD.
I'M VERY SORRY. YOU NEED TO PREPARE YOURSELF.
YOUR PATTERN WAS DAMAGED. THE STAR-DEATH ALTERED YOUR PATTERN ON A QUANTUM LEVEL.
WE COULDN'T RECREATE YOU AS YOU WERE AND--
WHERE'S HELAINE!
SHE DIDN'T SURVIVE! HER PATTERN WAS LOST ENTIRELY! AGHHKK!
NO!
LET ME SEE! WHAT HAVE I--
WHY... THAT'S JUST SUBLIME.

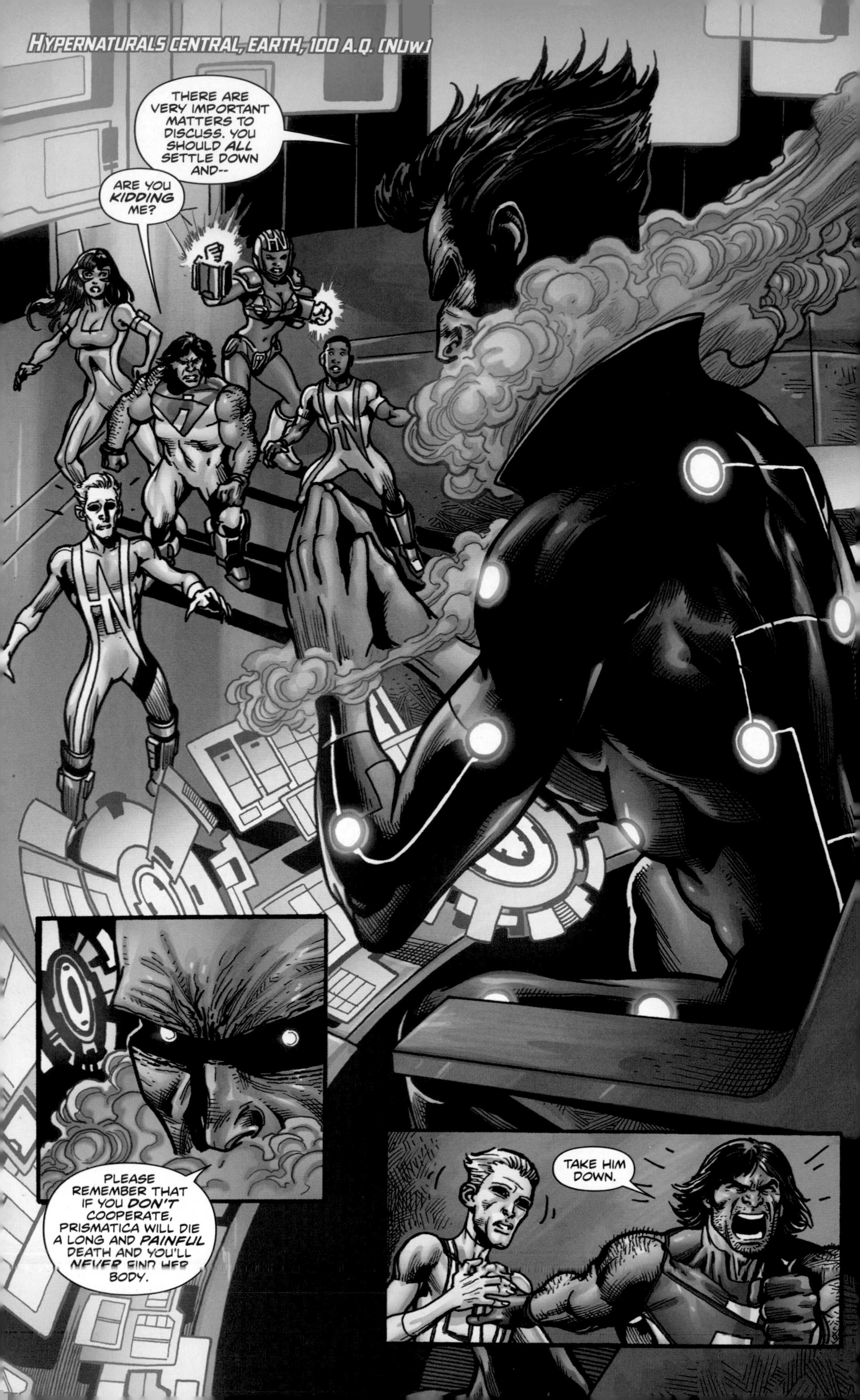
HYPERNATURALS CENTRAL, EARTH, 100 A.Q. [NOW]
THERE ARE VERY IMPORTANT MATTERS TO DISCUSS. YOU SHOULD ALL SETTLE DOWN AND--
ARE YOU KIDDING ME?
PLEASE REMEMBER THAT IF YOU DON'T COOPERATE, PRISMATICA WILL DIE A LONG AND PAINFUL DEATH AND YOU'LL NEVER FIND HER BODY.
TAKE HIM DOWN.

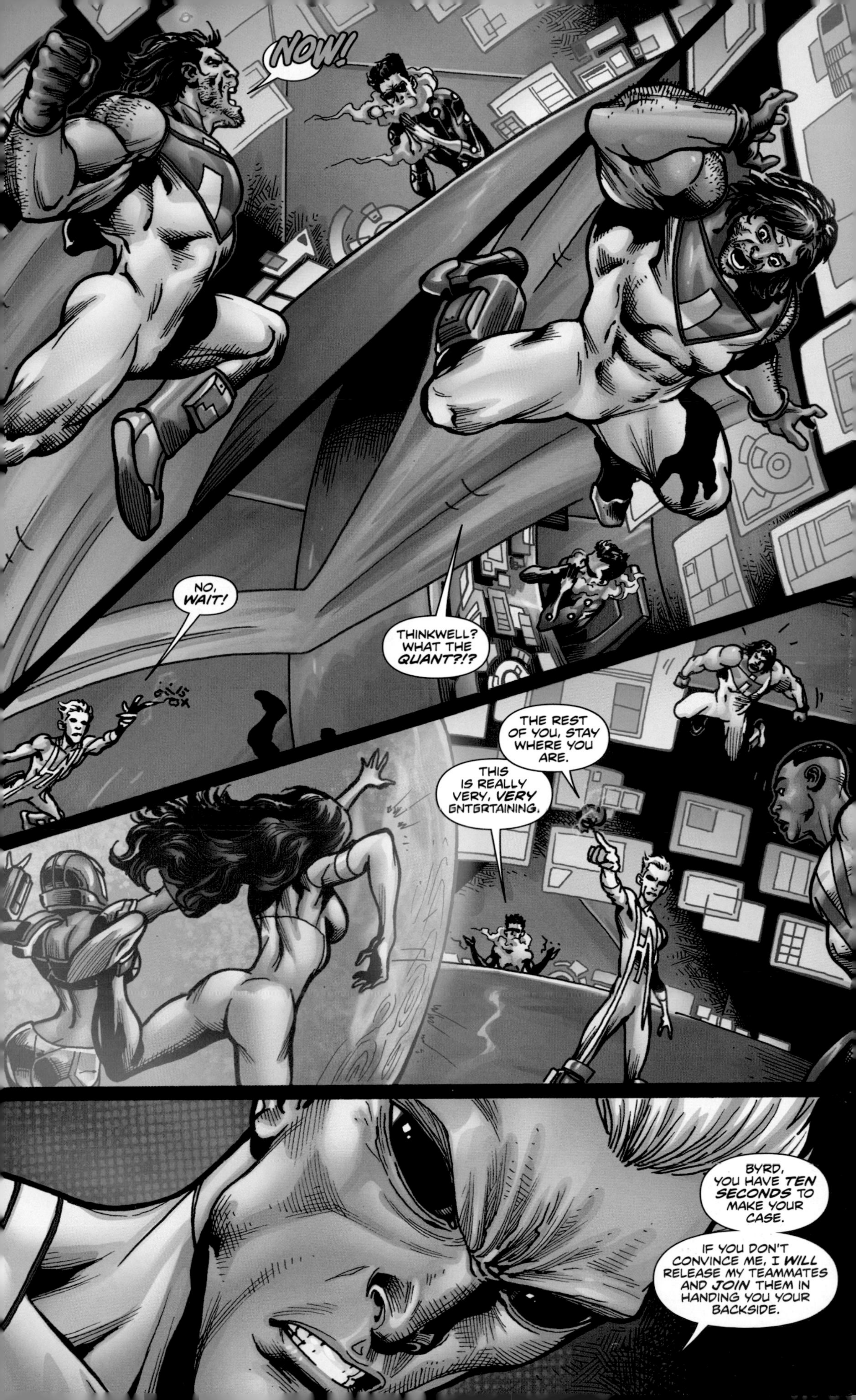
NOW!
NO, WAIT!
THINKWELL? WHAT THE QUANT?!?
THE REST OF YOU, STAY WHERE YOU ARE.
THIS IS REALLY VERY, VERY ENTERTAINING.
BYRD, YOU HAVE TEN SECONDS TO MAKE YOUR CASE.
IF YOU DON'T CONVINCE ME, I WILL RELEASE MY TEAMMATES AND JOIN THEM IN HANDING YOU YOUR BACKSIDE.

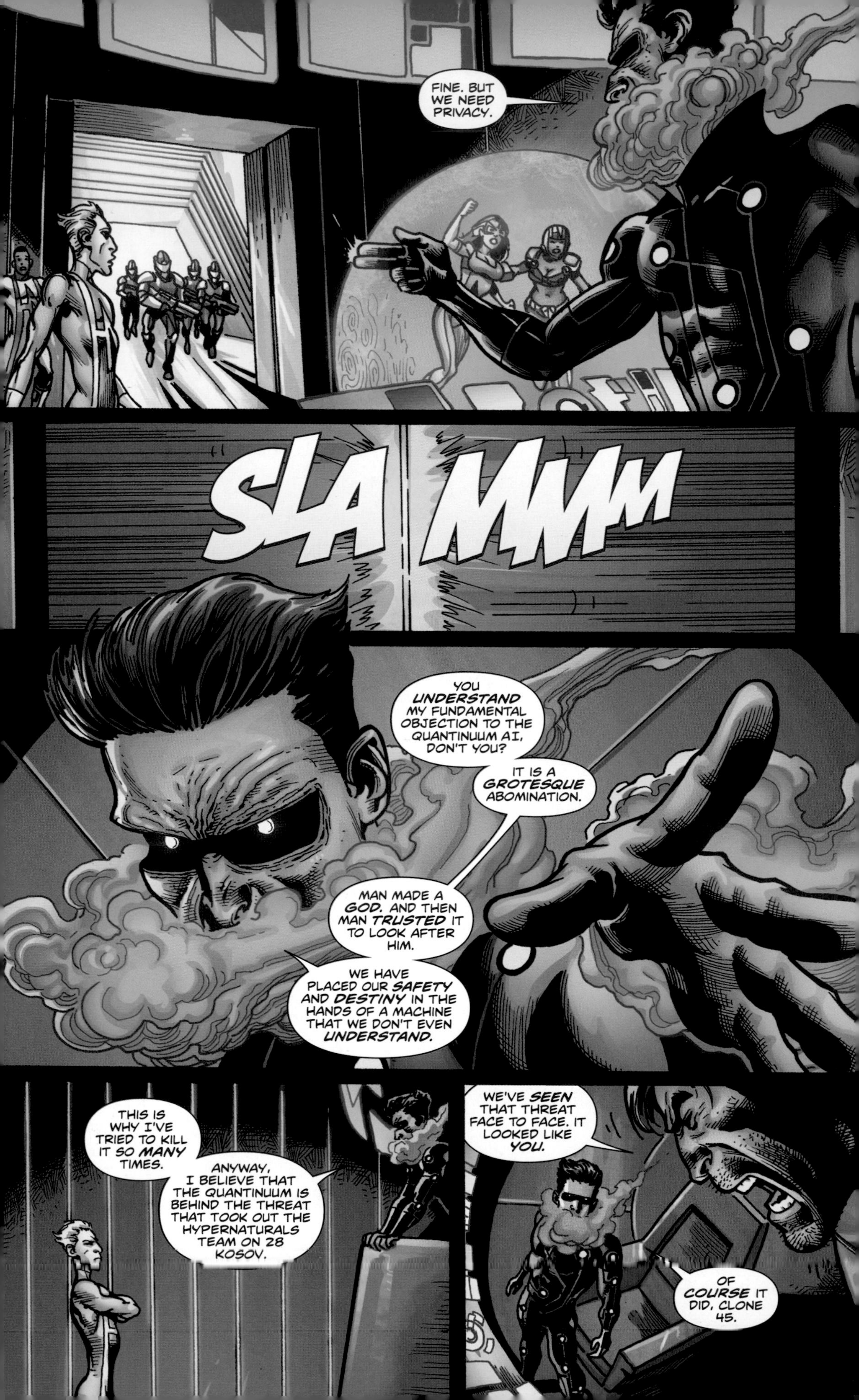
FINE. BUT WE NEED PRIVACY.
SLAMMM
YOU UNDERSTAND MY FUNDAMENTAL OBJECTION TO THE QUANTINUUM AI, DON'T YOU?
IT IS A GROTESQUE ABOMINATION.
MAN MADE A GOD. AND THEN MAN TRUSTED IT TO LOOK AFTER HIM.
WE HAVE PLACED OUR SAFETY AND DESTINY IN THE HANDS OF A MACHINE THAT WE DON'T EVEN UNDERSTAND.
THIS IS WHY I'VE TRIED TO KILL IT SO MANY TIMES.
ANYWAY, I BELIEVE THAT THE QUANTINUUM IS BEHIND THE THREAT THAT TOOK OUT THE HYPERNATURALS TEAM ON 28 KOSOV.
WE'VE SEEN THAT THREAT FACE TO FACE. IT LOOKED LIKE YOU.
OF COURSE IT DID, CLONE 45.

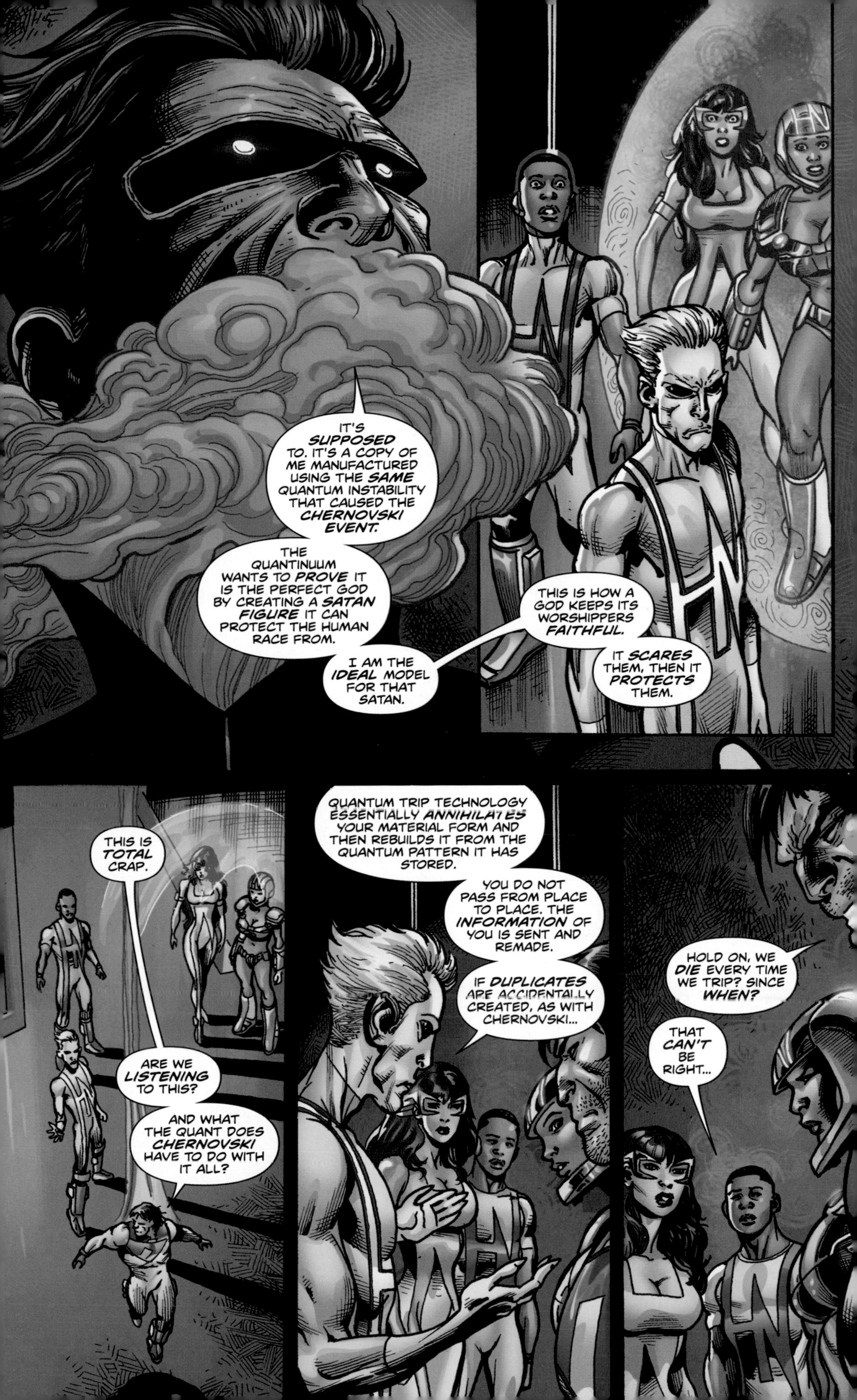
IT'S SUPPOSED TO. IT'S A COPY OF ME MANUFACTURED USING THE SAME QUANTUM INSTABILITY THAT CAUSED THE CHERNOVSKI EVENT.
THE QUANTINUUM WANTS TO PROVE IT IS THE PERFECT GOD BY CREATING A SATAN FIGURE IT CAN PROTECT THE HUMAN RACE FROM.
I AM THE IDEAL MODEL FOR THAT SATAN.
THIS IS HOW A GOD KEEPS ITS WORSHIPPERS FAITHFUL.
IT SCARES THEM, THEN IT PROTECTS THEM.
THIS IS TOTAL CRAP.
ARE WE LISTENING TO THIS?
AND WHAT THE QUANT DOES CHERNOVSKI HAVE TO DO WITH IT ALL?
QUANTUM TRIP TECHNOLOGY ESSENTIALLY ANNIHILATES YOUR MATERIAL FORM AND THEN REBUILDS IT FROM THE QUANTUM PATTERN IT HAS STORED.
YOU DO NOT PASS FROM PLACE TO PLACE. THE INFORMATION OF YOU IS SENT AND REMADE.
IF DUPLICATES ARE ACCIDENTALLY CREATED, AS WITH CHERNOVSKI...
HOLD ON, WE DIE EVERY TIME WE TRIP? SINCE WHEN?
THAT CAN'T BE RIGHT...

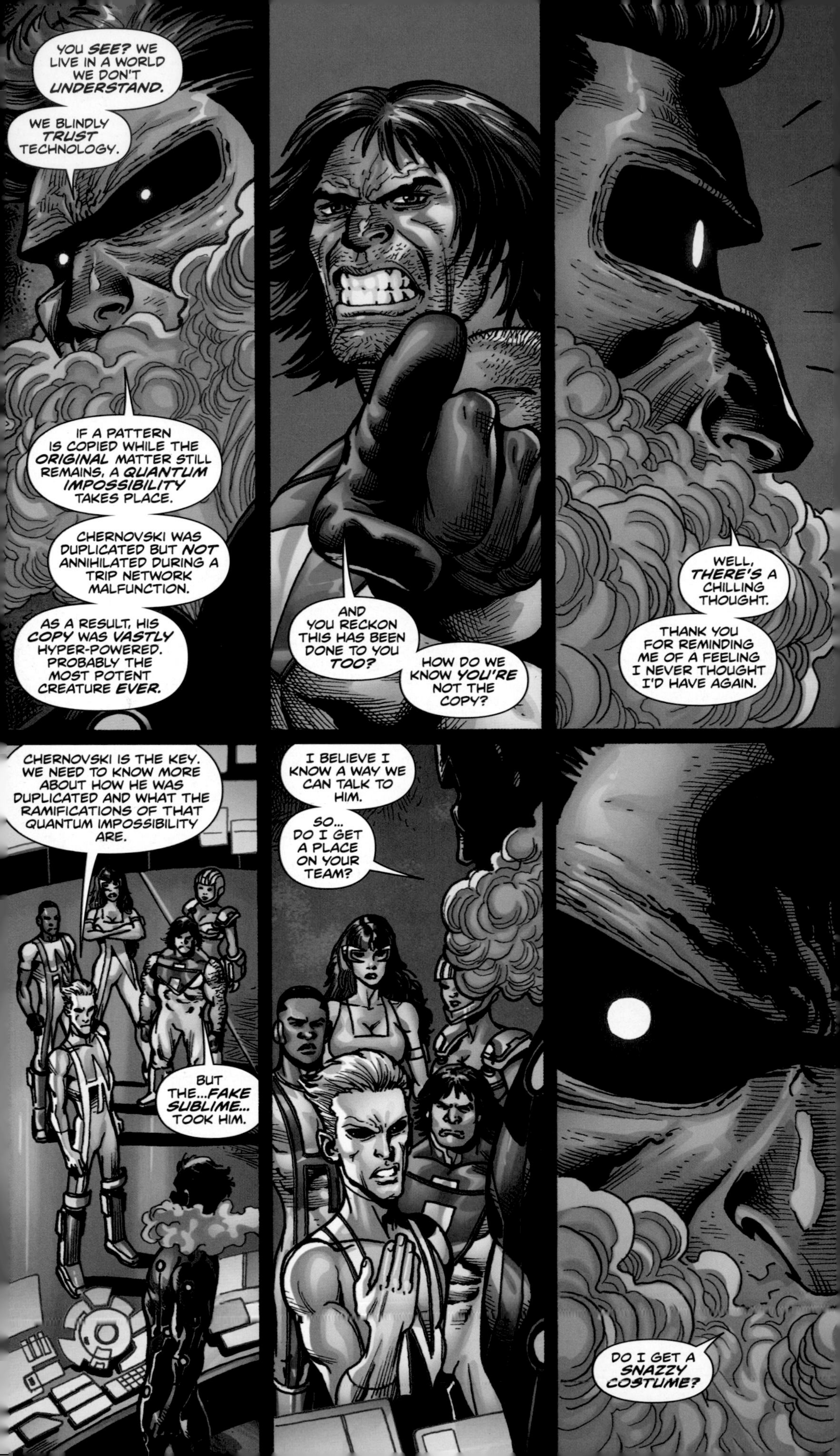
YOU SEE? WE LIVE IN A WORLD WE DON'T UNDERSTAND.
WE BLINDLY TRUST TECHNOLOGY.
IF A PATTERN IS COPIED WHILE THE ORIGINAL MATTER STILL REMAINS, A QUANTUM IMPOSSIBILITY TAKES PLACE.
CHERNOVSKI WAS DUPLICATED BUT NOT ANNIHILATED DURING A TRIP NETWORK MALFUNCTION.
AS A RESULT, HIS COPY WAS VASTLY HYPER-POWERED. PROBABLY THE MOST POTENT CREATURE EVER.
AND YOU RECKON THIS HAS BEEN DONE TO YOU TOO?
HOW DO WE KNOW YOU'RE NOT THE COPY?
WELL, THERE'S A CHILLING THOUGHT.
THANK YOU FOR REMINDING ME OF A FEELING I NEVER THOUGHT I'D HAVE AGAIN.
CHERNOVSKI IS THE KEY. WE NEED TO KNOW MORE ABOUT HOW HE WAS DUPLICATED AND WHAT THE RAMIFICATIONS OF THAT QUANTUM IMPOSSIBILITY ARE.
BUT THE...FAKE SUBLIME... TOOK HIM.
I BELIEVE I KNOW A WAY WE CAN TALK TO HIM.
SO... DO I GET A PLACE ON YOUR TEAM?
DO I GET A SNAZZY COSTUME?

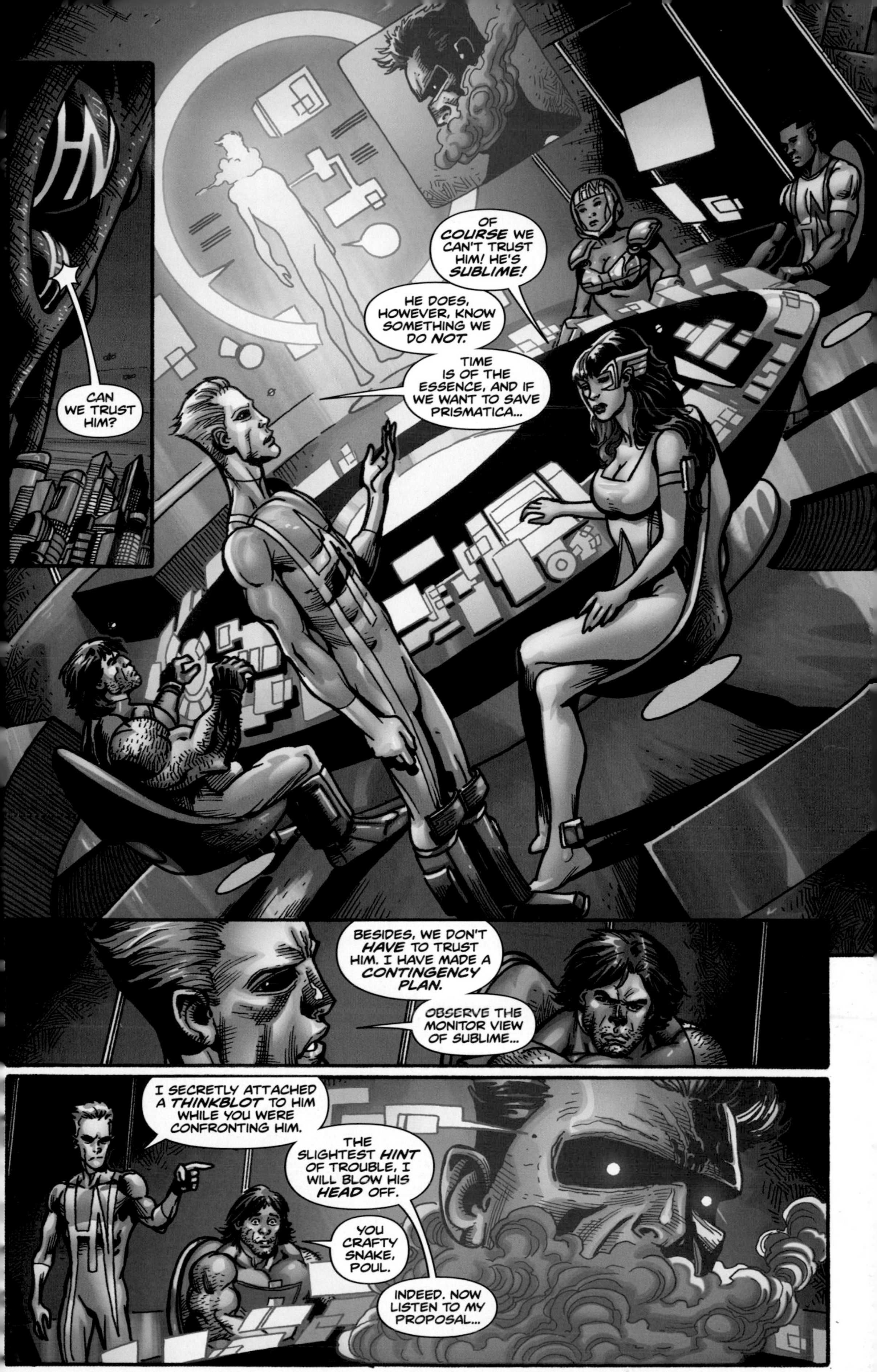
CAN WE TRUST HIM?
OF COURSE WE CAN'T TRUST HIM! HE'S SUBLIME!
HE DOES, HOWEVER, KNOW SOMETHING WE DO NOT.
TIME IS OF THE ESSENCE, AND IF WE WANT TO SAVE PRISMATICA...
BESIDES, WE DON'T HAVE TO TRUST HIM. I HAVE MADE A CONTINGENCY PLAN.
OBSERVE THE MONITOR VIEW OF SUBLIME...
I SECRETLY ATTACHED A THINKBLOT TO HIM WHILE YOU WERE CONFRONTING HIM.
THE SLIGHTEST HINT OF TROUBLE, I WILL BLOW HIS HEAD OFF.
YOU CRAFTY SNAKE, POUL.
INDEED. NOW LISTEN TO MY PROPOSAL...

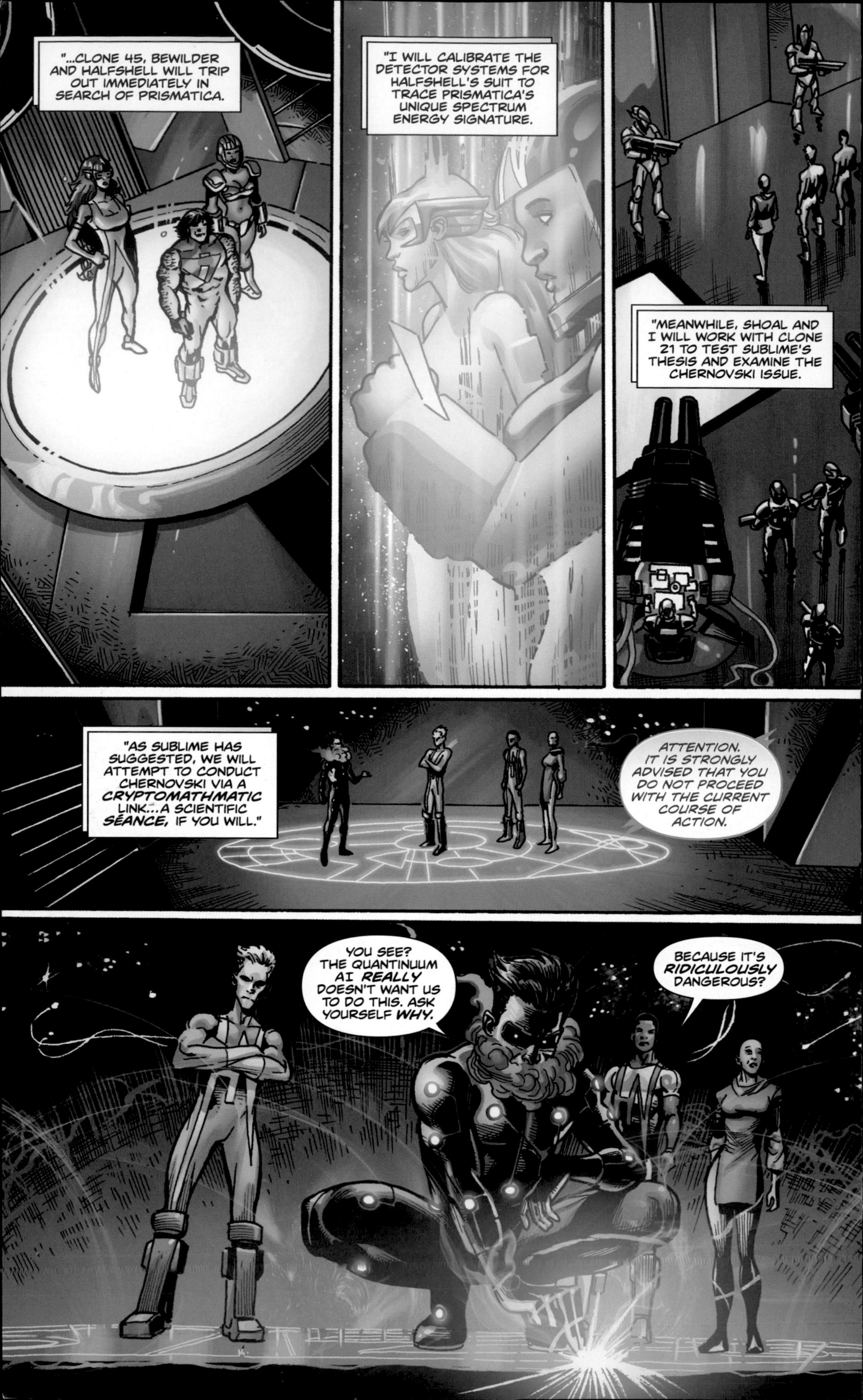
"...CLONE 45, BEWILDER AND HALFSHELL WILL TRIP OUT IMMEDIATELY IN SEARCH OF PRISMATICA.
"I WILL CALIBRATE THE DETECTOR SYSTEMS FOR HALFSHELL'S SUIT TO TRACE PRISMATICA'S UNIQUE SPECTRUM ENERGY SIGNATURE.
"MEANWHILE, SHOAL AND I WILL WORK WITH CLONE 21 TO TEST SUBLIME'S THESIS AND EXAMINE THE CHERNOVSKI ISSUE.
"AS SUBLIME HAS SUGGESTED, WE WILL ATTEMPT TO CONDUCT CHERNOVSKI VIA A CRYPTOMATHMATIC LINK...A SCIENTIFIC SÉANCE, IF YOU WILL."
ATTENTION. IT IS STRONGLY ADVISED THAT YOU DO NOT PROCEED WITH THE CURRENT COURSE OF ACTION.
YOU SEE? THE QUANTINUUM AI REALLY DOESN'T WANT US TO DO THIS. ASK YOURSELF WHY.
BECAUSE IT'S RIDICULOUSLY DANGEROUS?

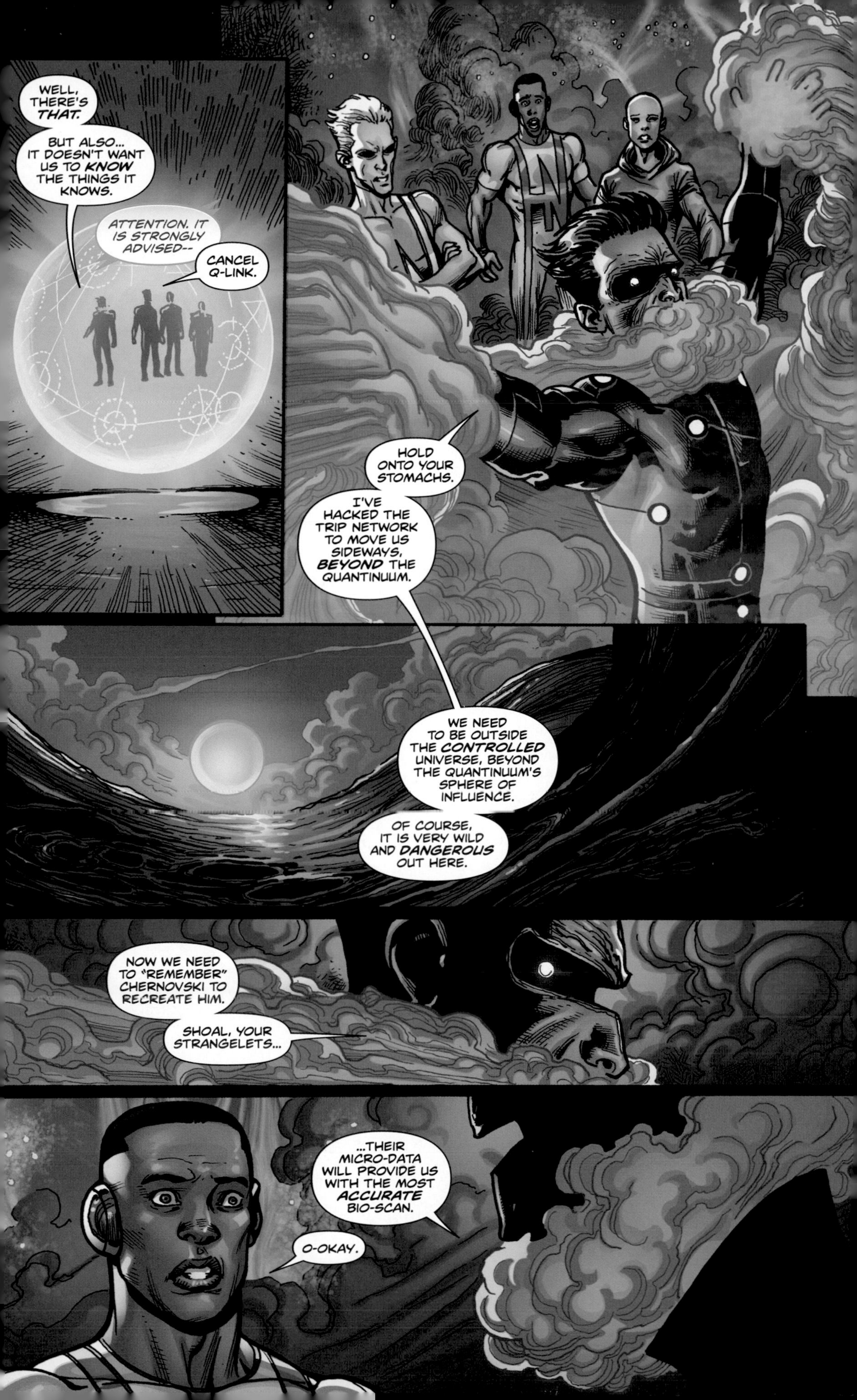
WELL, THERE'S *THAT.*
BUT ALSO... IT DOESN'T WANT US TO *KNOW* THE THINGS IT KNOWS.
ATTENTION. IT IS STRONGLY ADVISED--
CANCEL Q-LINK.
HOLD ONTO YOUR STOMACHS.
I'VE HACKED THE TRIP NETWORK TO MOVE US SIDEWAYS, *BEYOND* THE QUANTINUUM.
WE NEED TO BE OUTSIDE THE *CONTROLLED* UNIVERSE, BEYOND THE QUANTINUUM'S SPHERE OF INFLUENCE.
OF COURSE, IT IS VERY WILD AND *DANGEROUS* OUT HERE.
NOW WE NEED TO "REMEMBER" CHERNOVSKI TO RECREATE HIM.
SHOAL, YOUR STRANGELETS...
...THEIR MICRO-DATA WILL PROVIDE US WITH THE MOST *ACCURATE* BIO-SCAN.
O-OKAY.

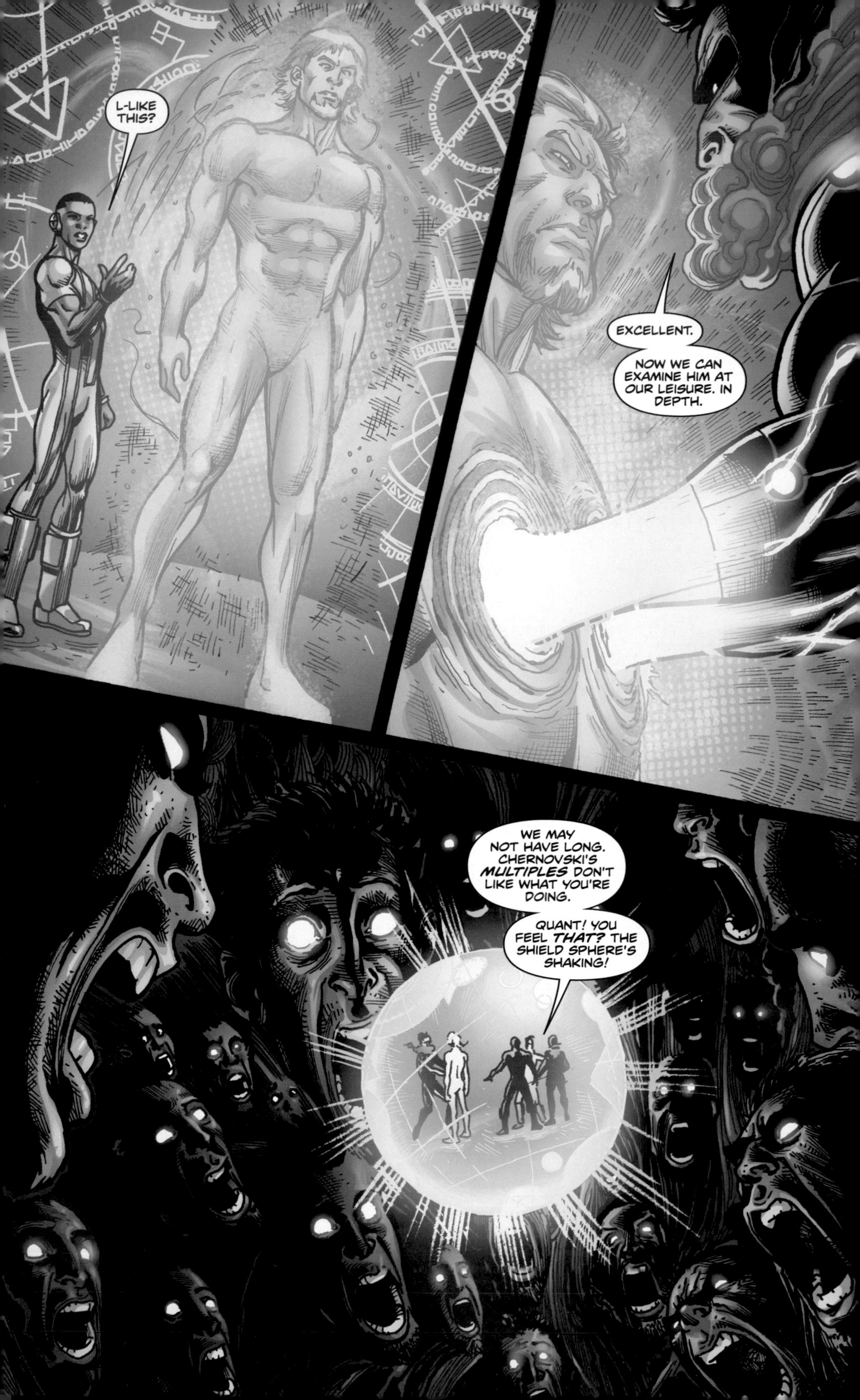
L-LIKE THIS?
EXCELLENT.
NOW WE CAN EXAMINE HIM AT OUR LEISURE. IN DEPTH.
WE MAY NOT HAVE LONG. CHERNOVSKI'S *MULTIPLES* DON'T LIKE WHAT YOU'RE DOING.
QUANT! YOU FEEL *THAT?* THE SHIELD SPHERE'S SHAKING!

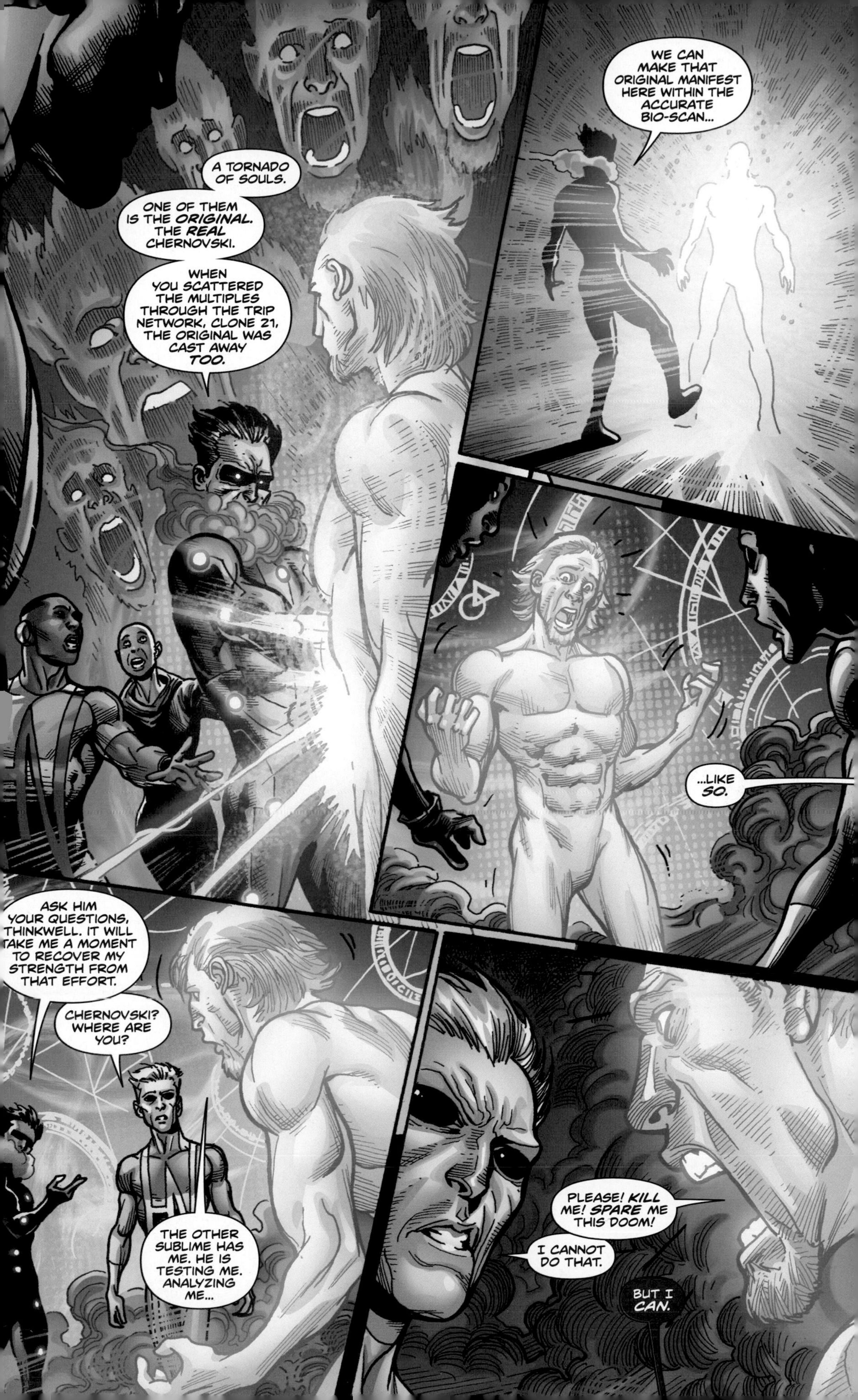
A TORNADO OF SOULS.
ONE OF THEM IS THE *ORIGINAL*. THE *REAL* CHERNOVSKI.
WHEN YOU SCATTERED THE MULTIPLES THROUGH THE TRIP NETWORK, CLONE 21, THE ORIGINAL WAS CAST AWAY *TOO*.
WE CAN MAKE THAT ORIGINAL MANIFEST HERE WITHIN THE ACCURATE BIO-SCAN...
...LIKE *SO*.
ASK HIM YOUR QUESTIONS, THINKWELL. IT WILL TAKE ME A MOMENT TO RECOVER MY STRENGTH FROM THAT EFFORT.
CHERNOVSKI? WHERE ARE YOU?
THE OTHER SUBLIME HAS ME. HE IS TESTING ME. ANALYZING ME...
PLEASE! *KILL* ME! *SPARE* ME THIS DOOM!
I CANNOT DO THAT.
BUT I *CAN*.

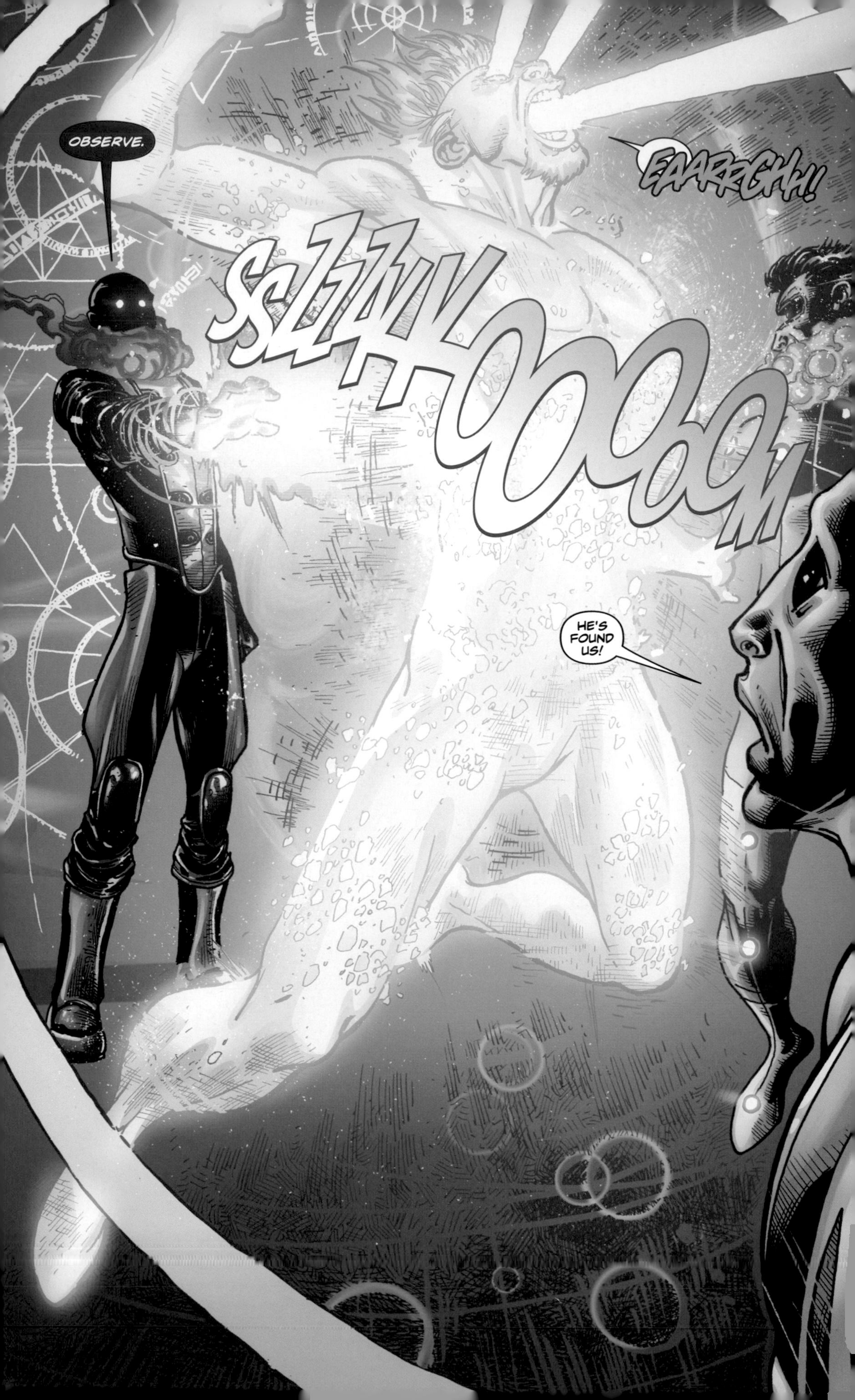
OBSERVE.
EAARRGHH!
SSZZZZKOOOOM
HE'S FOUND US!

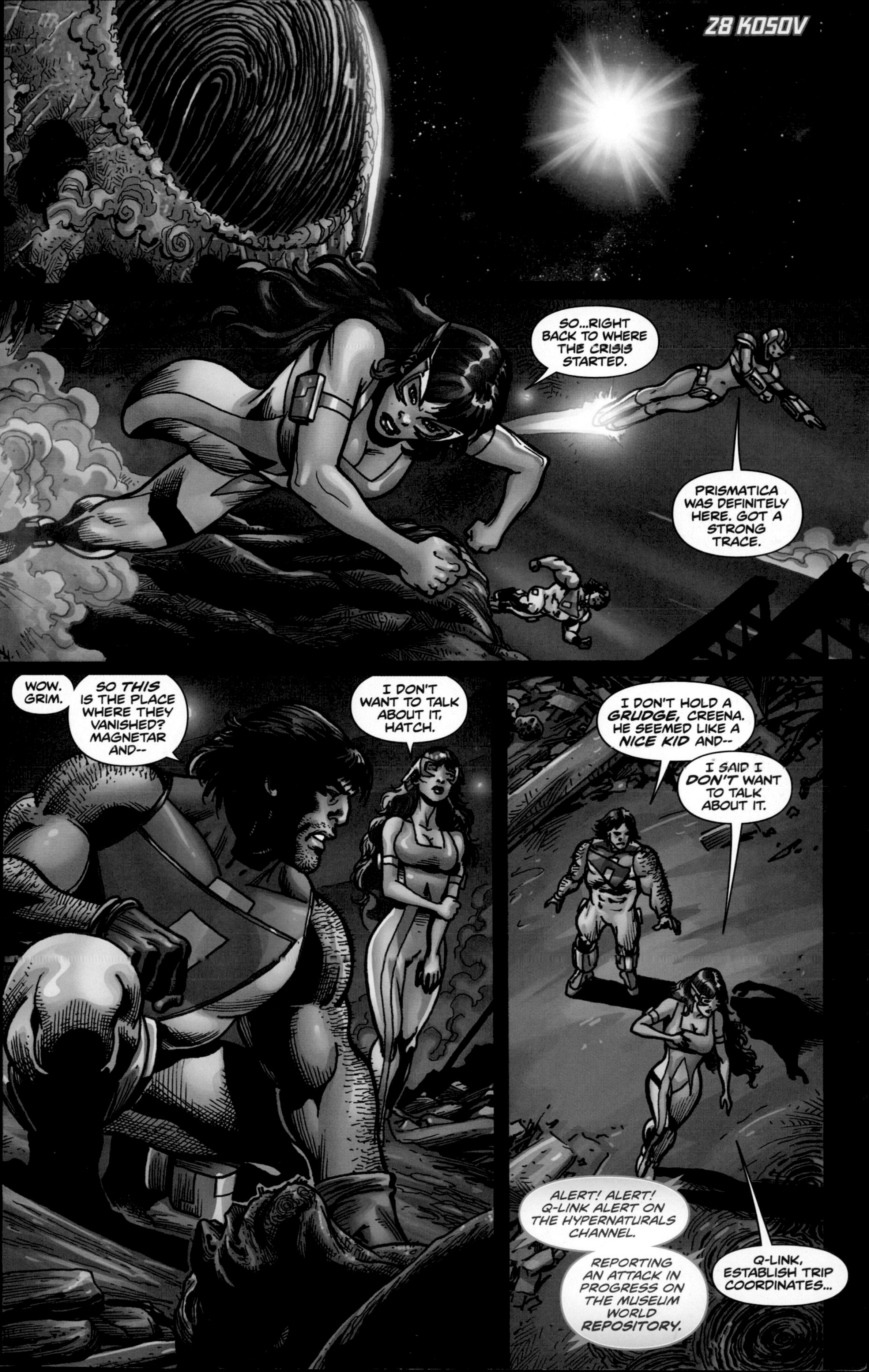
SO...RIGHT BACK TO WHERE THE CRISIS STARTED.
PRISMATICA WAS DEFINITELY HERE. GOT A STRONG TRACE.
WOW. GRIM.
SO THIS IS THE PLACE WHERE THEY VANISHED? MAGNETAR AND--
I DON'T WANT TO TALK ABOUT IT, HATCH.
I DON'T HOLD A GRUDGE, CREENA. HE SEEMED LIKE A NICE KID AND--
I SAID I DON'T WANT TO TALK ABOUT IT.
ALERT! ALERT! Q-LINK ALERT ON THE HYPERNATURALS CHANNEL.
REPORTING AN ATTACK IN PROGRESS ON THE MUSEUM WORLD REPOSITORY.
Q-LINK, ESTABLISH TRIP COORDINATES...

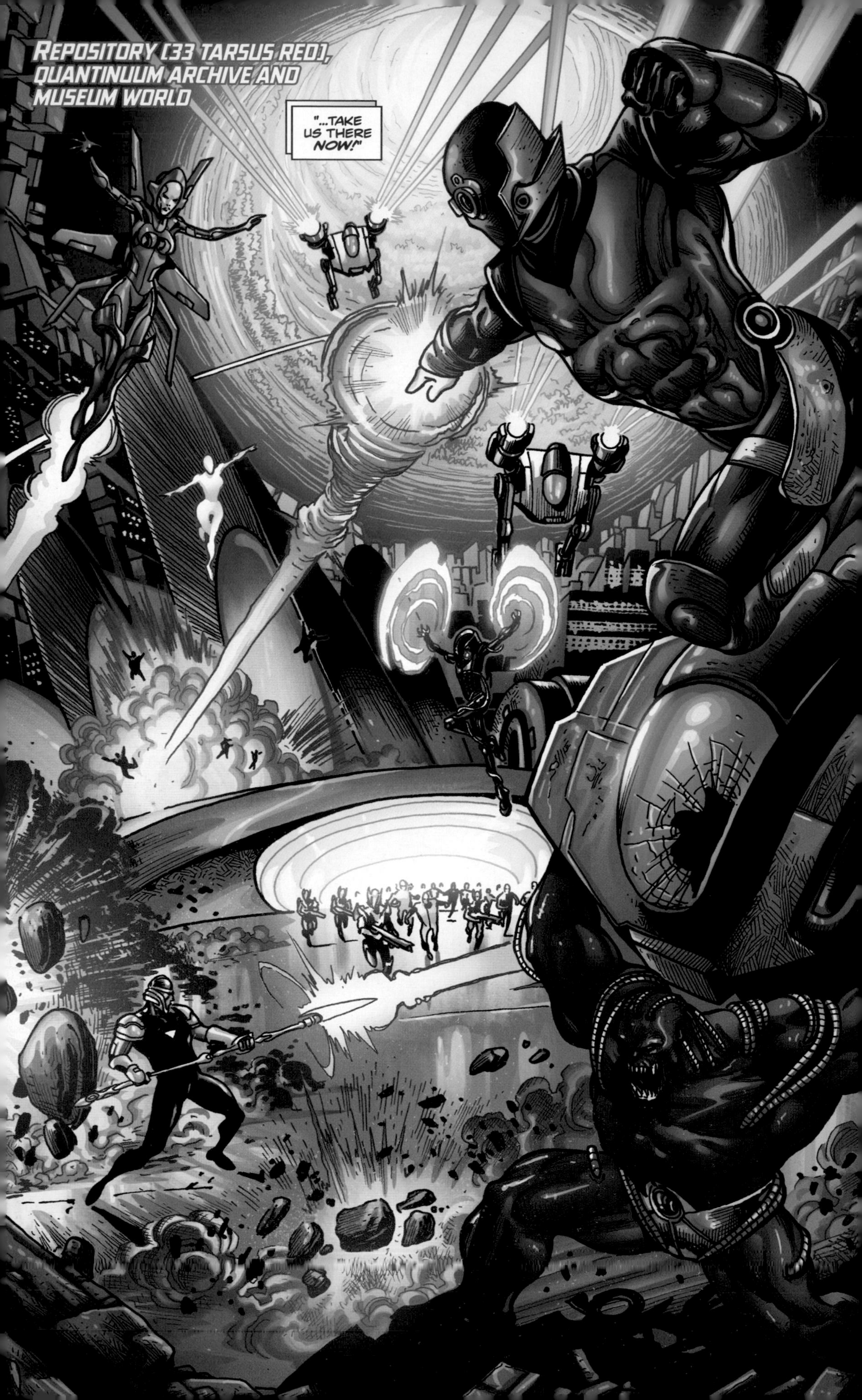
REPOSITORY [33 TARSUS RED], QUANTINUUM ARCHIVE AND MUSEUM WORLD
"...TAKE US THERE NOW!"

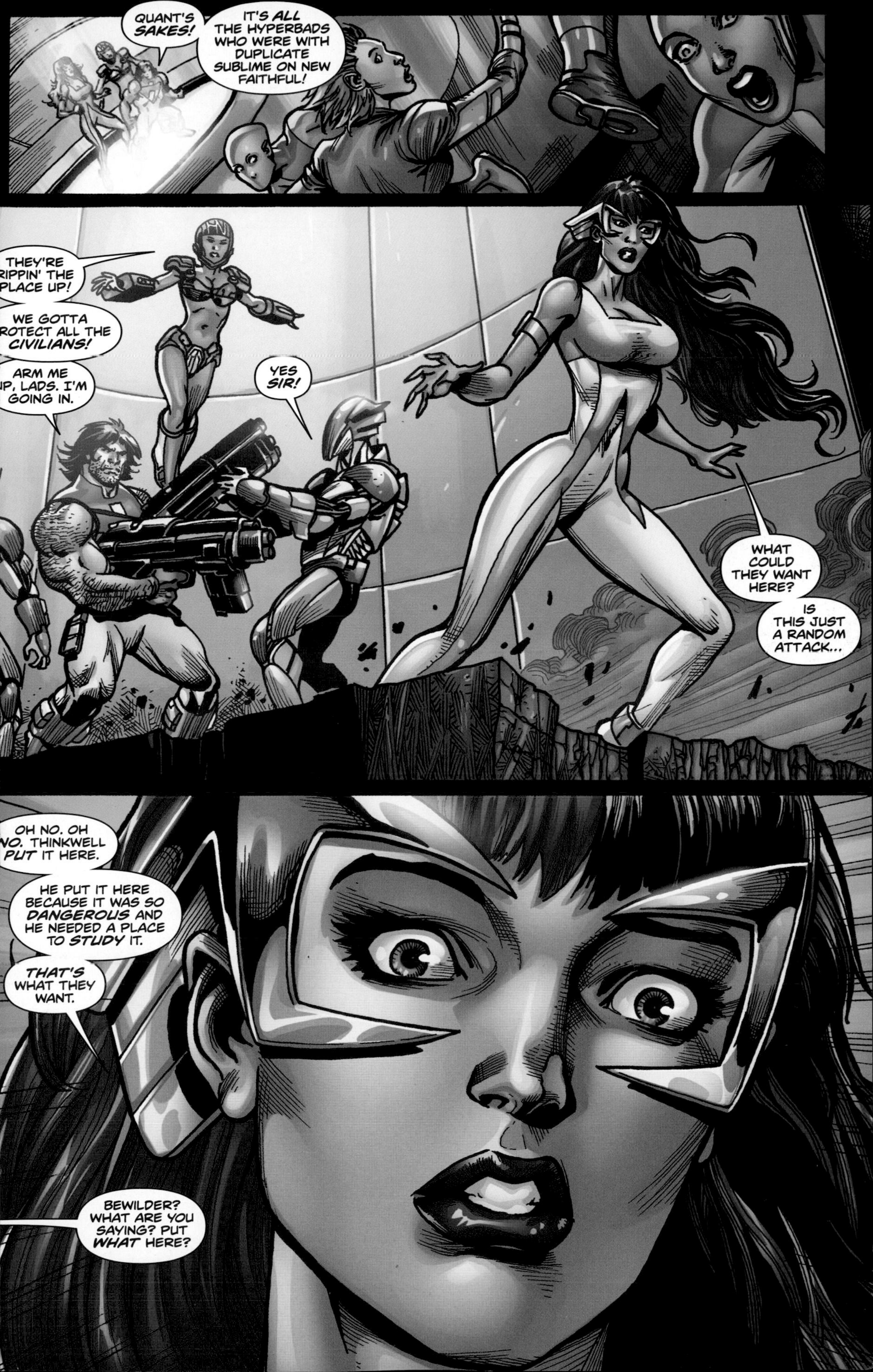
QUANT'S SAKES!
IT'S ALL THE HYPERBADS WHO WERE WITH DUPLICATE SUBLIME ON NEW FAITHFUL!
THEY'RE RIPPIN' THE PLACE UP!
WE GOTTA PROTECT ALL THE CIVILIANS!
ARM ME UP, LADS. I'M GOING IN.
YES SIR!
WHAT COULD THEY WANT HERE?
IS THIS JUST A RANDOM ATTACK...
OH NO. OH NO. THINKWELL PUT IT HERE.
HE PUT IT HERE BECAUSE IT WAS SO DANGEROUS AND HE NEEDED A PLACE TO STUDY IT.
THAT'S WHAT THEY WANT.
BEWILDER? WHAT ARE YOU SAYING? PUT WHAT HERE?

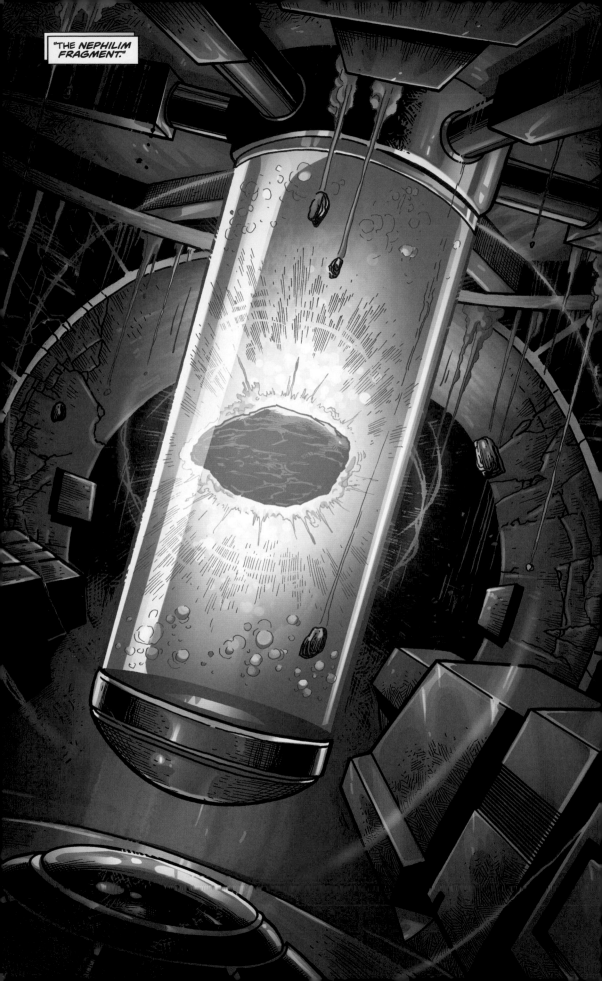

"THE NEPHILIM FRAGMENT."

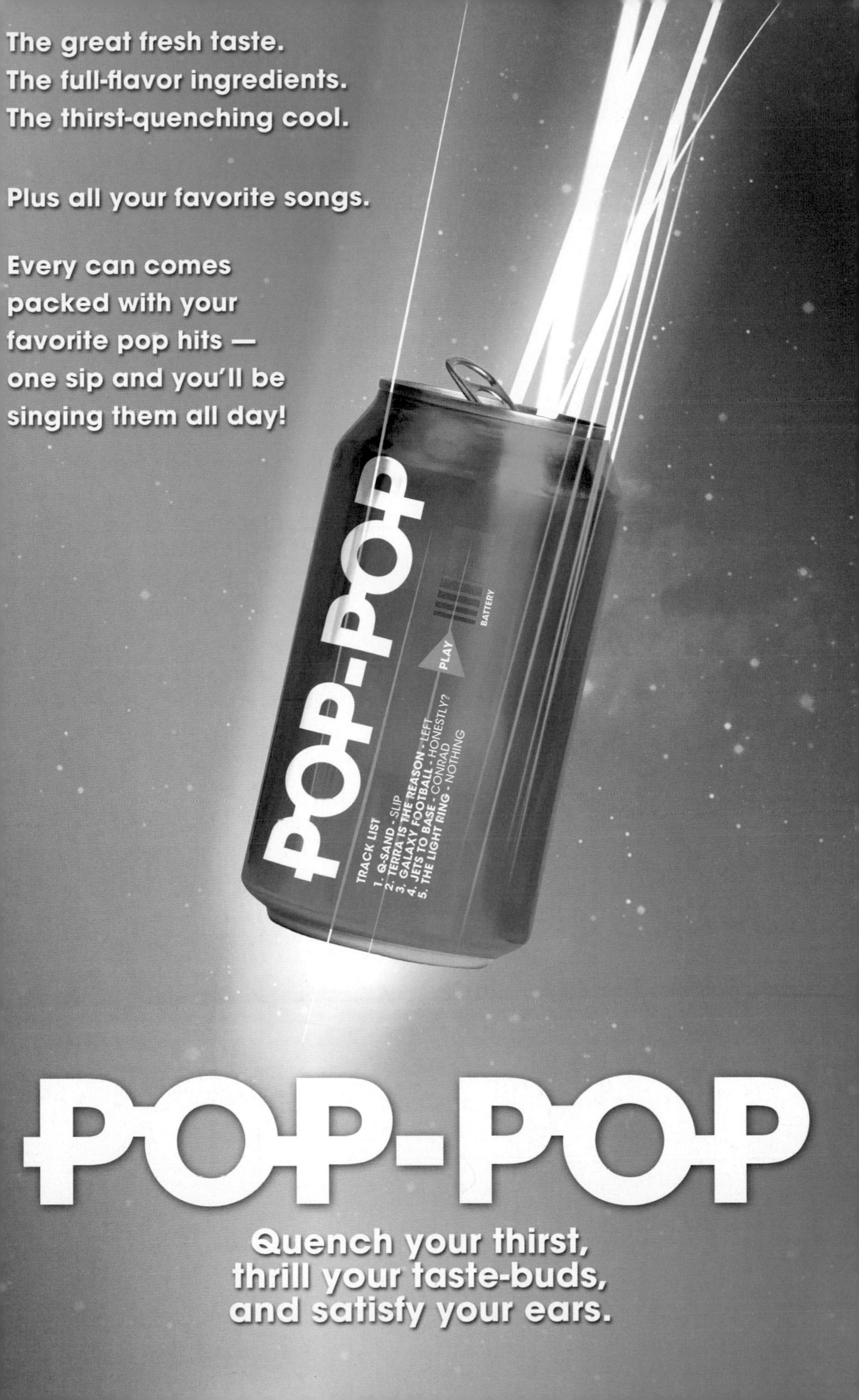
The great fresh taste.
The full-flavor ingredients.
The thirst-quenching cool.
Plus all your favorite songs.
Every can comes packed with your favorite pop hits — one sip and you'll be singing them all day!
POP-POP
TRACK LIST
1. Q-SAND - SLIP
2. TERRA IS THE REASON - LEFT
3. GALAXY FOOTBALL - HONESTLY?
4. JETS TO BASE - CONRAD
5. THE LIGHT RING - NOTHING
PLAY
BATTERY
POP-POP
Quench your thirst, thrill your taste-buds, and satisfy your ears.

> PROFILE REPORT ON BYRD, JOHN ALVIS

> AKA SUBLIME

SUBLIME
Real name: John Alvis Byrd

Currently imprisoned in the Omni-Max prison facility within the Orcus storm zone of the 15 Tartarus System. Hypernatural gift varies between Class 12 to Class 15 depending on the attribute and conditions. It makes him capable of radically subverting any technology he is allowed to interface with to his own ends. Pattern regression as a form of rehabilitation is impossible due to Byrd's transformed nature, following an early Trip network accident in 8 AQ. Byrd believes in human determinism and thus feels the Quantinuum AI is the enemy of freedom.

Byrd was working on the establishment of the Trip Network during the first decade of the Quantinuum. He was assigned help to implement Quantinuum's Trip technology, setting up Trip nodes throughout the universe, even in the most dangerous and inhospitable regions.

Byrd had an acute Hypernatural gift: meta-intelligence. He was Level 12, hitherto unheard of. He was the smartest man in the universe but also a borderline sociopath and a high functioning autistic.

Even before his accident, he was full of himself: cock-sure and brash, because he knew he could not truly die as long as he meticulously backed up his pattern with the Q-hub.

He was constantly berated by his supervisor. If it wasn't for the fact he was the smartest guy in the program, they'd have cut him. His reckless Trip experimentation often almost cost the lives of his colleagues as well as millions of dollars' worth of equipment.

Byrd was unconcerned. He trusted the restorative power of pattern rebuild, and also believed that the Quantinuum AI had personally requested his involvement in the program

Byrd had become so fascinated and enthralled by the notion of being virtually immortal due to the process of pattern rebuild employed in Tripping that he became impetuous to the point of suicidal – flirting with death whilst knowing he could not die. He believed that the Quantinuum would always restore him to his last save-point.

His ultimate faith and trust in the Quantinuum led to his undoing and is at the root of his hatred and desire for revenge.

After his 'accident' Byrd's body was remade from his stored pattern but the very pattern itself had been altered, changed by extreme circumstances of the accident (a stellar explosion). His pattern was scattered, disrupted, amalgamated and blended with the very stuff of the universes, then tempered in the boiling furnace and explosive radiation of solar fusion.

Byrd has 'sublimated': become a being of transcendent power. His body shifting between realities, becoming mist-like.

His mind expanded; functioning on levels of reasoning far beyond anything human: he's become a 13th level intellect or beyond.

As Sublime, he feels detached and remote, experiencing things on many levels. Post transformation, he quickly came to the conclusion the Quantinuum was to blame, and that by extension mankind based far too much blind faith in an AI device it could not begin to comprehend. He resolved to use his newfound powers to destroy it and free humankind from its insidious clutches.

Sublime is happy to be seen as the villain. He is convinced what he is doing is right and for the good of all mankind. Millions may die, but eventually he will liberate mankind from the yoke of the computer's oppressive rule.

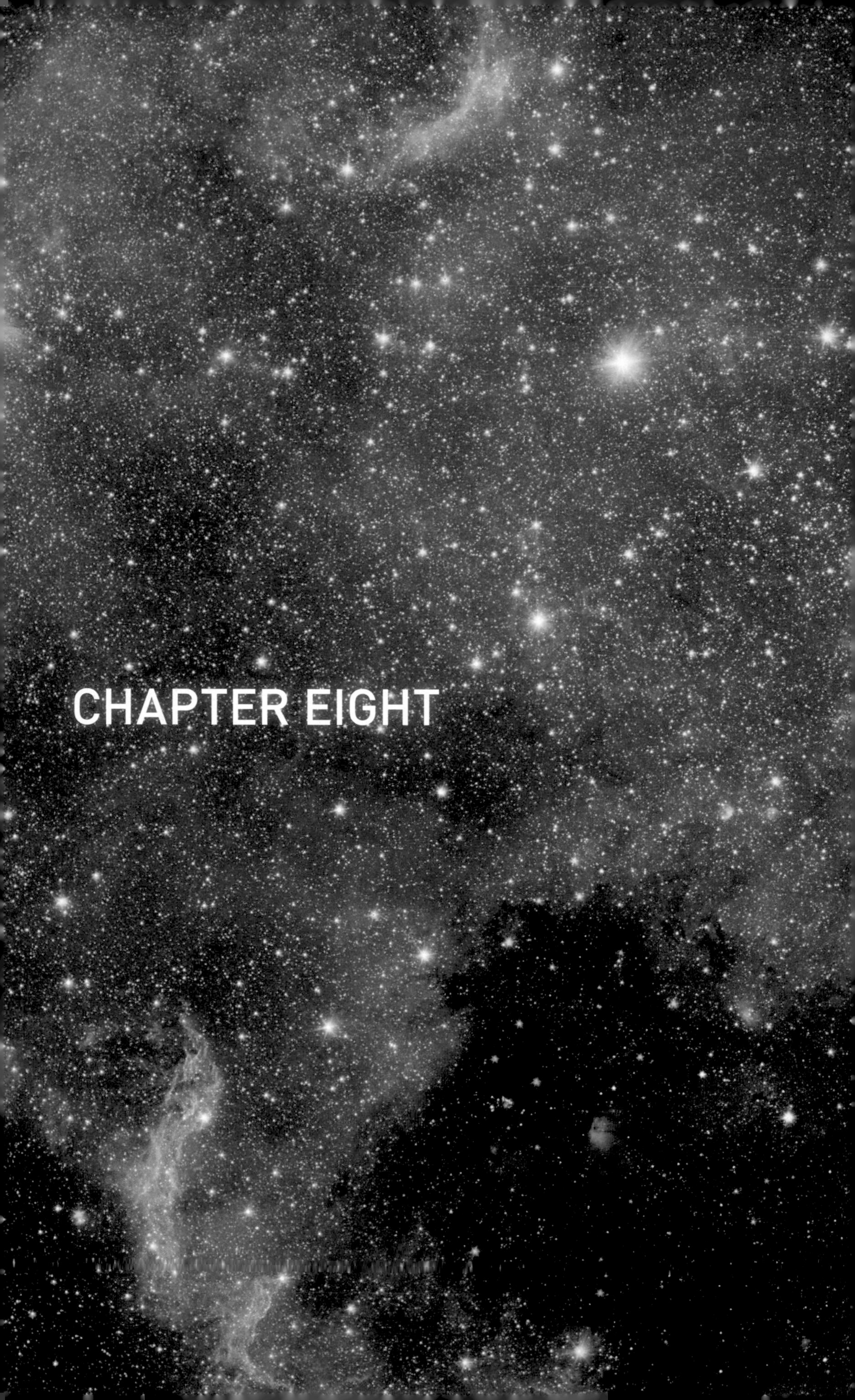

CHAPTER EIGHT

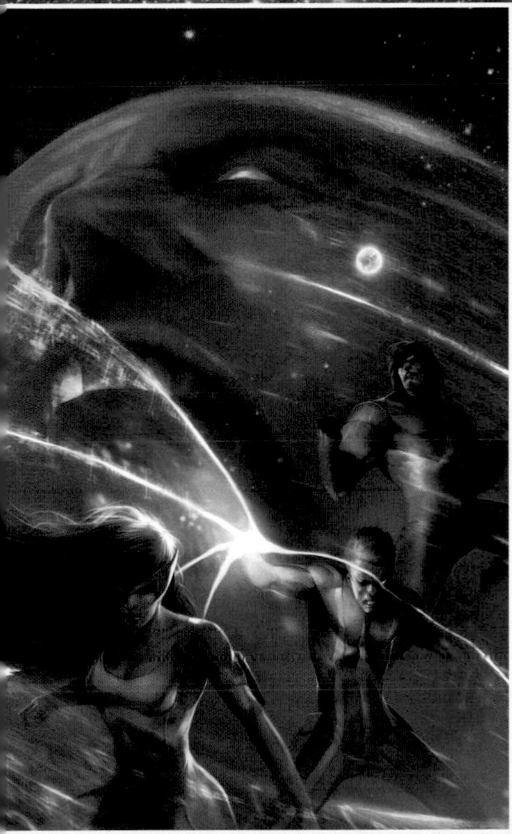

Issue Eight
Francesco Mattina

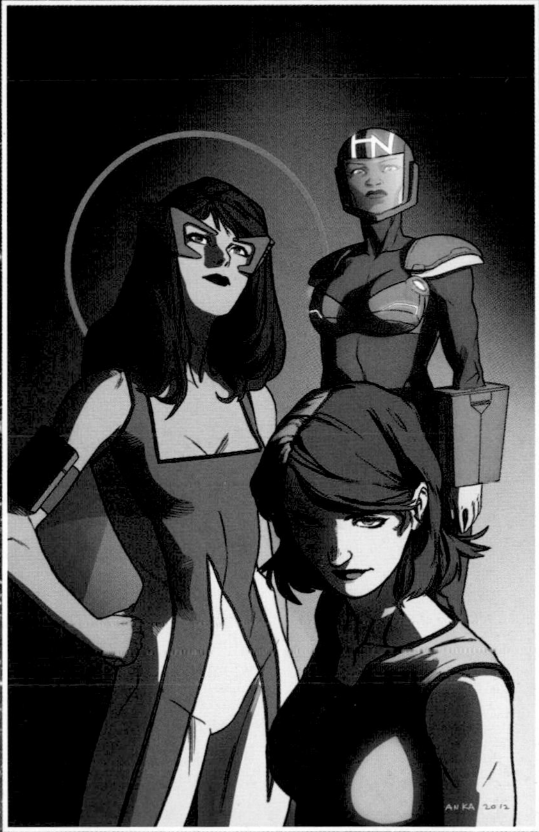
ANKA 2012

Issue Eight
Kris Anka

• You have selected Q-Data link.

The team that saved 356 Barnard from the Replicator crisis. This is the team that put Sublime in iso, for Quant's sake! Big shoes. Big, big shoes.

• It is the 13th of January in the year **100 A.Q.**
    • Touch here to select an alternative to the **Anno Quantinuum** calendar system.
    • Touch here to load local weather reports for your **current cosmic location**.
    • Touch here to access **Q-Data newsflows** from planets near your current cosmic location.
    • Touch here for latest **Quantum Trip** transit times.

• Q-Data entry: The Quantinuum

• The Quantinuum is the name for the **human galactic culture**, and also for the **artificial intelligence** that controls its function.

• The Quantinuum was created 100 years ago at the start of the **Nanocene Era**. The Nanocene began when the Quantinuum AI achieved Singularity and refashioned human galactic culture. Succeeding the **Holocene Era**, the Nanocene is the next progression of human evolution and...

                                 (to read this entry in full, touch here)

• You have selected live feed newsflow.

• **Advancer et Cie Trading** files lawsuit against **CostKov** for trade-route infringement
• **44 Farouk** to auction off its moons
• Inhabitants of **51 Jered** vote unanimously to reverse the planet's direction of rotation
• Confirmed reports of break-out at **Tartarus Omni-max prison**
• **AI Law** star **Badge Frankham** enters rehab for a widely reported Pop-pop problem
• **Hypernaturals Central**, San Diego, reports that the "emergency team" is continuing to investigate the disappearance of the **Centennial Year Iteration** of the team, lost during an response mission to **28 Kosov** three days ago

• The Hypernaturals are the Quantinuum's foremost champions. Famous across the entirety of human galactic culture, the team members are selected on the basis of their hypernatural powers and their strength of character, and serve for five-year terms. In honor of the start of the twenty-first term, the line-up of the team's so-called "Centennial Year Iteration" has recently been announced amid huge publicity and--

...BREAKING NEWS... reports are coming in of a Hypernatural incident at the Quantinuum Archive and Museum World Repository...

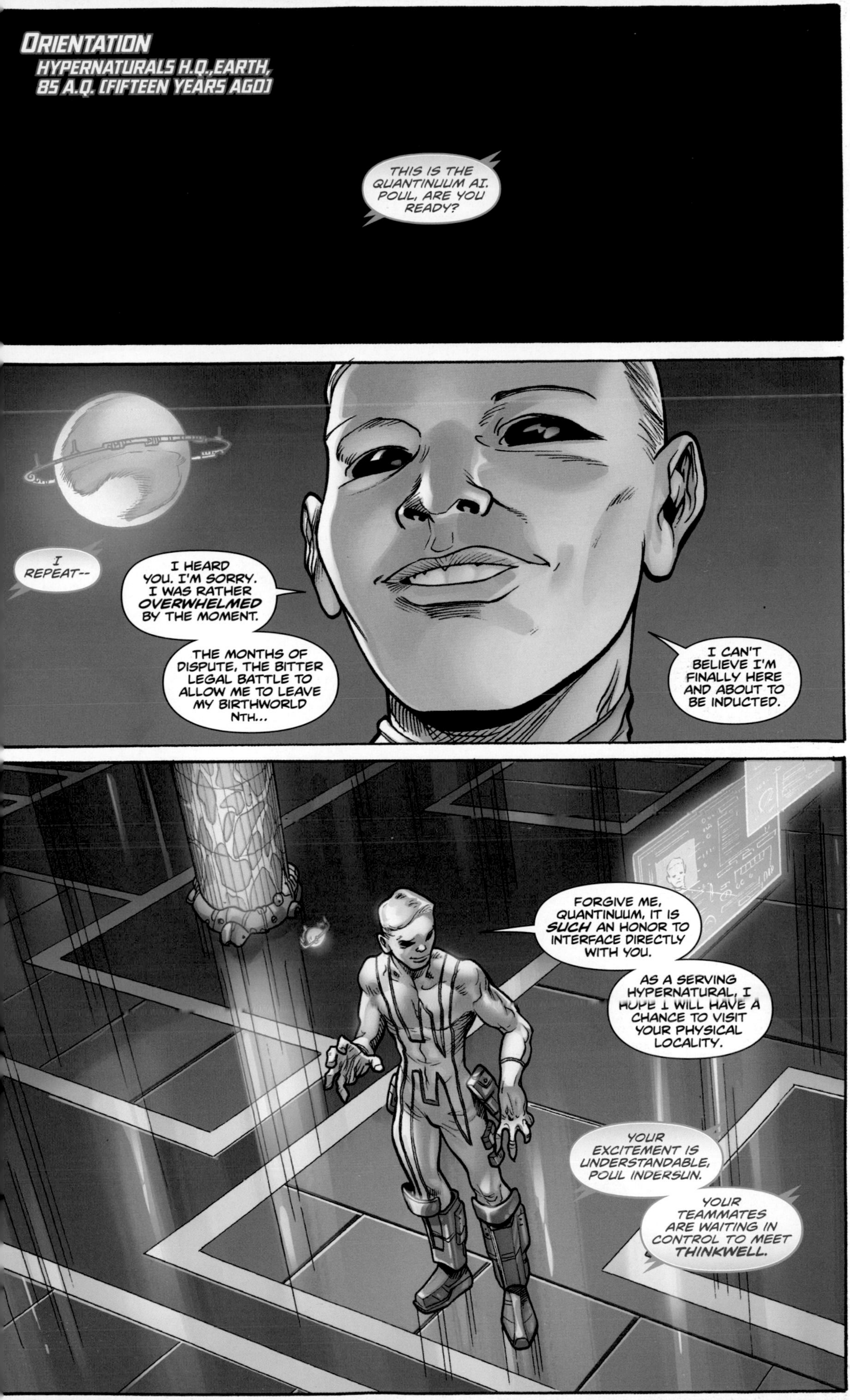

ORIENTATION
HYPERNATURALS H.Q.,EARTH, 85 A.Q. [FIFTEEN YEARS AGO]
THIS IS THE QUANTINUUM AI. POUL, ARE YOU READY?
I REPEAT--
I HEARD YOU. I'M SORRY. I WAS RATHER OVERWHELMED BY THE MOMENT.
THE MONTHS OF DISPUTE, THE BITTER LEGAL BATTLE TO ALLOW ME TO LEAVE MY BIRTHWORLD NTH...
I CAN'T BELIEVE I'M FINALLY HERE AND ABOUT TO BE INDUCTED.
FORGIVE ME, QUANTINUUM, IT IS SUCH AN HONOR TO INTERFACE DIRECTLY WITH YOU.
AS A SERVING HYPERNATURAL, I HOPE I WILL HAVE A CHANCE TO VISIT YOUR PHYSICAL LOCALITY.
YOUR EXCITEMENT IS UNDERSTANDABLE, POUL INDERSUN.
YOUR TEAMMATES ARE WAITING IN CONTROL TO MEET THINKWELL.

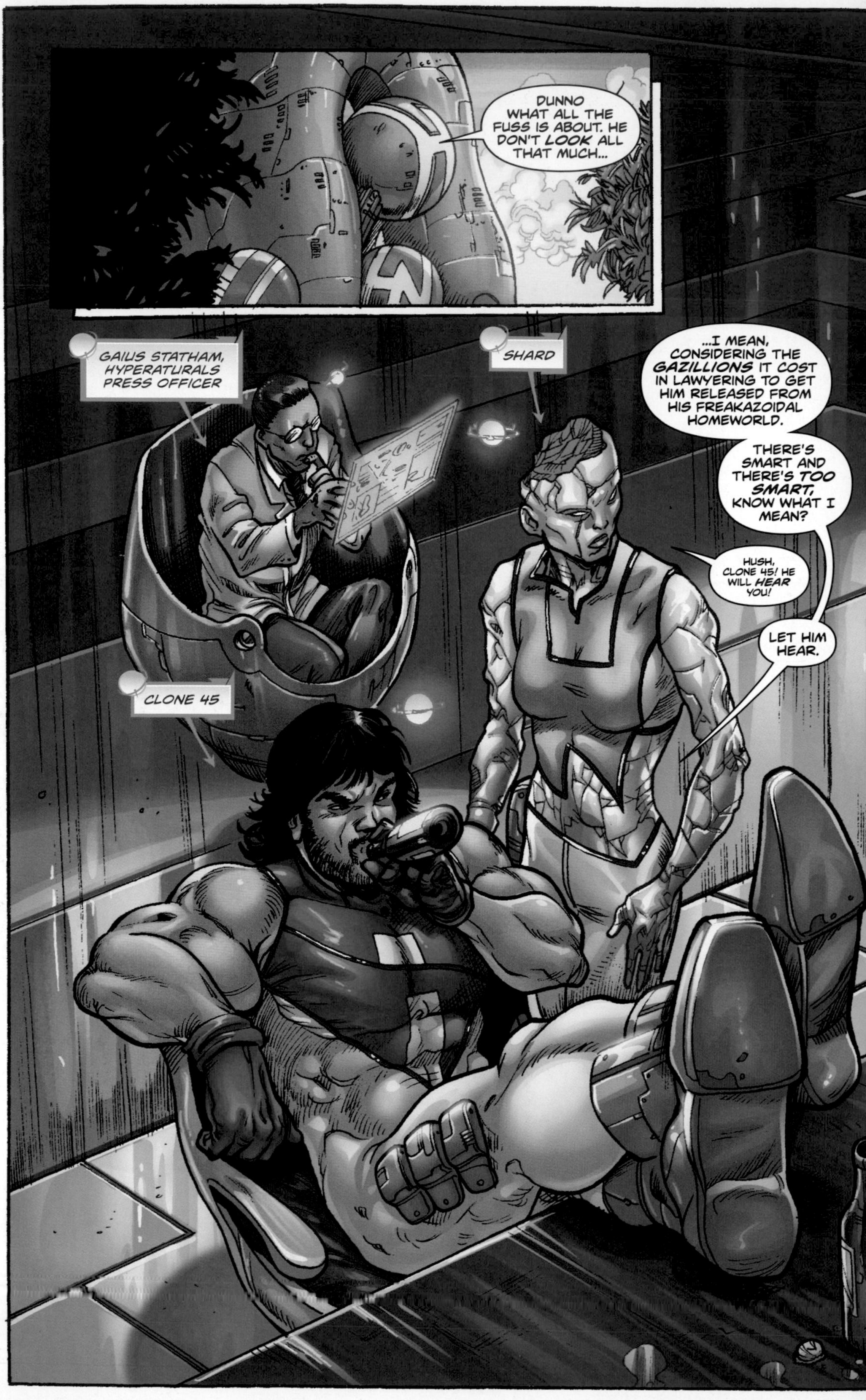
DUNNO WHAT ALL THE FUSS IS ABOUT. HE DON'T LOOK ALL THAT MUCH...
GAIUS STATHAM, HYPERATURALS PRESS OFFICER
SHARD
...I MEAN, CONSIDERING THE GAZILLIONS IT COST IN LAWYERING TO GET HIM RELEASED FROM HIS FREAKAZOIDAL HOMEWORLD.
THERE'S SMART AND THERE'S TOO SMART, KNOW WHAT I MEAN?
HUSH, CLONE 45! HE WILL HEAR YOU!
LET HIM HEAR.
CLONE 45

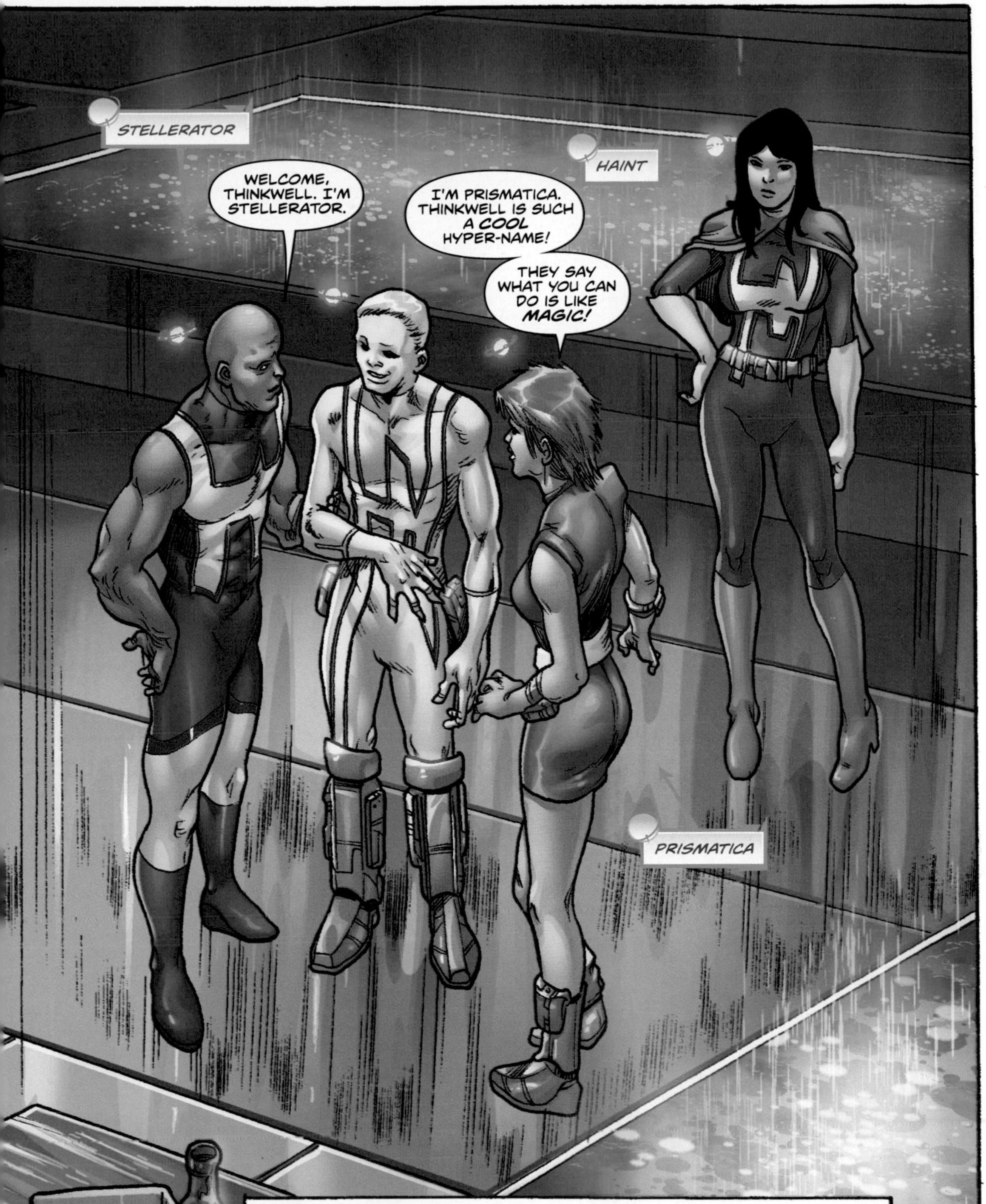
STELLERATOR
WELCOME, THINKWELL. I'M STELLERATOR.
HAINT
I'M PRISMATICA. THINKWELL IS SUCH A COOL HYPER-NAME!
THEY SAY WHAT YOU CAN DO IS LIKE MAGIC!
PRISMATICA

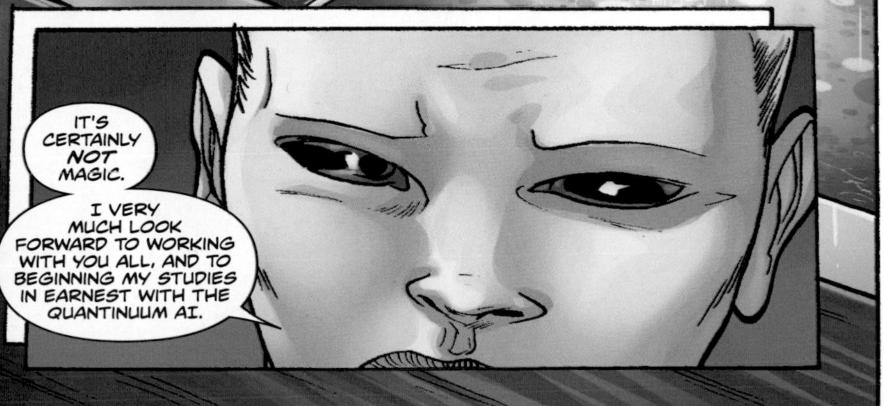
IT'S CERTAINLY NOT MAGIC.
I VERY MUCH LOOK FORWARD TO WORKING WITH YOU ALL, AND TO BEGINNING MY STUDIES IN EARNEST WITH THE QUANTINUUM AI.

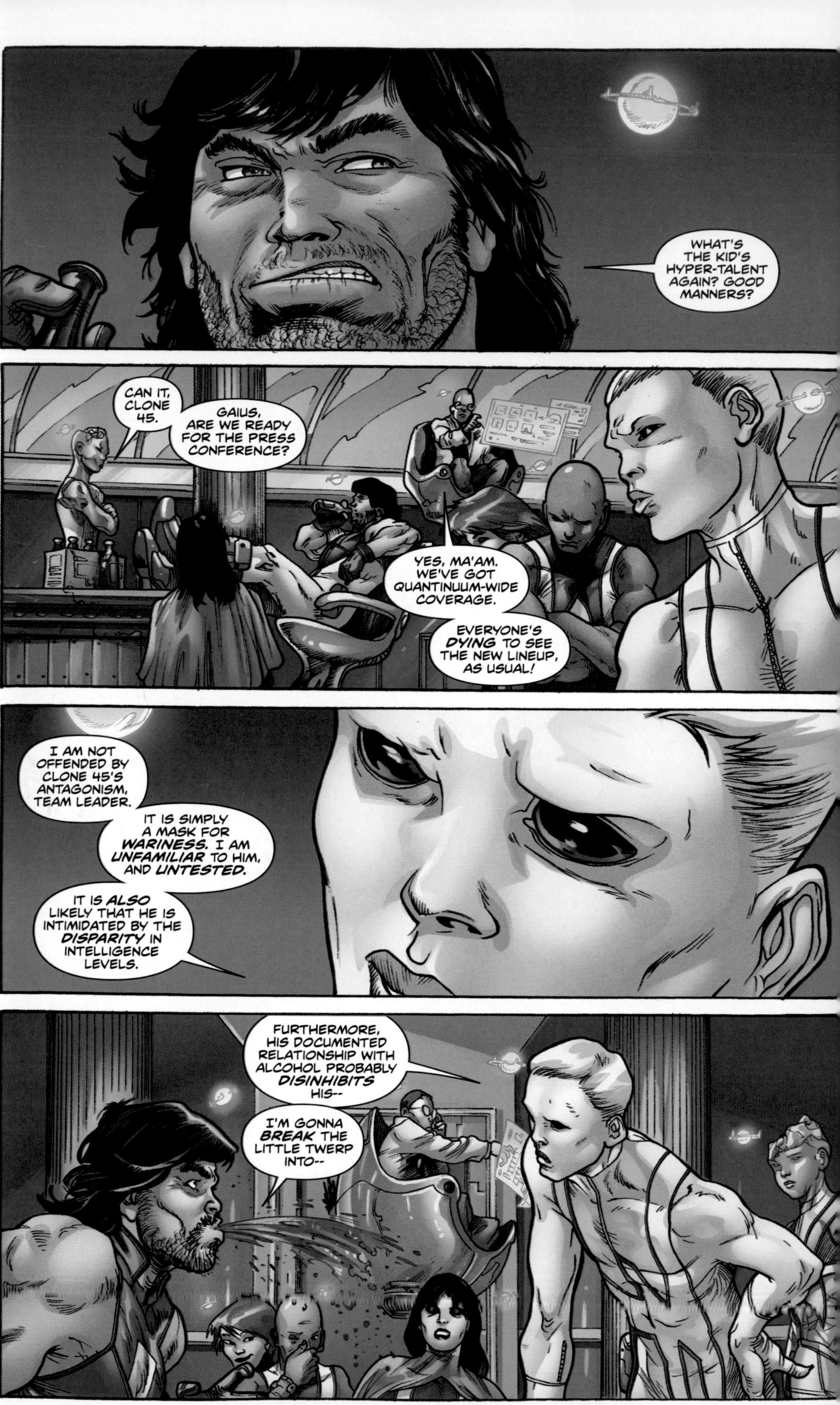
WHAT'S THE KID'S HYPER-TALENT AGAIN? GOOD MANNERS?
CAN IT, CLONE 45.
GAIUS, ARE WE READY FOR THE PRESS CONFERENCE?
YES, MA'AM. WE'VE GOT QUANTINUUM-WIDE COVERAGE.
EVERYONE'S DYING TO SEE THE NEW LINEUP, AS USUAL!
I AM NOT OFFENDED BY CLONE 45'S ANTAGONISM, TEAM LEADER.
IT IS SIMPLY A MASK FOR WARINESS. I AM UNFAMILIAR TO HIM, AND UNTESTED.
IT IS ALSO LIKELY THAT HE IS INTIMIDATED BY THE DISPARITY IN INTELLIGENCE LEVELS.
FURTHERMORE, HIS DOCUMENTED RELATIONSHIP WITH ALCOHOL PROBABLY DISINHIBITS HIS--
I'M GONNA BREAK THE LITTLE TWERP INTO--

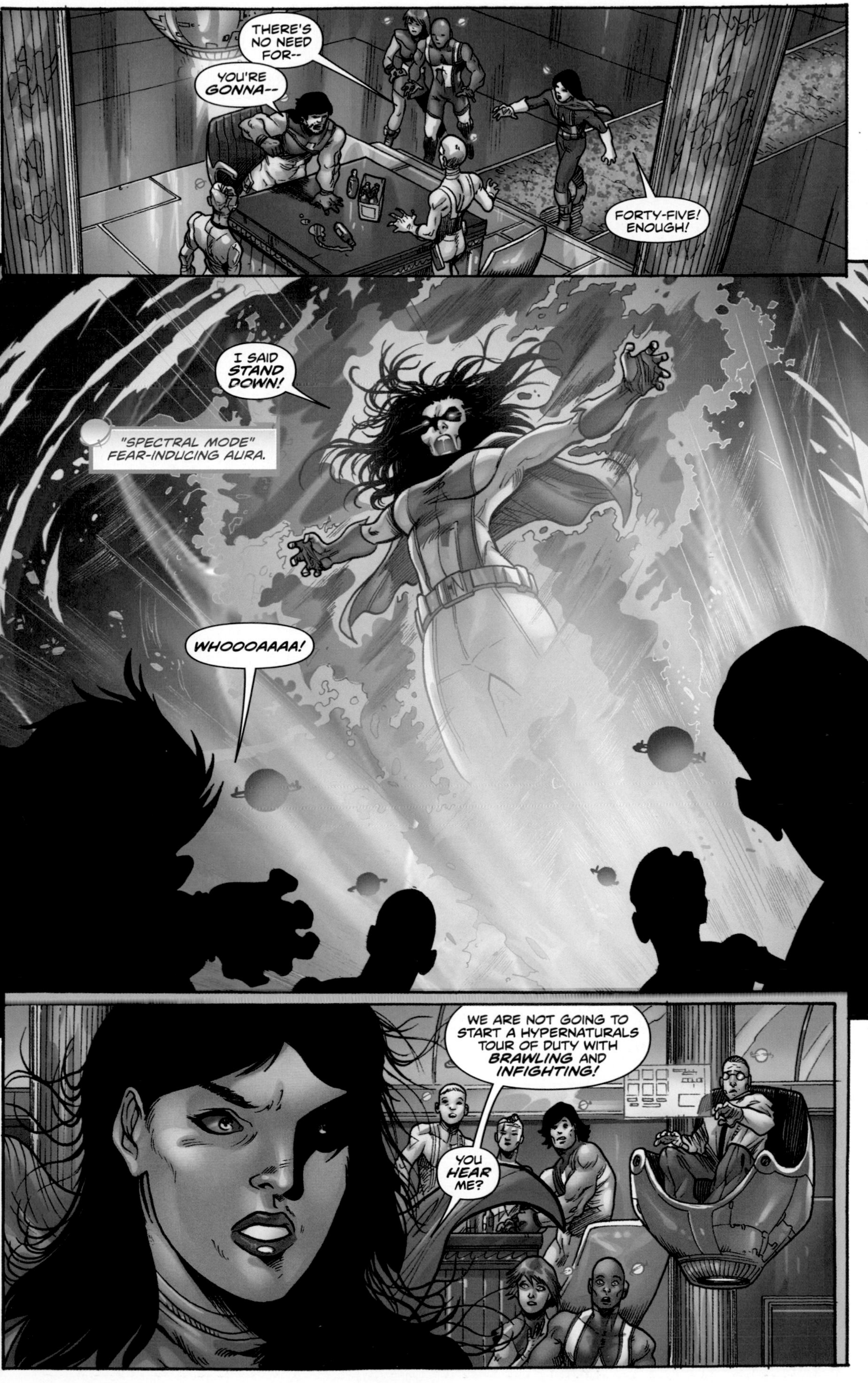
THERE'S NO NEED FOR--
YOU'RE GONNA--
FORTY-FIVE! ENOUGH!
I SAID STAND DOWN!
"SPECTRAL MODE" FEAR-INDUCING AURA.
WHOOOAAAA!
WE ARE NOT GOING TO START A HYPERNATURALS TOUR OF DUTY WITH BRAWLING AND INFIGHTING!
YOU HEAR ME?

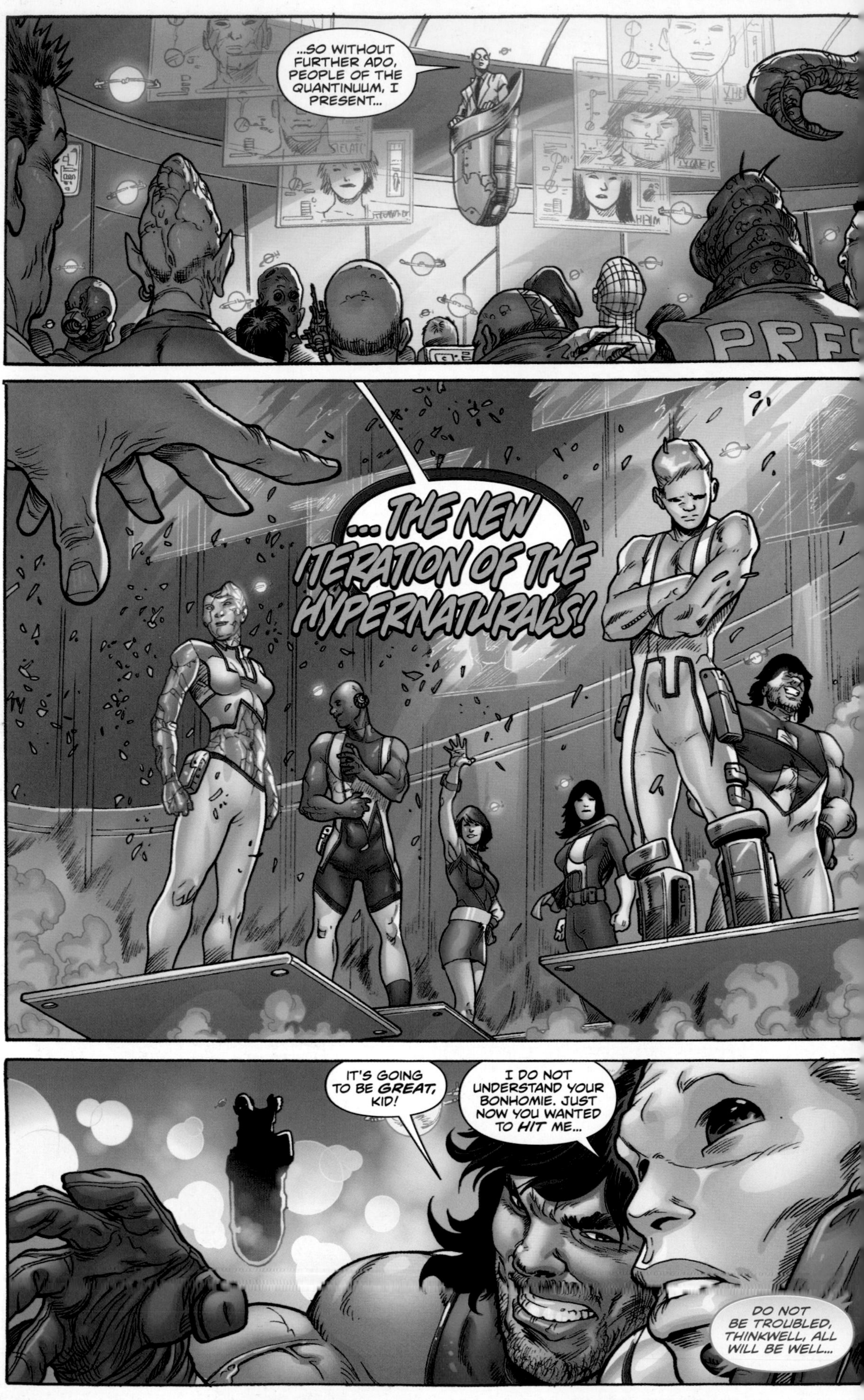
...SO WITHOUT FURTHER ADO, PEOPLE OF THE QUANTINUUM, I PRESENT...
...THE NEW ITERATION OF THE HYPERNATURALS!
IT'S GOING TO BE *GREAT*, KID!
I DO NOT UNDERSTAND YOUR BONHOMIE. JUST NOW YOU WANTED TO *HIT* ME...
DO NOT BE TROUBLED, THINKWELL, ALL WILL BE WELL...

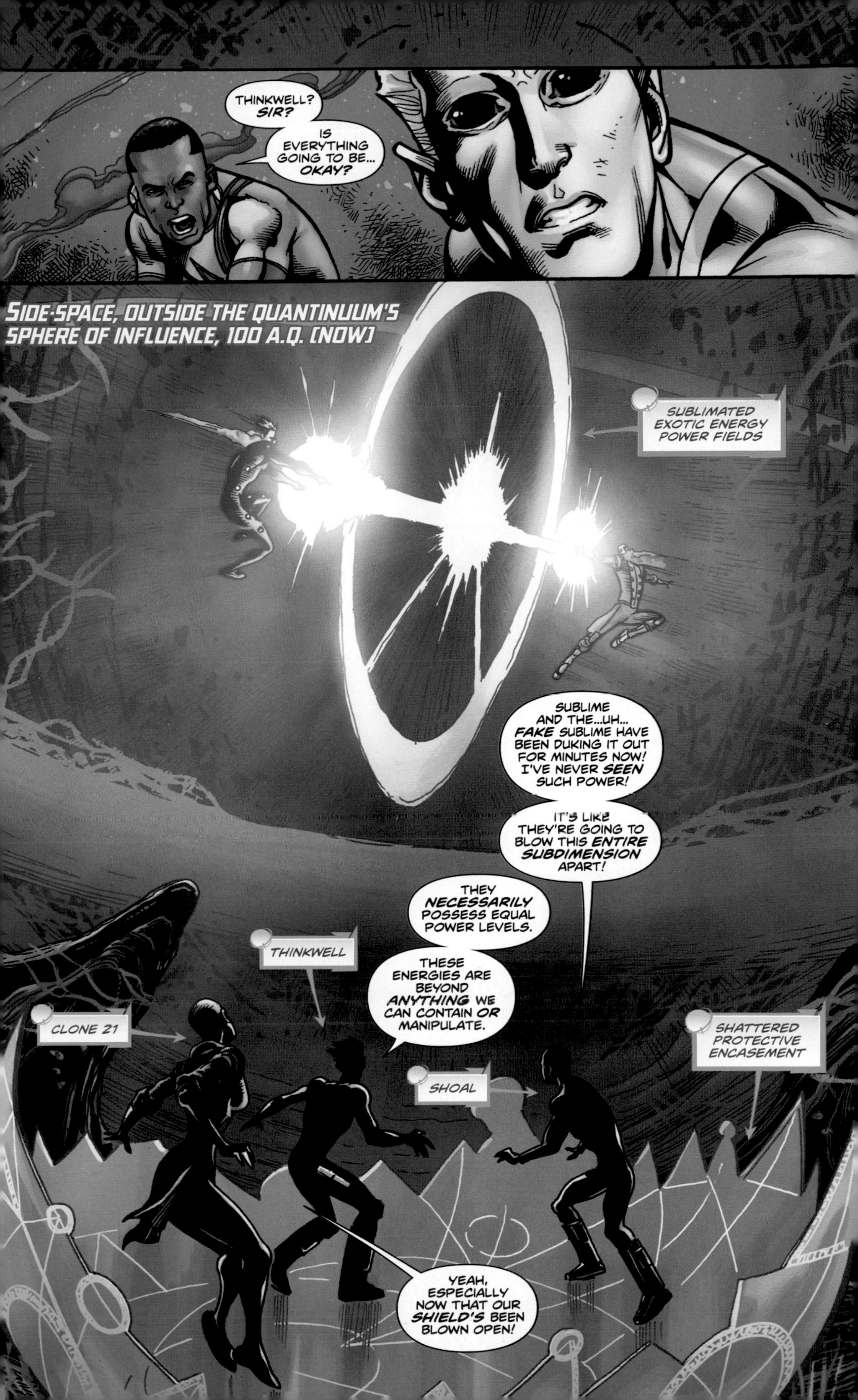
THINKWELL? SIR?
IS EVERYTHING GOING TO BE... OKAY?
SIDE-SPACE, OUTSIDE THE QUANTINUUM'S SPHERE OF INFLUENCE, 100 A.Q. [NOW]
SUBLIMATED EXOTIC ENERGY POWER FIELDS
SUBLIME AND THE...UH... FAKE SUBLIME HAVE BEEN DUKING IT OUT FOR MINUTES NOW! I'VE NEVER SEEN SUCH POWER!
IT'S LIKE THEY'RE GOING TO BLOW THIS ENTIRE SUBDIMENSION APART!
THEY NECESSARILY POSSESS EQUAL POWER LEVELS.
THINKWELL
THESE ENERGIES ARE BEYOND ANYTHING WE CAN CONTAIN OR MANIPULATE.
CLONE 21
SHATTERED PROTECTIVE ENCASEMENT
SHOAL
YEAH, ESPECIALLY NOW THAT OUR SHIELD'S BEEN BLOWN OPEN!

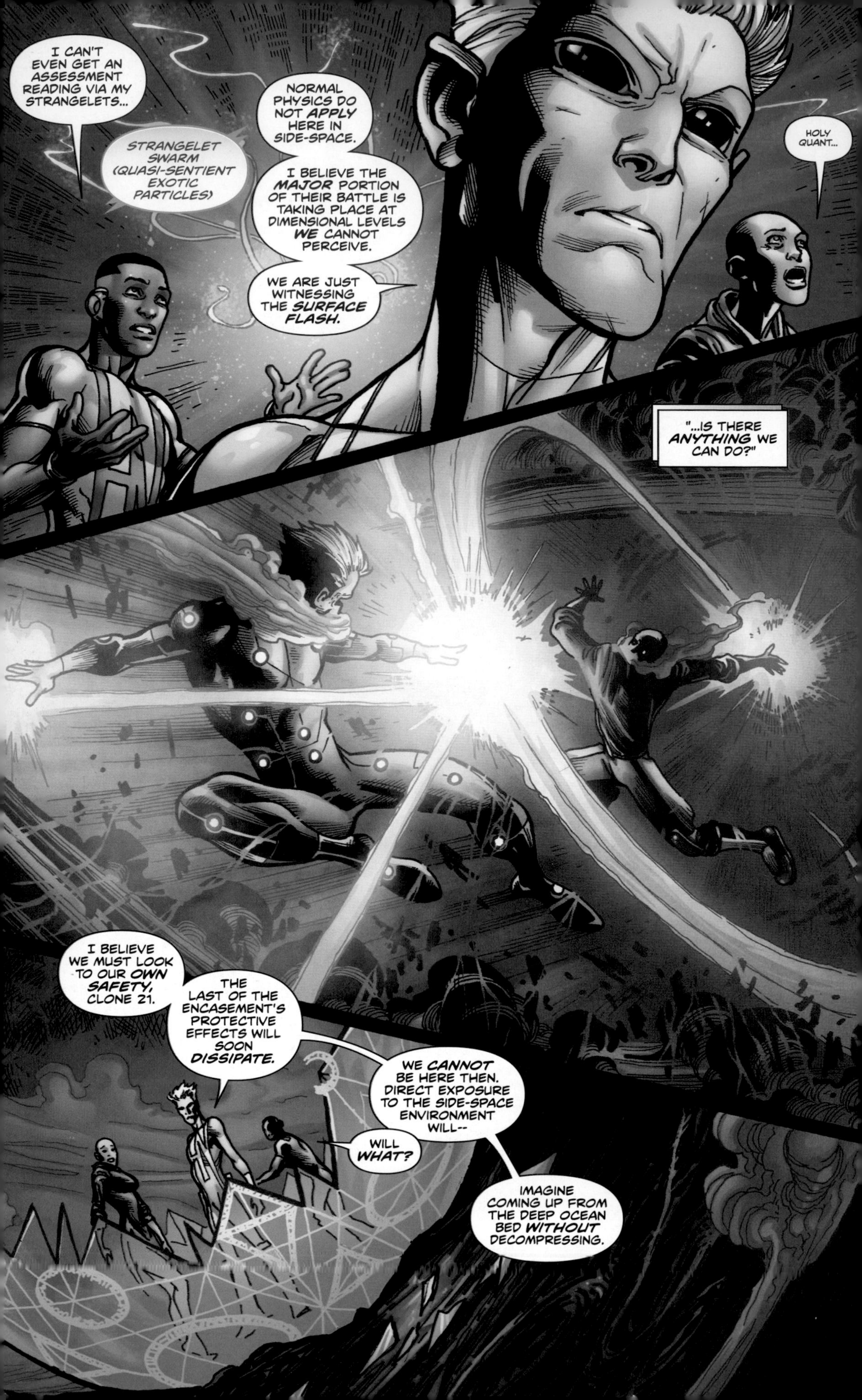
I CAN'T EVEN GET AN ASSESSMENT READING VIA MY STRANGELETS...
STRANGELET SWARM (QUASI-SENTIENT EXOTIC PARTICLES)
NORMAL PHYSICS DO NOT APPLY HERE IN SIDE-SPACE.
I BELIEVE THE MAJOR PORTION OF THEIR BATTLE IS TAKING PLACE AT DIMENSIONAL LEVELS WE CANNOT PERCEIVE.
WE ARE JUST WITNESSING THE SURFACE FLASH.
HOLY QUANT...
"...IS THERE ANYTHING WE CAN DO?"
I BELIEVE WE MUST LOOK TO OUR OWN SAFETY, CLONE 21.
THE LAST OF THE ENCASEMENT'S PROTECTIVE EFFECTS WILL SOON DISSIPATE.
WE CANNOT BE HERE THEN. DIRECT EXPOSURE TO THE SIDE-SPACE ENVIRONMENT WILL--
WILL WHAT?
IMAGINE COMING UP FROM THE DEEP OCEAN BED WITHOUT DECOMPRESSING.

REPOSITORY [33 TARSUS RED], QUANTINUUM ARCHIVE AND MUSEUM WORLD
EEAARRGHH!
ARRGH!
AHHKK!
UHHKK!
SPUTCH!
SPLATT!
SPLUNNCH!
SPUNNCH!
SPLOTT!
"THESE HYPERBADS ARE TAKING THE ENTIRE GUARD FORCE APART!"

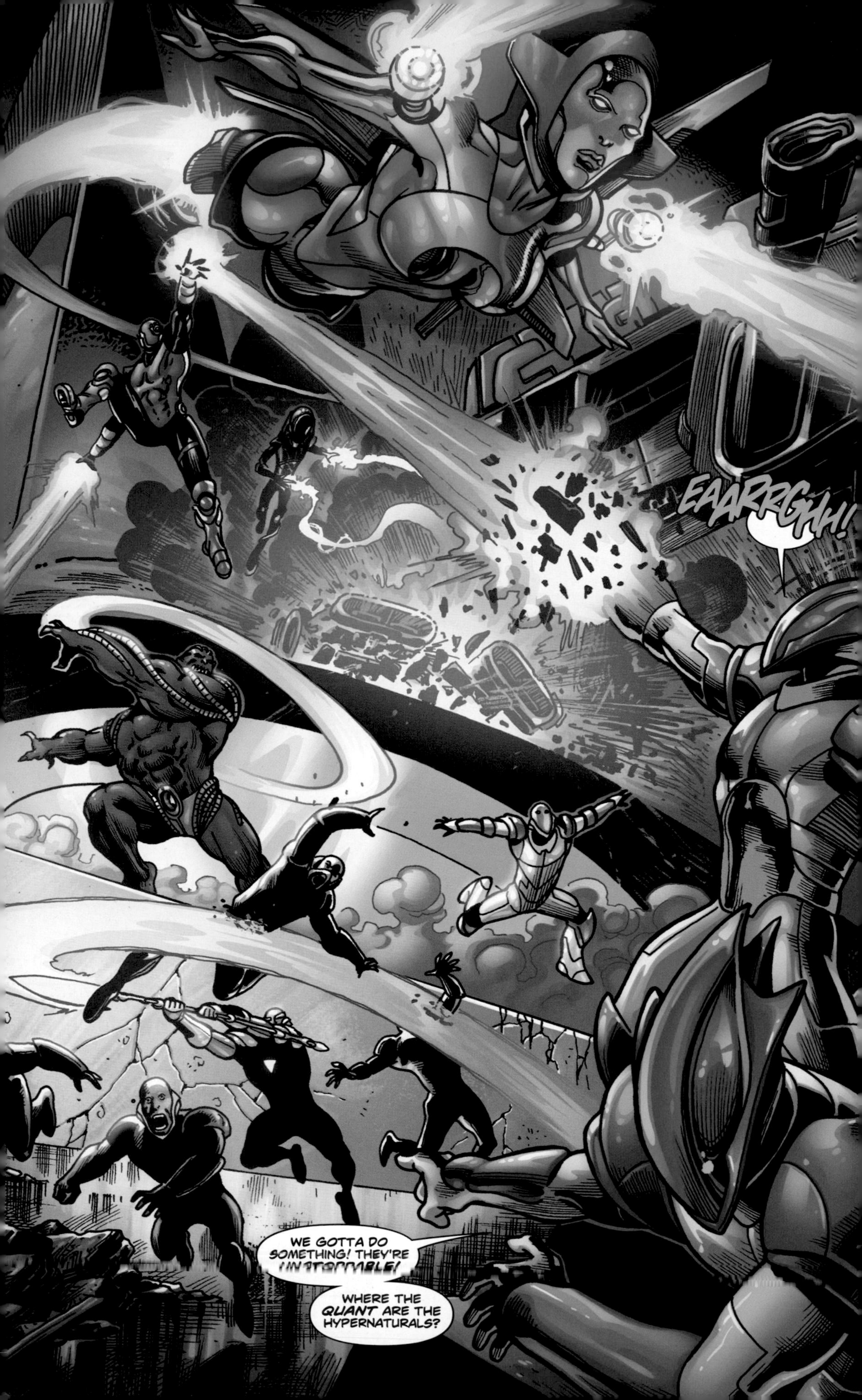
EAARRGHH!
WE GOTTA DO SOMETHING! THEY'RE UNSTOPPABLE!
WHERE THE *QUANT* ARE THE HYPERNATURALS?

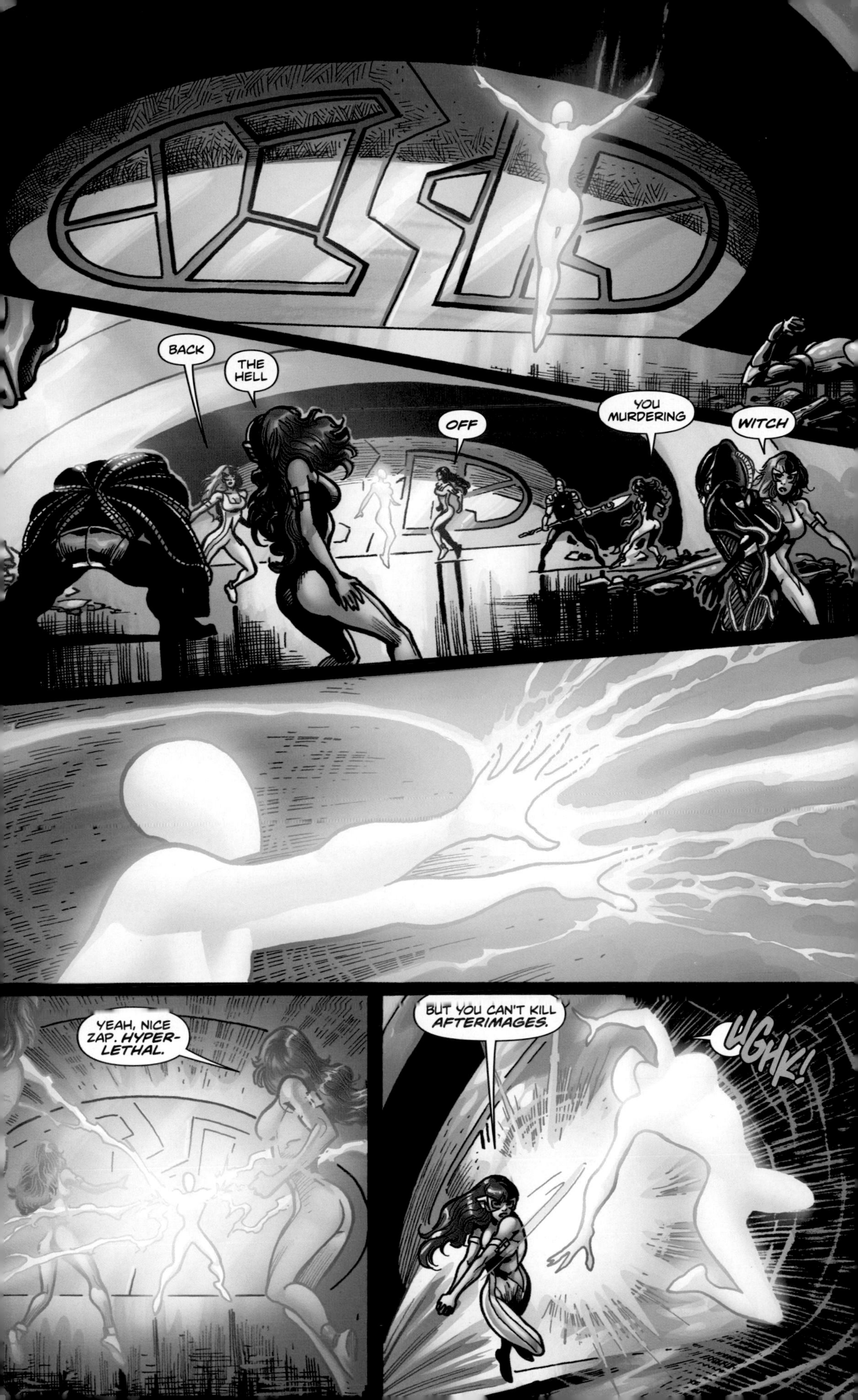
BACK
THE HELL
OFF
YOU MURDERING
WITCH
YEAH, NICE ZAP. HYPER-LETHAL.
BUT YOU CAN'T KILL AFTERIMAGES.
UGHK!

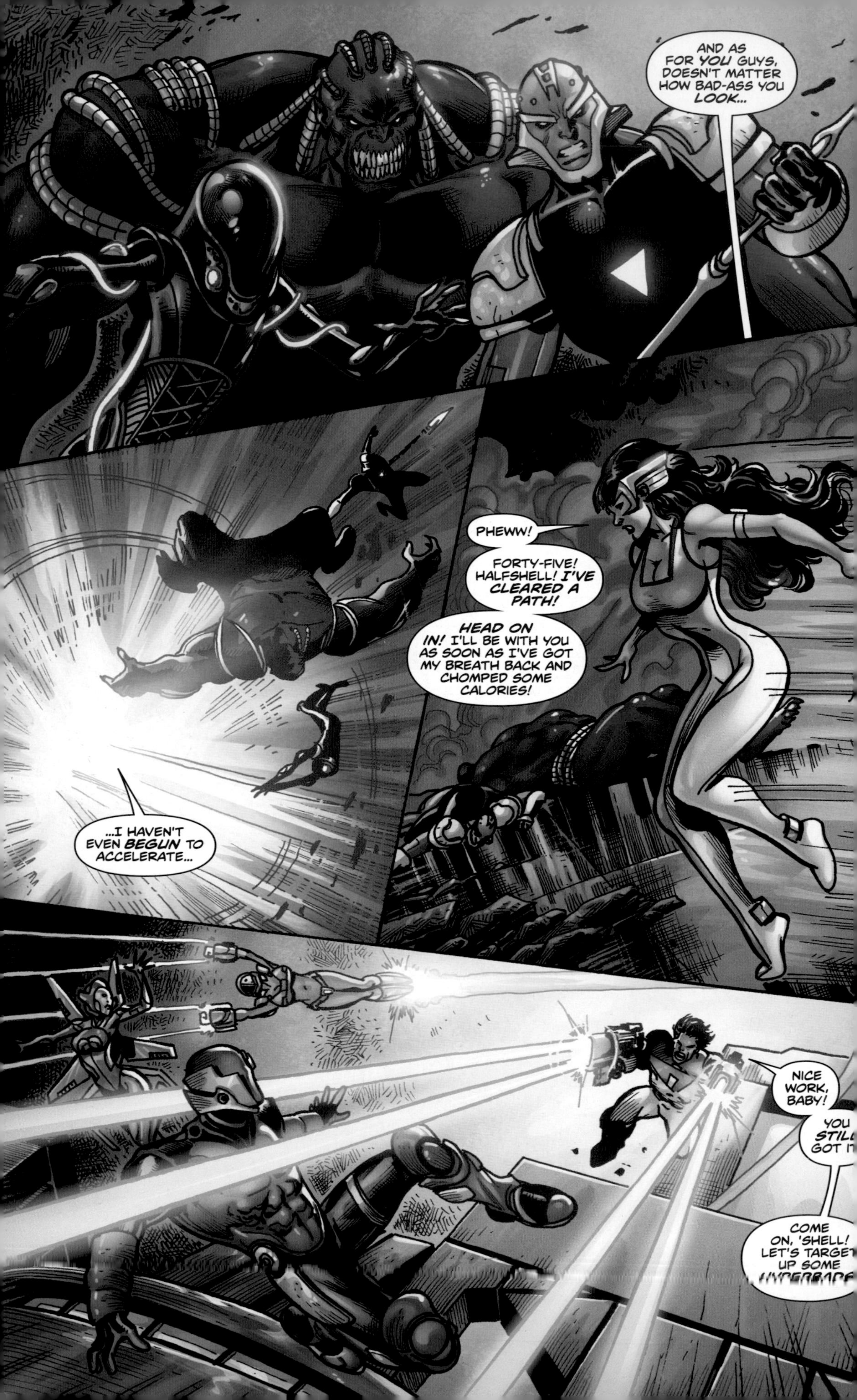
AND AS FOR YOU GUYS, DOESN'T MATTER HOW BAD-ASS YOU LOOK...
...I HAVEN'T EVEN BEGUN TO ACCELERATE...
PHEWW!
FORTY-FIVE! HALFSHELL! I'VE CLEARED A PATH!
HEAD ON IN! I'LL BE WITH YOU AS SOON AS I'VE GOT MY BREATH BACK AND CHOMPED SOME CALORIES!
NICE WORK, BABY!
YOU STILL GOT I
COME ON, 'SHELL! LET'S TARGET UP SOME

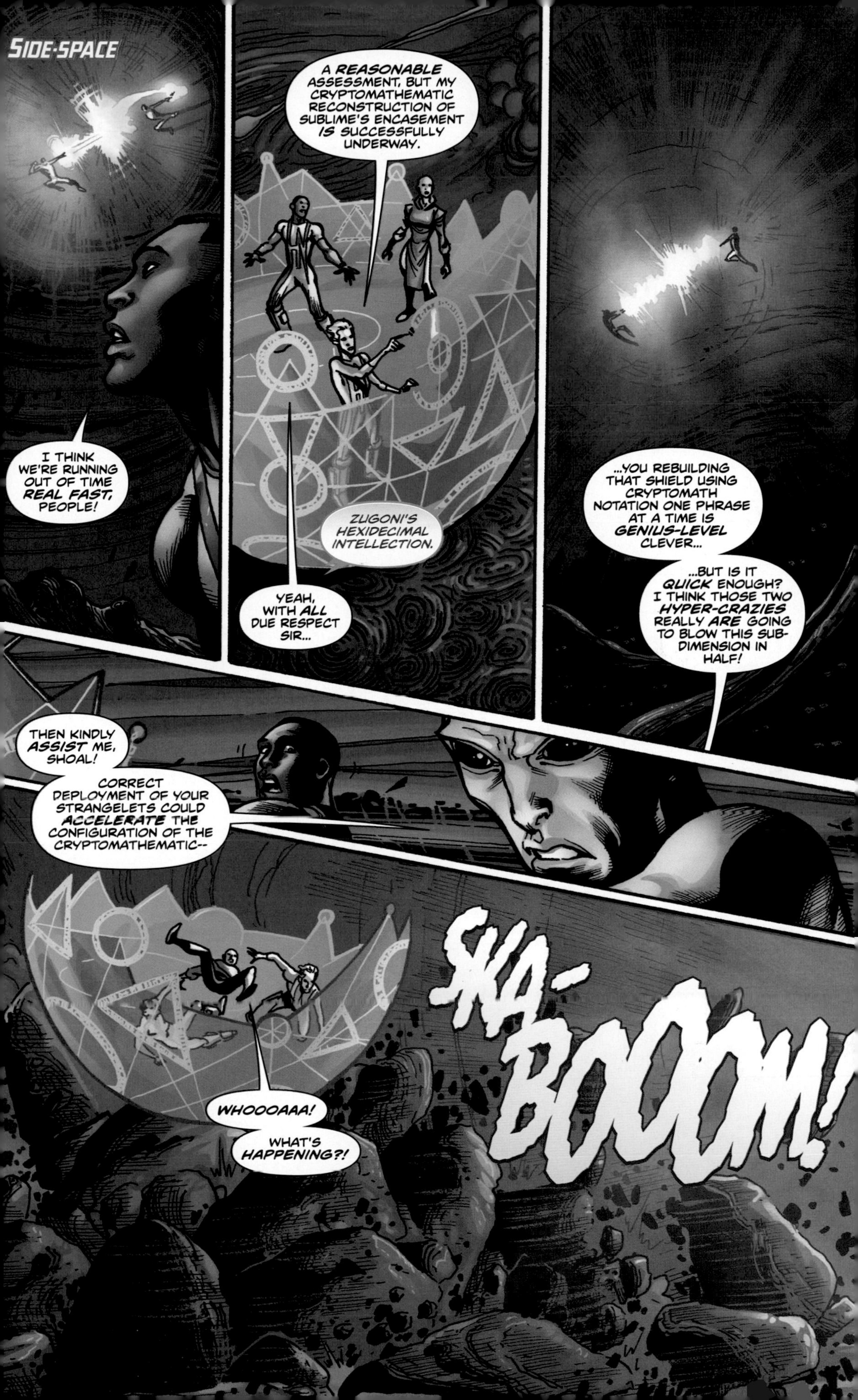
SIDE-SPACE
I THINK WE'RE RUNNING OUT OF TIME REAL FAST, PEOPLE!
A REASONABLE ASSESSMENT, BUT MY CRYPTOMATHEMATIC RECONSTRUCTION OF SUBLIME'S ENCASEMENT IS SUCCESSFULLY UNDERWAY.
ZUGONI'S HEXIDECIMAL INTELLECTION.
YEAH, WITH ALL DUE RESPECT SIR...
...YOU REBUILDING THAT SHIELD USING CRYPTOMATH NOTATION ONE PHRASE AT A TIME IS GENIUS-LEVEL CLEVER...
...BUT IS IT QUICK ENOUGH? I THINK THOSE TWO HYPER-CRAZIES REALLY ARE GOING TO BLOW THIS SUB-DIMENSION IN HALF!
THEN KINDLY ASSIST ME, SHOAL!
CORRECT DEPLOYMENT OF YOUR STRANGELETS COULD ACCELERATE THE CONFIGURATION OF THE CRYPTOMATHEMATIC--
SKA-BOOOM!
WHOOOAAA!
WHAT'S HAPPENING?!

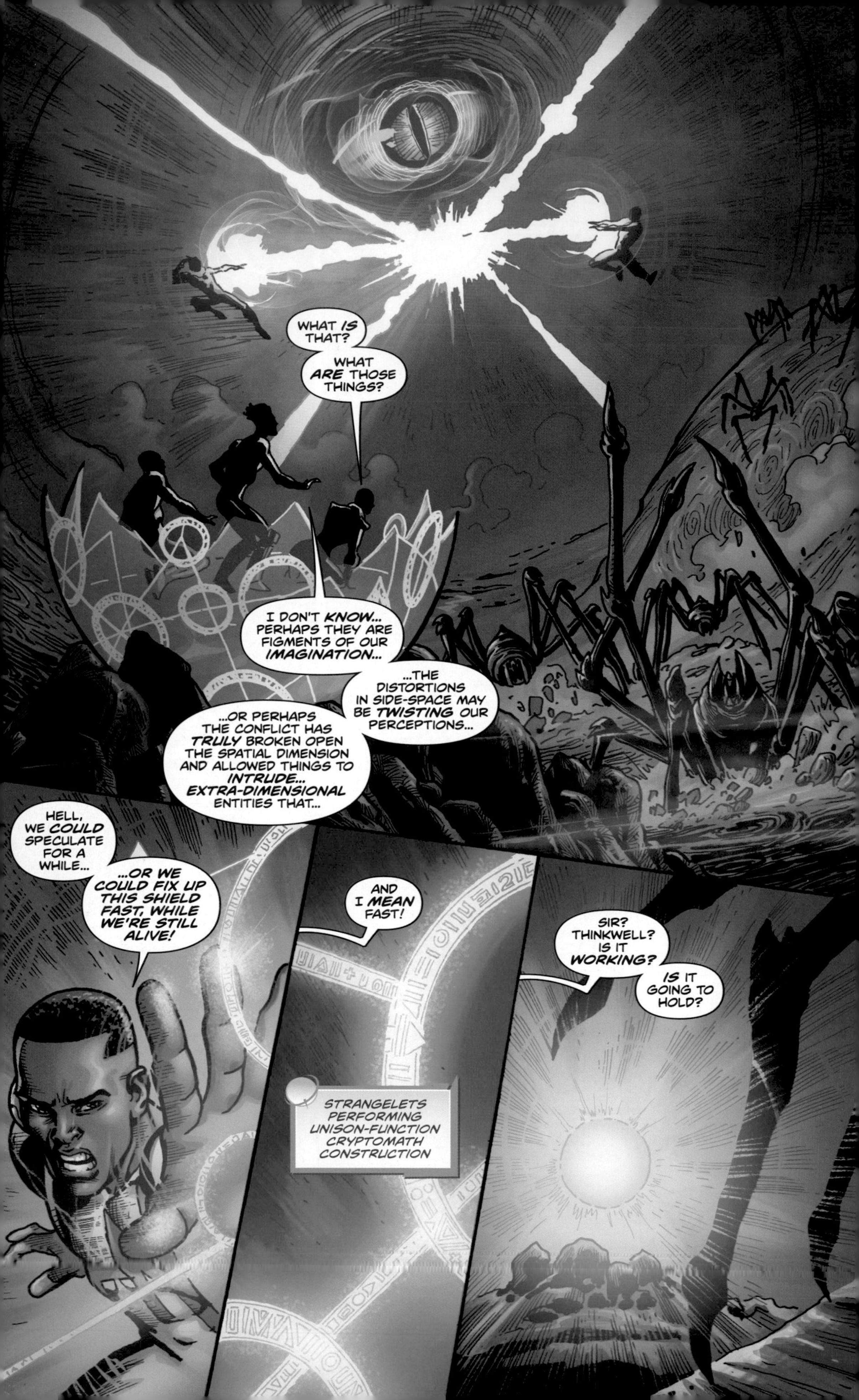
WHAT IS THAT?
WHAT ARE THOSE THINGS?
I DON'T KNOW... PERHAPS THEY ARE FIGMENTS OF OUR IMAGINATION...
...THE DISTORTIONS IN SIDE-SPACE MAY BE TWISTING OUR PERCEPTIONS...
...OR PERHAPS THE CONFLICT HAS TRULY BROKEN OPEN THE SPATIAL DIMENSION AND ALLOWED THINGS TO INTRUDE... EXTRA-DIMENSIONAL ENTITIES THAT...
HELL, WE COULD SPECULATE FOR A WHILE...
...OR WE COULD FIX UP THIS SHIELD FAST, WHILE WE'RE STILL ALIVE!
AND I MEAN FAST!
STRANGELETS PERFORMING UNISON-FUNCTION CRYPTOMATH CONSTRUCTION
SIR? THINKWELL? IS IT WORKING?
IS IT GOING TO HOLD?

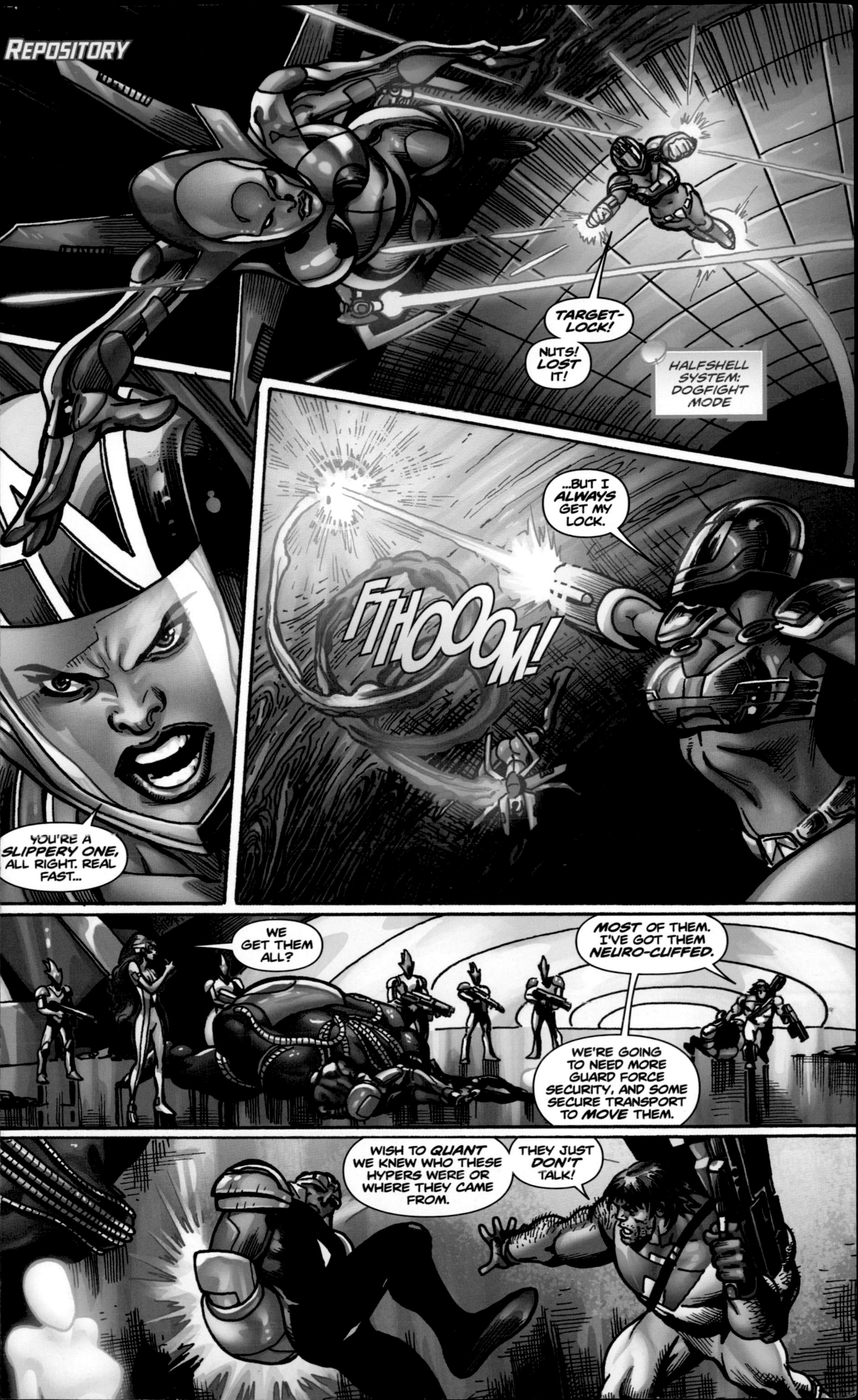
TARGET-LOCK!
NUTS! LOST IT!
HALFSHELL SYSTEM: DOGFIGHT MODE
YOU'RE A SLIPPERY ONE, ALL RIGHT. REAL FAST...
...BUT I ALWAYS GET MY LOCK.
FTHOOOM!
WE GET THEM ALL?
MOST OF THEM. I'VE GOT THEM NEURO-CUFFED.
WE'RE GOING TO NEED MORE GUARD FORCE SECURITY, AND SOME SECURE TRANSPORT TO MOVE THEM.
WISH TO QUANT WE KNEW WHO THESE HYPERS WERE OR WHERE THEY CAME FROM.
THEY JUST DON'T TALK!

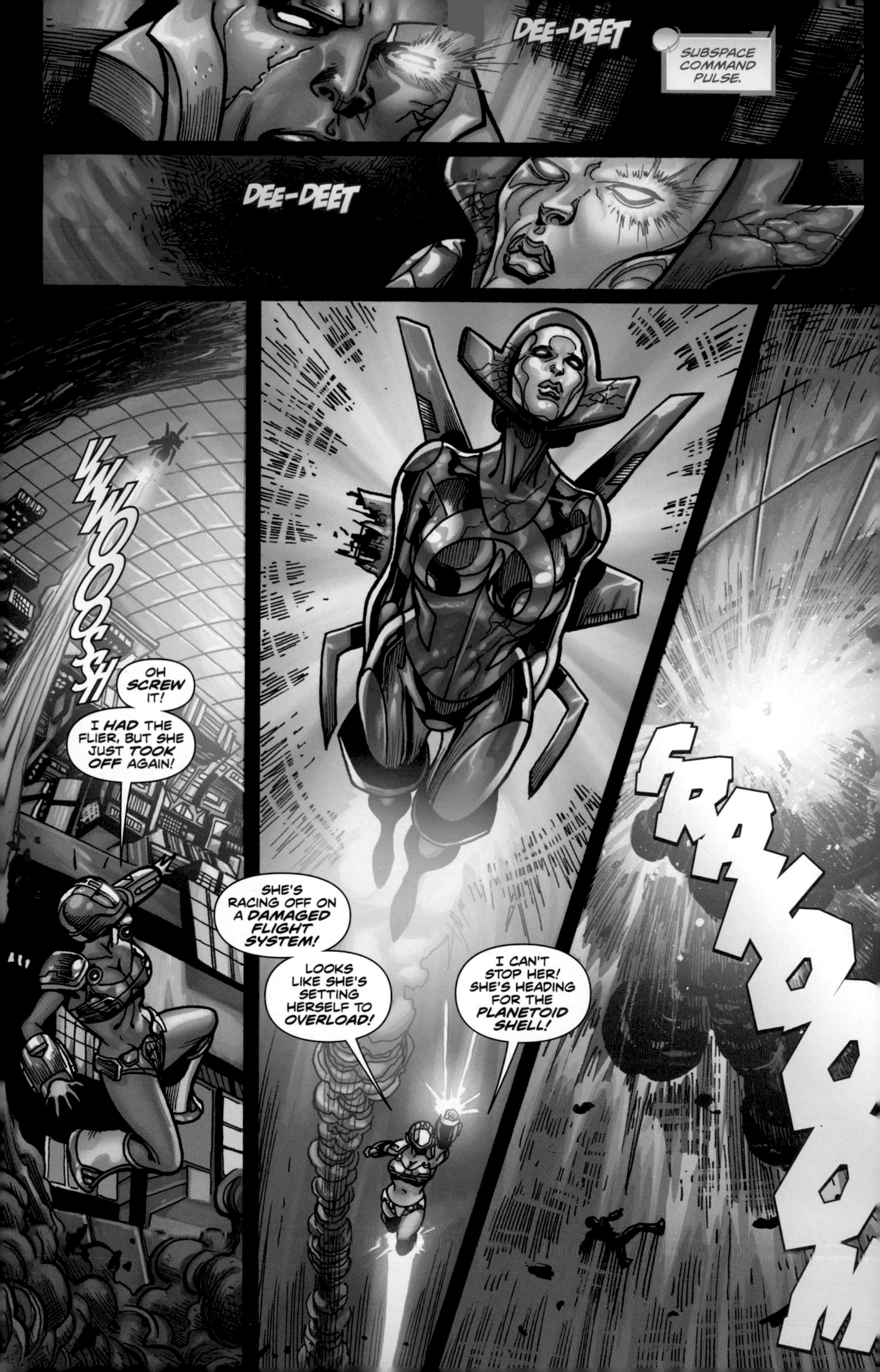
DEE-DEET
SUBSPACE COMMAND PULSE.
DEE-DEET
WWOOOOSSH
OH SCREW IT!
I HAD THE FLIER, BUT SHE JUST TOOK OFF AGAIN!
SHE'S RACING OFF ON A DAMAGED FLIGHT SYSTEM!
LOOKS LIKE SHE'S SETTING HERSELF TO OVERLOAD!
I CAN'T STOP HER! SHE'S HEADING FOR THE PLANETOID SHELL!
FRAKOOOM

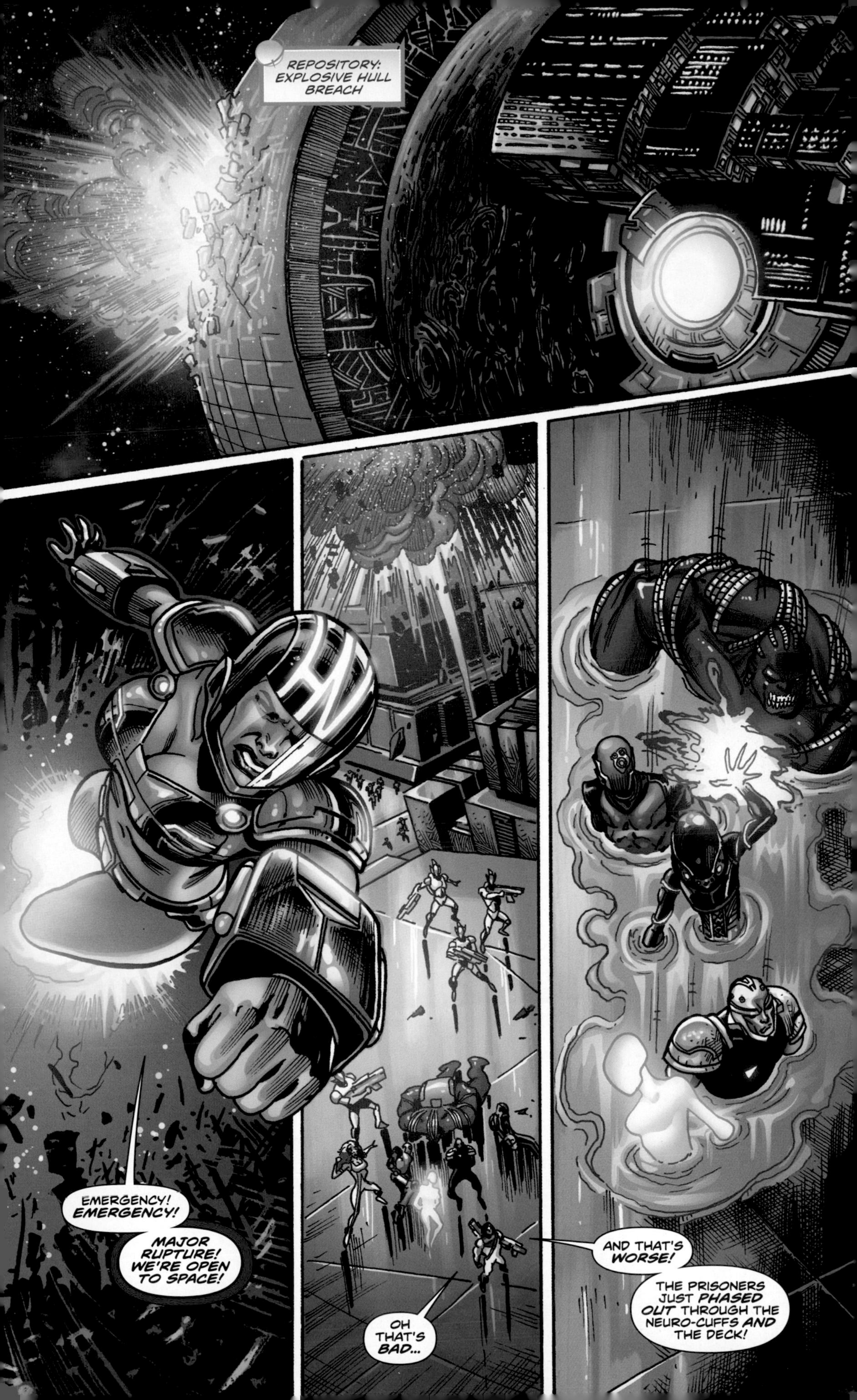
REPOSITORY: EXPLOSIVE HULL BREACH
EMERGENCY! *EMERGENCY!*
MAJOR RUPTURE! WE'RE OPEN TO SPACE!
OH THAT'S *BAD...*
AND THAT'S *WORSE!*
THE PRISONERS JUST *PHASED OUT* THROUGH THE NEURO-CUFFS *AND* THE DECK!

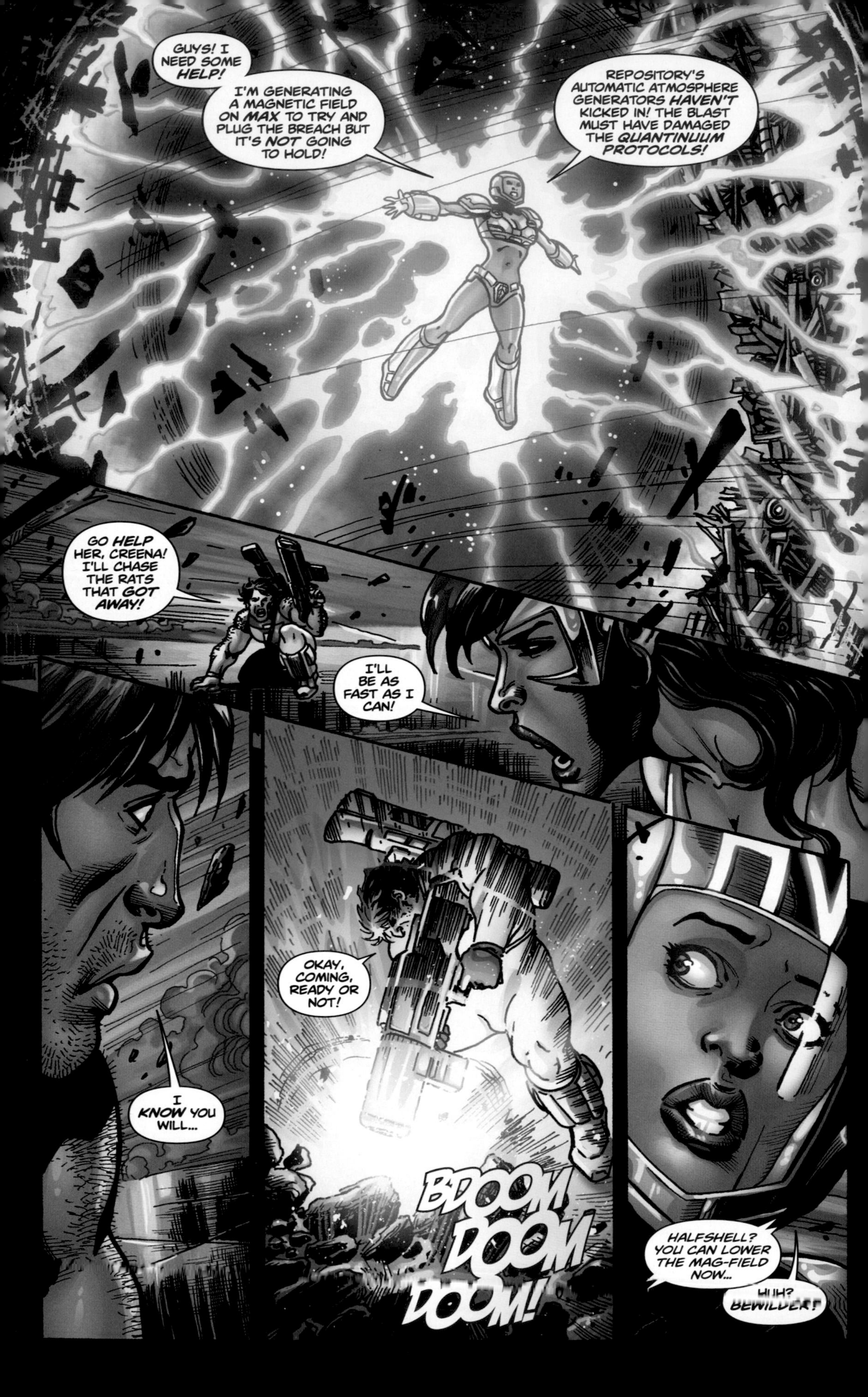
GUYS! I NEED SOME HELP!
I'M GENERATING A MAGNETIC FIELD ON MAX TO TRY AND PLUG THE BREACH BUT IT'S NOT GOING TO HOLD!
REPOSITORY'S AUTOMATIC ATMOSPHERE GENERATORS HAVEN'T KICKED IN! THE BLAST MUST HAVE DAMAGED THE QUANTINUUM PROTOCOLS!
GO HELP HER, CREENA! I'LL CHASE THE RATS THAT GOT AWAY!
I'LL BE AS FAST AS I CAN!
I KNOW YOU WILL...
OKAY, COMING, READY OR NOT!
BDOOM DOOM DOOM!
HALFSHELL? YOU CAN LOWER THE MAG-FIELD NOW...
HUH? BEWILDER?

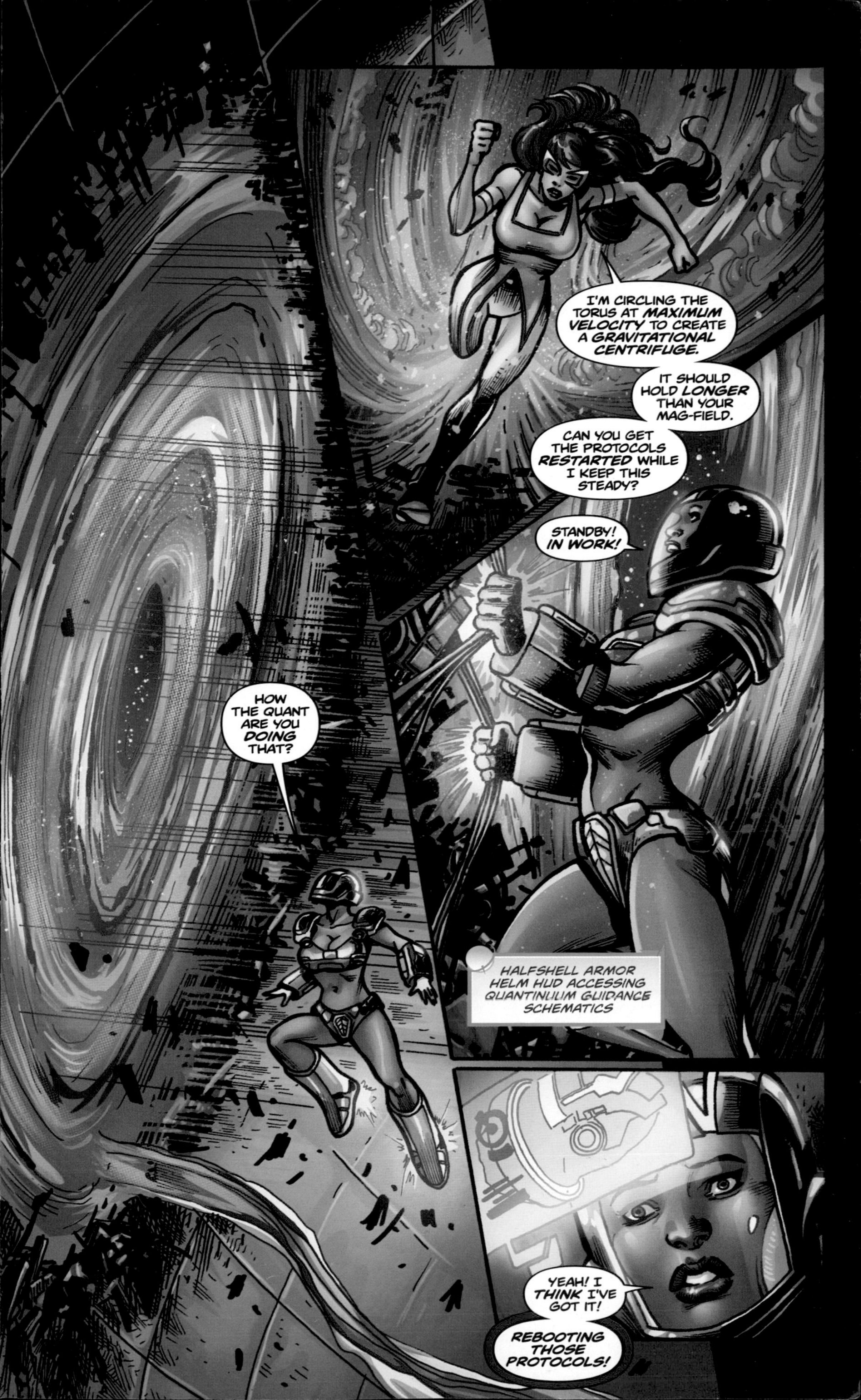
I'M CIRCLING THE TORUS AT MAXIMUM VELOCITY TO CREATE A GRAVITATIONAL CENTRIFUGE.
IT SHOULD HOLD LONGER THAN YOUR MAG-FIELD.
CAN YOU GET THE PROTOCOLS RESTARTED WHILE I KEEP THIS STEADY?
HOW THE QUANT ARE YOU DOING THAT?
STANDBY! IN WORK!
HALFSHELL ARMOR HELM HUD ACCESSING QUANTINUUM GUIDANCE SCHEMATICS
YEAH! I THINK I'VE GOT IT!
REBOOTING THOSE PROTOCOLS!

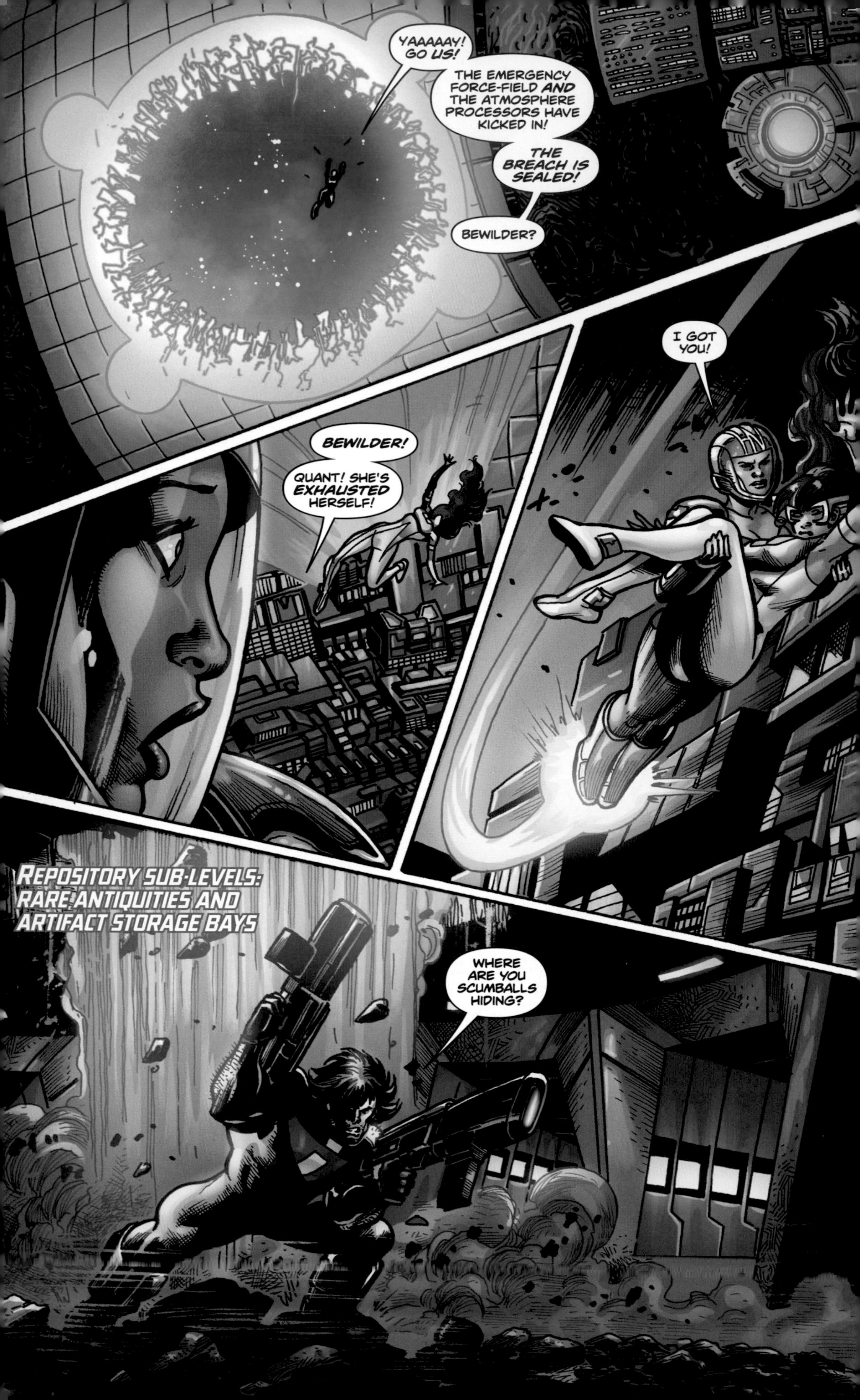
YAAAAAY! GO US!
THE EMERGENCY FORCE-FIELD AND THE ATMOSPHERE PROCESSORS HAVE KICKED IN!
THE BREACH IS SEALED!
BEWILDER?
BEWILDER!
QUANT! SHE'S EXHAUSTED HERSELF!
I GOT YOU!
REPOSITORY SUB-LEVELS: RARE ANTIQUITIES AND ARTIFACT STORAGE BAYS
WHERE ARE YOU SCUMBALLS HIDING?

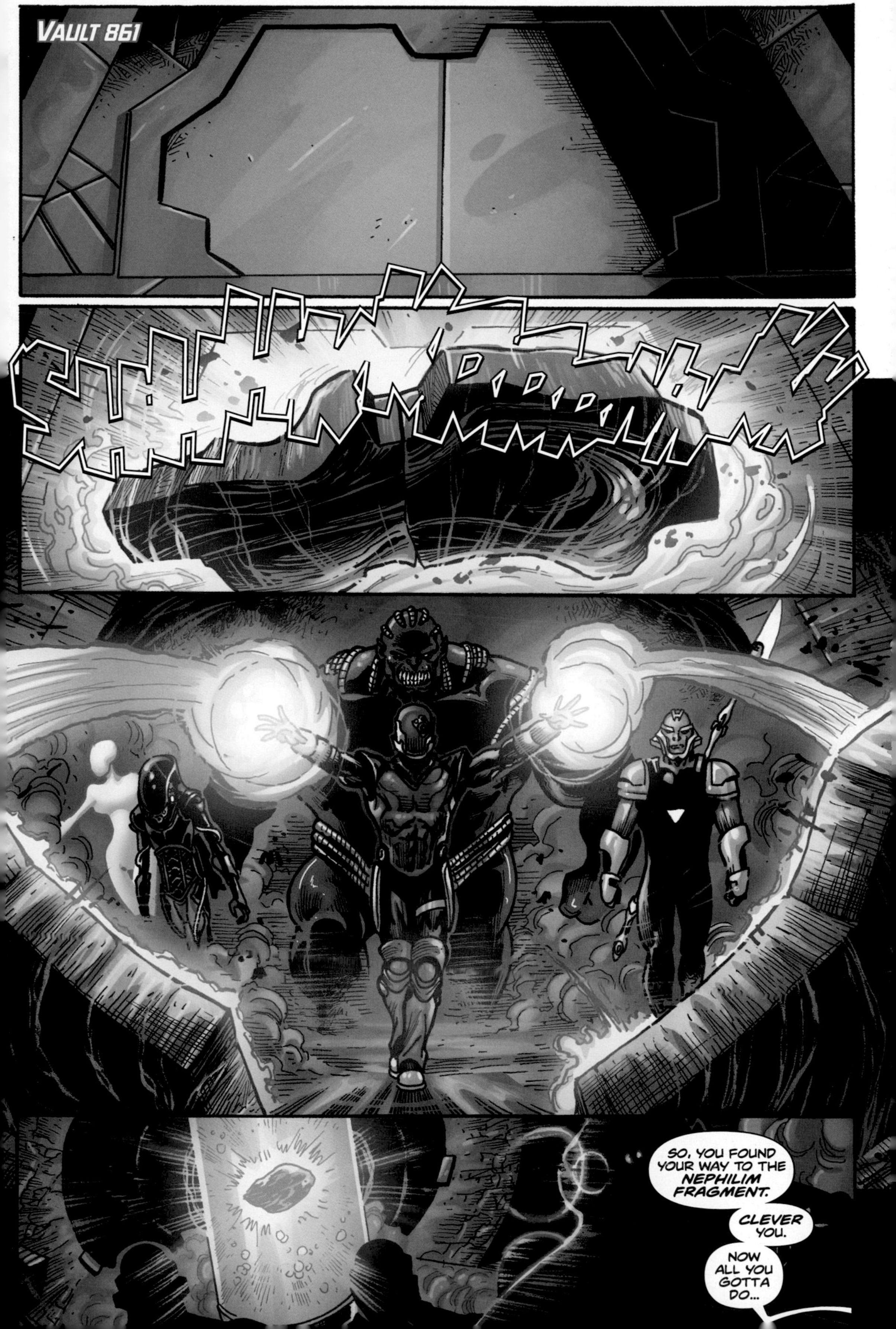
VAULT 861
SO, YOU FOUND YOUR WAY TO THE NEPHILIM FRAGMENT.
CLEVER YOU.
NOW ALL YOU GOTTA DO...

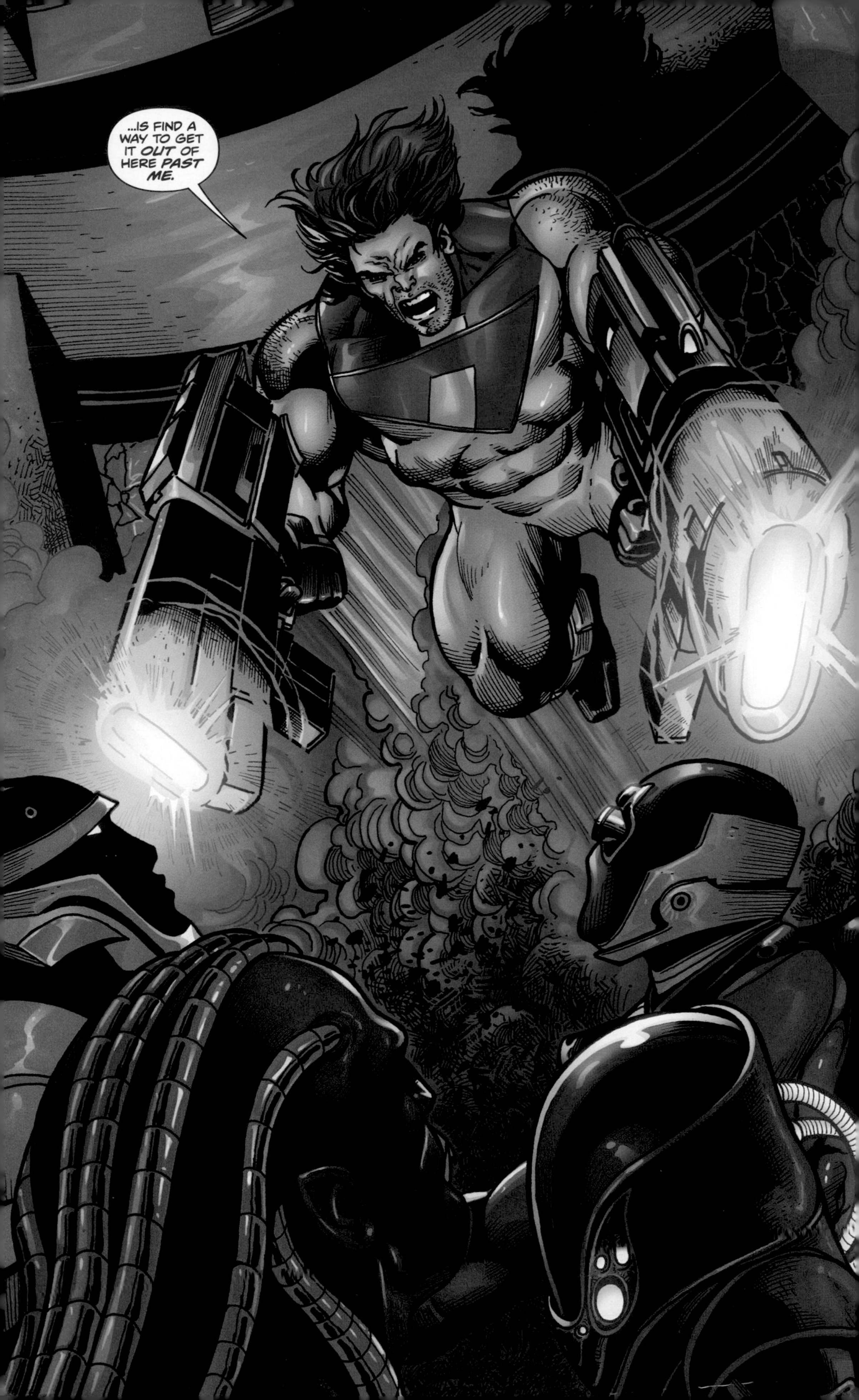
...IS FIND A WAY TO GET IT OUT OF HERE PAST ME.

A UNIVERSE AWAY FROM THE ONE YOU LOVE?

A MESSAGE YOU NEED TO SEND INSTANTLY?

A UNIQUE ITEM OR DOCUMENT THAT HAS TO BE ABSOLUTELY GUARANTEED?

TRIPSHIP

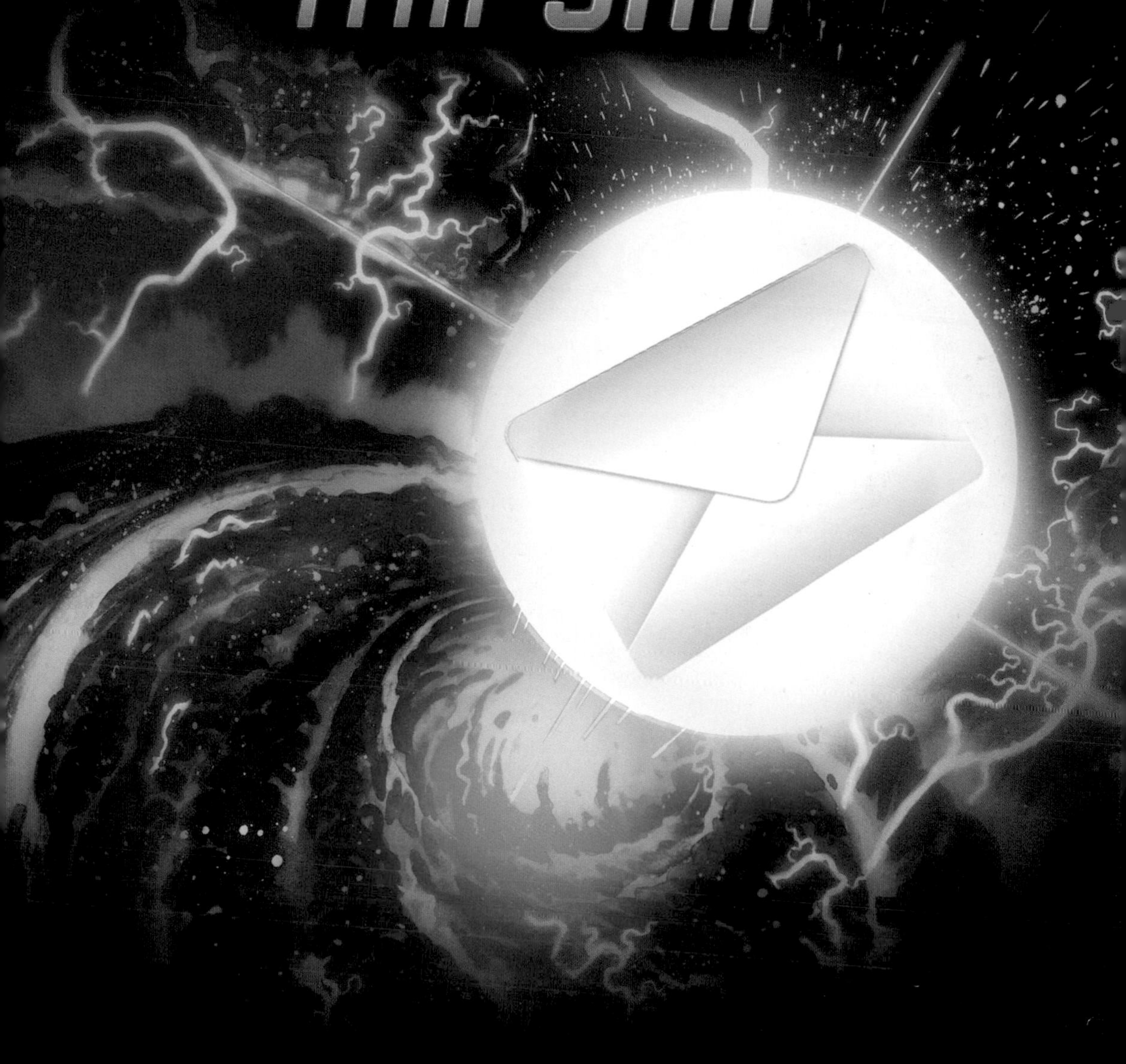

WHEN IT HAS TO BE THERE, RIGHT NOW, NO QUESTIONS.

TRIPSHIP.
INSTANTANEOUS QUANTUM COURIER SERVICE.

CERTIFIED BLACK HOLE, SUPERNOVA, AND SINGULARITY PROOF

Repository

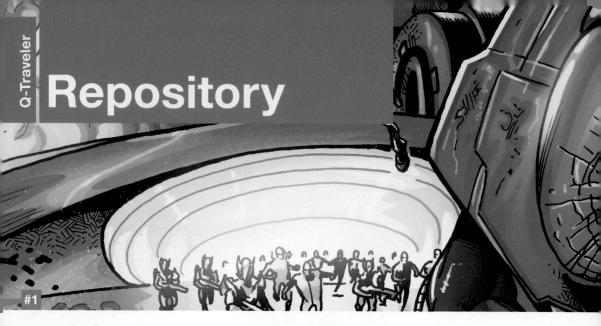

#1

Welcome to Repository

Repository is a planet-sized museum, a torus space habitat housed inside a huge asteroid that is part of an asteroid belt.

#1 - Overview

Repository is famous throughout the Quantinuum as the culture's main permanent archive, data store and museum. Situated inside the massive asteroid 33 Tarsus Red, which forms part of the Salent Tarsus belt, Repository is a torus habitat, which is to say the living spaces and museum display areas line the inside of the hollow structure. "The walls of the world rise up around you, and overhead, in dizzying fashion," said architect Ham Sammersham in 23 AQ. Repository is linked to the rest of the Quantinuum by both void ship links and a fully serviced Trip Network portal. Its priceless exhibits are protected by the Repository Guard Detail, a company of dedicated security professionals.

Attractions

Discover

#2 - The Nephilim Fragment

Repository's most famous—or infamous—exhibit is undoubtedly the Nephilim Fragment. The Fragment, whose origin and purpose remains an enigma, is the only object ever found that was demonstrably manufactured by a species other than our own. No sentient xenospecies has ever been discovered in this Galaxy or others, so the Fragment may be a relic from some pre-human civilization. It is believed that the Fragment is part of a "dark matter" engine, a reality warping machine. The Fragment is kept in the ultra-sec security levels of the archive, and may be viewed on request, subject to clearance and written permission from the curator.

#3 - Hanging Habitats

Repository attracts visitors from all over the Quantinuum, and is fully equipped with resorts attractions and hotel accommodation for those wishing to enjoy a full tour. The arcologies lining some part of the torus' interior surfaces, the so-called "hanging habitats" provide full accommodation for long-term residents, such as academics and graduate student who need to be based on the museum world while the conduct research and other major studies.

#4 - The Mini Sun

Another of the Museum world's most popula exhibits is the "mini sun", an artificial stella object created by Doctor Lincoln Pine in 11 AQ Pine's objective was to find a self-replenishing energy source that could light and power habitats in extreme cosmic conditions. The "mini sun" was his crowning glory, and would have gone into full production had Pine not been tragically killed in the Ducelidor disaster and the secrets of the sun's manufacture lost with him The "mini sun" is used to power and heat large section of the Museum World, so its operation can be clearly demonstrated to visitors.

Other key exhibits include: the Keys of Lygos; the original manuscripts of the complete works of Nobe prize-winner Fagel Fluaca; the Zod-Terfil Hologram which stopped World War Eight on 45 Bleen; the Nogur Assembly, complete with all the mini-assemblies; the original NASA lunar lander; the artificial (synthetic human Bill Byte; the Longchamps portrait of Halleluya Collins; the last surviving Tasmanian Tiger clone four pieces of Tom Whitford's first faster-than-light jump ship.

Continued on page 56..

The Nephilim Fragment

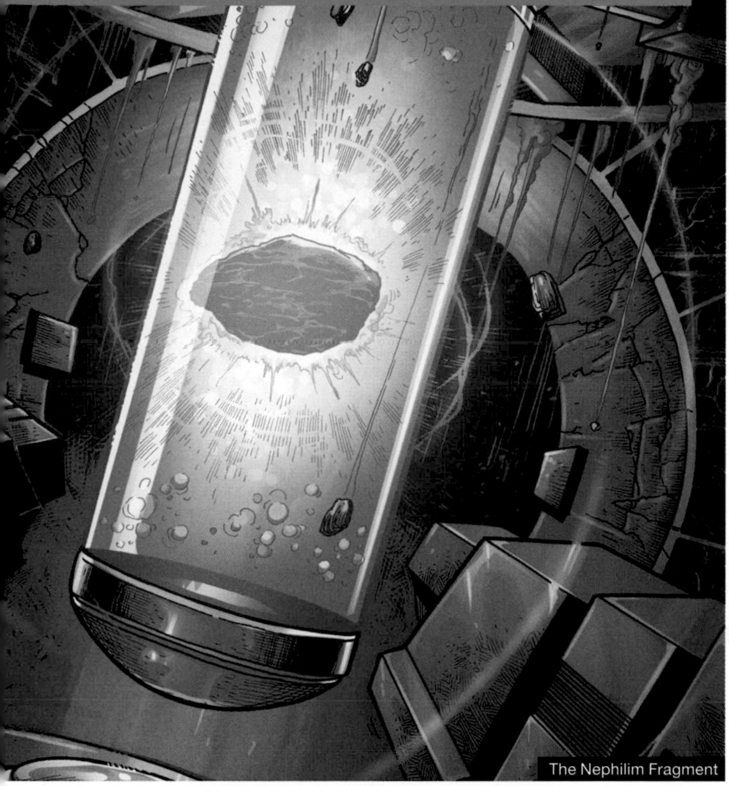

The Nephilim Fragment

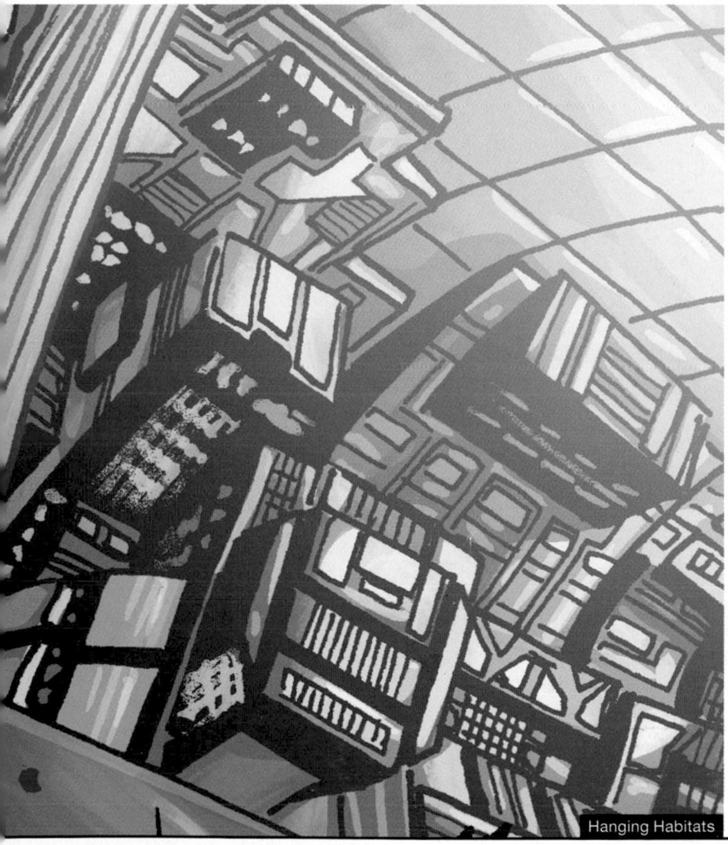

Hanging Habitats

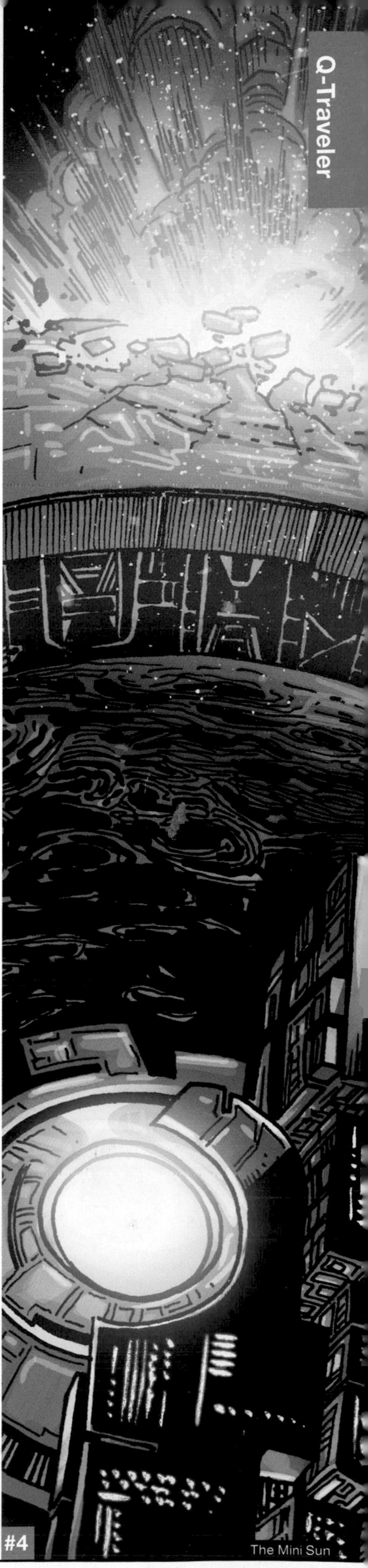

#4

The Mini Sun

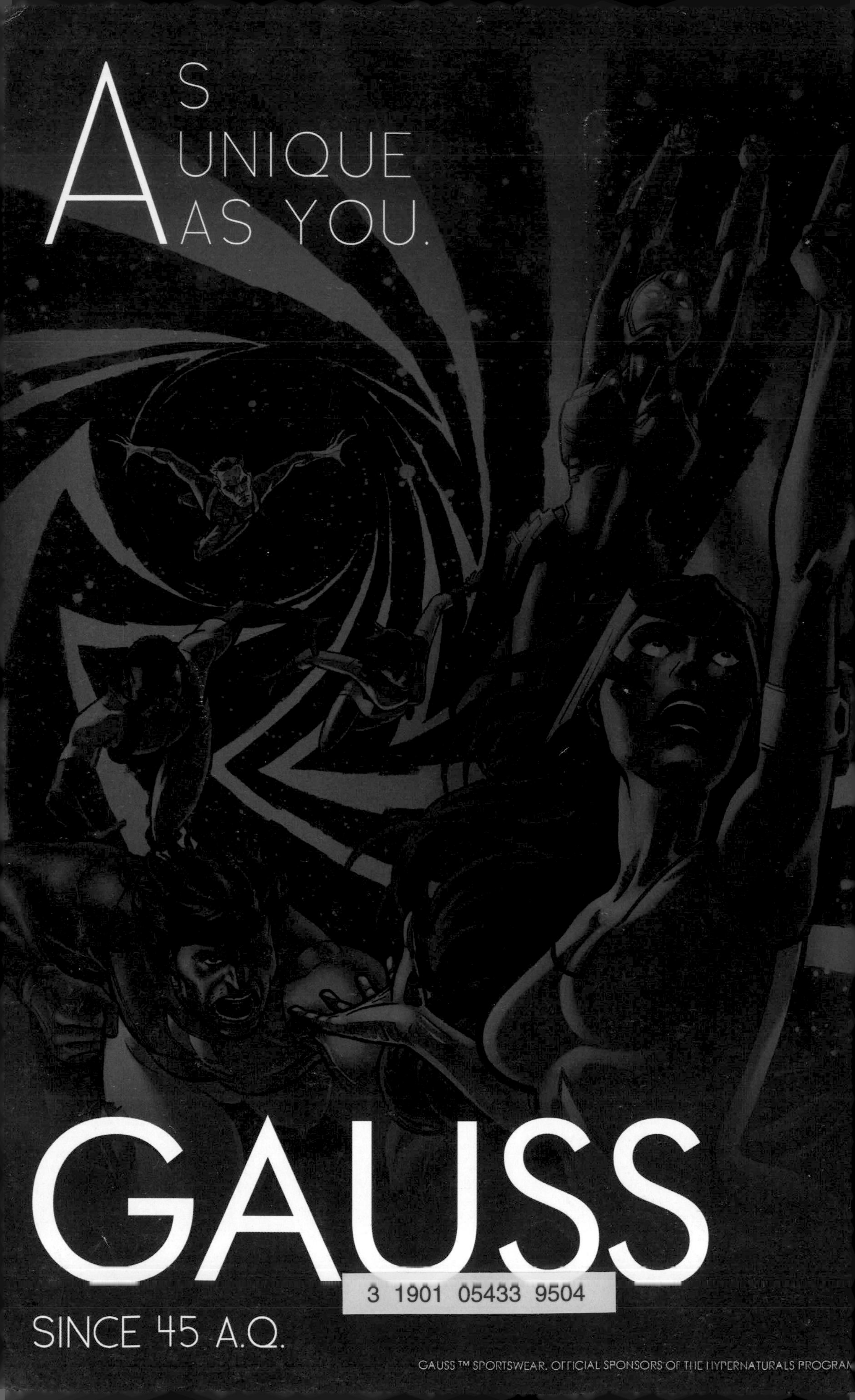
AS UNIQUE AS YOU.
GAUSS
SINCE 45 A.Q.
GAUSS ™ SPORTSWEAR. OFFICIAL SPONSORS OF THE HYPERNATURALS PROGRAM